I0759610

THE MAKING OF

AVATAR

AVATAR | AVATAR: THE WAY OF WATER | AVATAR: FIRE AND ASH

THE MAKING OF AVATAR

AVATAR | AVATAR: THE WAY OF WATER | AVATAR: FIRE AND ASH

Written by JOE FORDHAM

CONTENTS

FOREWORD

Cinema: from the Greek *kinema*, meaning "motion."

Virtual Cinema: "We would be capturing not just the motion, but the emotion, of actors in a new way. Just not with a camera."

James Cameron

Avatar movies are not made by computers.

They are made by people. By actors, by artists. Imaginers. Actors' performances are preserved as sacred in their computer-generated characters. Actors are not replaced. They are celebrated. Computers serve the artists' creativity.

Computers do not create.

No generative AI has ever created an image for an Avatar movie. This is the story of the making of the first three films in the Avatar saga.

It is a story of human creativity.

INTRODUCTION

The 2009 film *Avatar* is the cinematic tale of a former-Marine, Jake Sully, who transfers his consciousness into the heart and soul of an alien culture. Wrapped in a spectacular adventure, the story explored the impact of the human colonization of a new world—Pandora—and the fate of its indigenous people, the Na'vi.

To create the exo-moon Pandora, together with the people and creatures that inhabit its rainforests, floating mountains, oceans, skies, and volcanic terrain, the filmmakers created every biome from the ground up. No detail was too fine-grained for the Avatar designers across all realms—biology, geology, ecology, spirituality, language, clothing, diet, crafts, the traditions of multiple Na'vi cultures, and their relationship with the invading "Sky People." This book reveals how filmmaker James Cameron, producer Jon Landau, and their teams built that immersive world, from its early days through its evolution as the story has expanded across an epic, multi-part cinematic canvas.

With firsthand accounts from those who were there, those who made it happen, we explore the creative process across all three films—*Avatar* (2009), *Avatar: The Way of Water* (2022), and *Avatar: Fire and Ash* (2025.) The story will be told through the lens of five crucial production phases, as detailed in the book's five chapters.

The decades-long journey is illustrated with contributions from some of the world's top visual effects, creature effects, and filmmaking artisans. Behind-the-scenes imagery includes details from art department, costume, props and special effects teams, performance capture stages, virtual cinema and live-action shoots in Los Angeles and New Zealand, editing suites, sound-mixing and scoring stages. As the world-building continues, the filmmakers reflect on the saga's deeper themes—social, environmental, and spiritual—in an unfolding vision of paradise and apocalypse, where, as James Cameron has promised, "You ain't seen nothing yet."

Chapter 1
VISION

Vision

Fade in: flying through mist, a dimly glimpsed forest below. A male voice-over intones, "I started having these dreams of flying..."

The opening words of James Cameron's 2006 *Avatar* screenplay set the stage for the journey of a young paraplegic former Marine, Jake Sully (Sam Worthington), whose adventure will take him to another world, light-years away. There he will be able to live and walk—and fly—as an avatar, a hybrid body genetically engineered from human DNA combined with the DNA of an alien humanoid species. It has been 40 years since the discovery of a rich, living environment on Pandora, the fifth moon of the gas giant Polyphemus in the Alpha Centauri star system. Now, the human forces of the RDA (Resources Development Administration) are fighting to establish a new foothold for humanity beyond their dying Earth. Sully's awakening to the mysteries of the exo-moon he has been sent to exploit gives wings to what will ultimately be a five-film saga—beginning with *Avatar*, *Avatar: The Way of Water*, and continuing with *Avatar: Fire and Ash*.

Serial feature films have created detailed universes before, in the genres of fantasy, science-fiction, and comic books. But none have been so richly conceived, with ravishing depictions of an otherworldly ecosystem. And none have resonated so strongly with audiences worldwide.

The statistics are formidable.

Less than three weeks after its release in December 2009, *Avatar* became the fastest motion picture to earn one billion dollars worldwide, which it achieved in 19 days. The release set new standards for stereoscopic 3D and large-format IMAX presentation, and broke attendance records in more than 30 countries. Sixteen years later, *Avatar* remains the highest-grossing motion picture in history, with theatrical revenues a whisker shy of three billion dollars.

The film had its roots in James Cameron's passion for science and science fiction while growing up in the 60s in the shadow of the Cold War, but also during the dawn of both space and underwater exploration. Rebecca Keegan's

biography, *The Futurist*, described Cameron as a "cerebrally rambunctious" young man with an inclination for invention sparked by the imaginative fiction of Robert Heinlein, Arthur C. Clarke, and the other science-fiction authors of the Golden Age of SF. Every scrap of science-fiction and fantasy that Cameron could lay his hands on was grist for the mill, from the classics to pulp novels and magazines to comic books (especially Marvel!) as well as movies and television. These early influences inspired Cameron's artwork and short stories. "I loved science, history, and storytelling," said Cameron. "I was always a fan of science fiction, in literature and in movies." He grew up in the tiny rural Canadian town of Chippawa, Ontario. Attending high school in nearby Niagara Falls, he rode a bus for an hour each way. Every day, while jolting along, he would read a new science-fiction book—literally one a day if they were slim pulp novels, though more massive tomes like *Dune* might take a few days. If the story was really good, he'd continue reading in class, with the paperback propped behind his math or history text.

In 1978, Cameron's first attempt at screenwriting, working with his college friend Randall Frakes, was a feature script called *Xenogenesis*, in which interstellar travelers flee a dying Earth and genetically modify their offspring to become blue-skinned beings capable of living on an alien planet. In 1977 and '78, while hoping to actually get the film financed, Cameron generated a profusion of paintings and drawings of spacecraft and exotic worlds, complete with their alien inhabitants. These worlds included a bioluminescent planet that would become Pandora, years later. The original inspiration for that world was a dream Cameron had at the age of 19. In the dream he walked through a glowing forest with trees like fiber-optic lamps and purple moss that reacted to his footsteps by lighting up. Bioluminescent orange lizards snapped open like Chinese fans and spun lazily across the scene like living frisbees. When Cameron awoke, he quickly sketched that wondrous landscape, in colored oil-pastel on black paper. That little drawing was the true inception of what would become a multi-billion-dollar movie franchise. The scene it depicted would come to life, almost identically, 36 years later in *Avatar*.
Avatar's creative DNA continued to evolve in Cameron's first films. The *Terminator* (1984), *Aliens* (1986), *The Abyss* (1989) and *Terminator 2: Judgment Day* explored his fascination with futuristic tech, extraterrestrial intelligence, and the mysteries of underwater realms.

In 1993, after pioneering CG (computer generated) scenes for *The Abyss* and *Terminator 2*, Cameron co-founded visual effects studio Digital Domain with legendary creature designer Stan Winston. He drafted a 13-page "Digital Manifesto" that presaged the creative possibilities of the emerging digital tools. In addition to predicting that computer animation would replace conventional visual effects, the document proposed capturing actors' performances and applying that facial and body-motion data to synthetic characters in CG environments.

In 1995, to initiate a project that would drive that massive development at Digital Domain, Cameron wrote an 80-page treatment called *Avatar*. It was so dense and detailed that everyone referred to it as a "scriptment"—more script than treatment. That seminal document, written in only three weeks, contained every element of the story—the paraplegic marine, the overbearing Colonel, all the AMP Suits and rotorcraft, Grace the scientist, the Na'vi and their world, complete with all the various creatures—everything that was eventually brought to life in the movie.

Previous pages: Omatikaya rainforest, concept art by Robert Stromberg.

Opposite page, far left: One of the first conceptual paintings that production designer Robert Stromberg created to help define the mystery and wonder of Pandora.

Left: An alien bioluminescent rainforest first took form in James Cameron's imagination in an oil pastel sketch based on a lucid dream, c. 1973.

"I was always a fan of science-fiction, in literature and in movies."

James Cameron

Top: After a journey of more than five-and-a-half years, traversing 4.37 light-years from Earth, RDA Interstellar Space Vehicle *Venture Star* enters orbit above Pandora. Concept art by Dylan Cole.

Above: Pandora's jagged peaks wreathed in mist. Concept art by Robert Stromberg.

Opposite page, top : As Na'vi designs evolved, James Cameron created many conceptual sketches to guide the design process. These included a haunting Prismacolor pencil rendering made before casting Zoe Saldaña.

Opposite page, bottom: Cameron's early pencil sketches explored Na'vi facial features and hair designs that were underway with other artists in the Lightstorm collective and at Stan Winston Studios.

"To drive technical innovation, you create the need first," said Cameron. "I thought, if I write a big science-fiction film, I could challenge my team to figure out how to create environments and creatures, and use performance to create human-based characters. I went through all my old story ideas. I had a manila folder of what I called 'Planet Stories.' There was some old stuff from *Xenogenesis*, some early ideas that I developed for *Aliens*. I put this all in a pot, to make the "soup" that became *Avatar*. So I said, 'Okay, we're going to have all these elements in this new planet story. Now, what's my story?'"

The story coalesced around the idea of projecting one's consciousness into an alien body, and walking among the native people of another world. It was the classic alien-invader-disguised-as-human story, but told in reverse. Our hero would infiltrate the indigenous people, and even fall in love with one, in a body not truly his own.

But in 1995 it was still the dawn of CG character animation and performance capture. At Digital Domain, Cameron's treatment was deemed too ambitious for the state of the art of these nascent technologies at the time.

In fact, another 10 years would pass, during which Cameron made the historical epic romance *Titanic* and embarked on a series of six deep ocean expeditions. In 2005, seeing the rapid advances in CG technology being done by others, he was ready to return to filmmaking, and revisit *Avatar*.

Jon Landau, Cameron's producing partner on *Titanic*, was the COO of their company, Lightstorm Entertainment. He agreed with the director that the time was ripe to make Cameron's dream project. They put together a small team of engineers and VFX people to start creating the suite of tools needed to make the film: a "head-rig" to capture an actor's facial performance, a motion-capture Volume to capture their body movement, and a virtual camera that would allow the director to work in a world that was invisible to the naked eye—that existed only within a vamped-up game engine. Under the code name Project 880 (chosen, like the best passwords, because it was absolutely random and meant nothing at all) the team began to climb the insanely steep learning curve of how to make an entirely new form of cinema.

In parallel, Cameron embarked on a design phase, working out of his Malibu home with concept artists Wayne Barlow, Yuri Bartoli, Neville Page, and Jordu Schell. Working from the 1995 scriptment, these diverse artists began exploring character and creature design. Veteran visual-effects designer Robert Stromberg was also brought in to do concept landscapes. For a presentation to show to Fox executives, Stromberg created an image that catalyzed the look of the rainforest of Pandora. "I created one image that included a vista of an alien world with giant trees and floating mountains," Robert Stromberg recalled. "This image was certainly, for me, the 'eureka' moment in that James responded to it with great enthusiasm. I knew then that we had something special, and we began designing Pandora." Stromberg's painting captured the majesty of the "Great

Trees," rising a thousand feet above the already oversized jungle canopy of Pandora, their upper branches shrouded in clouds. Beyond, filling the sky, were the awe-inspiring Hallelujah Mountains, floating miles above the ground. Stromberg became the key production designer for the world of Pandora and all its inhabitants. He brought in other artists—including Dylan Cole and Steven Messing—to build an art deck. Conceptual artists Rob Stromberg, Ryan Church, Kasra Farahani, Francois Audouy, Neville Page, Joe Pepe, TyRuben Ellingson, Seth Engstrom, and James Clyne contributed renderings that Cameron assembled into a 17-minute pitch reel with a music track and voices. Key images included the polluted nightmare of Earth 2148, the interstellar technologies of the Resources Development Administration (RDA), the exotic creatures of Pandora, and the exo-moon's intelligent species—the 10-foot-tall, blue-skinned, golden-eyed Na'vi.

The elegant and mysterious Na'vi were a focus for design, particularly Neytiri, a huntress of the forest-dwelling Omatikaya clan. "Jordu Schell, Neville Page, and all the Malibu artists took some early cracks at the Na'vi," commented Dylan Cole. "That helped solidify the design in Jim's mind. And Jim did a couple of very definitive drawings."

The artists began with Cameron's original vision for the Na'vi, as described in the 1995 treatment:

"Its skin is blue... two shades of blue in a banded pattern. The waist is narrow and elongated, the shoulders very wide, giving a V shaped upper back... The hands are graceful, with three very long fingers, and one opposed thumb... The faces are exquisite... large wise eyes, maybe twice the size of ours... like those of a cat, or a lemur... The teeth are white, with pronounced canines... They have a tail... like the tail of a panther... A complex pattern of iridescent dots and lines, perfectly symmetrical, runs over the body... these glow in the dark like fireflies... there is what looks like a black ponytail, or queue... hanging down almost to the waist. This is not hair, but actually an external part of the nervous system."

Though this description remains accurate to the Na'vi in the final film, there were many details that needed to be brought into focus, and many varied interpretations emerged amongst the artists. The early work focused largely on Neytiri, who would ultimately be played by Zoe Saldaña. But at the time, not knowing who would play her, the designs roamed freely, exploring many different looks. Most of these proved too alien.

"When we started designing the Na'vi in July 2005," Cameron recalled, "everybody was coming back with insectile, amphibious, or fish-like Na'vi designs. It was difficult to relate to those. I decided to play more with proportion, scale, color, and pigmentation. We played with structures of tails and ears. But I didn't want to lose contact with the emotional affect of the actors." Cameron guided the artists back toward the original concept,

Left: To explore Na'vi photorealism, Stan Winston Studio designer Joe Pepe used reference of his pet cat Spooky, a member of the hairless sphynx breed, whose distinguished feline countenance inspired skin texture concepts.

focusing on nuances of design that would not interfere with the actors' expression of emotions, which he believed were critical for the audience to relate to. And it was also important for Neytiri to be attractive, not a fish-girl.

Stan Winston Studio—Cameron's collaborators in character creation dating back to *The Terminator*, *Aliens*, and *Terminator 2*—also produced studies of Na'vi physiognomy, defining their feline qualities, physique, and empathetic features. "Stan Winston Studios did some of the first really good Na'vi adaptations using photography of real people," noted Dylan Cole. "Joe Pepe was one of the main artists over there, who came to work with us at Lightstorm on *The Way of Water*. With every Na'vi, a lot of the character has to do with casting. Our basic Na'vi formula is to use the performer's mouth and chin almost as-is. And then, we widen the Na'vi eyes and do the leonine nose." Stan Winston Studio took the design of the Na'vi characters to a new level, using techniques of photomontage, based on reference photos and even photo shoots with human models. "Jim had hit a wall," says Lightstorm's lead character designer Joseph C. Pepe, who was then part of the Winston team. "That's how Stan had described it to us: Jim needed a new perspective. We didn't know what that was, but it was an opportunity, and Jim knew that Stan always brought a sense of life and realism to his films. Fortunately, my methodology involved compositing and collaging photographs, rather than drawing with a pencil, or painting in a purely digital medium." Pepe's first Photoshop concept applied organic details of skin imperfections to a Na'vi elder. "I randomly selected a high-resolution photo of an elderly female from Stan's archive of sculpting reference. I included skin pores, scars, moles, and fine wrinkles around the eyes that naturally existed in the photos."

Pepe explored a biologically plausible blue skin tone using subtle striations of pigment, depth, translucency, and feline qualities. "I had recently bought a hairless sphynx cat," Pepe recalled. "His name was Spooky. I realized this was the perfect reference for a feline without hair. I photographed and took video of Spooky, and I was able to sample all the subsurface scattering of light shining through his ears. Those were real details, and I put them in my artwork. I'm sure Weta had their own reference, but Spooky was my muse."

But the challenge was far greater than just designing the central characters.

Opposite page, below: James Clyne's conceptual art of Hell's Gate.

Left: Stephen Lang, in character as Quaritch, addresses new arrivals in the Hell's Gate cafeteria set. Greenscreen backings facilitated composites of the RDA landing strip and Pandora rainforest perimeter, visible beyond the mess hall windows.

An entire world needed to be conjured. Over the next year, the art department created renderings for hundreds of Pandoran plants and creatures. Production designer Rick Carter—a veteran of Steven Spielberg and Robert Zemeckis films, including *Jurassic Park* (1993) and *Forrest Gump* (1994)—joined the team. He would spearhead the design of the human world—the RDA base with its mining and military technology—allowing Robert Stromberg's team to focus on Pandora's organic elements. "We became two forces of design," said Stromberg. "My initial two weeks working with the group turned into three years and during that time I developed a wonderful relationship with Rick. We were able to integrate our design styles and lead our teams to build the contrast in the visuals that followed the storyline."

Carter homed in on narrative themes. He proposed design motifs for the RDA that had strong thematic subtext. For example, in a scene where Colonel Miles Quaritch (Stephen Lang) addresses the new arrivals in the base commissary, he stands before a louvered window that looks out onto the Pandoran rainforest. "That window was designed to look like the American flag," observed Rick Carter. "The way slats are against the scenery is like the flag." This was meant to be a subtle reflection of American colonial history, during which the indigenous Native Americans were displaced and decimated as their land was colonized. Though Cameron never explicitly states that the RDA or "the Marines" to which Jake and Quaritch formerly belonged, are American, there was meant to be a definite connection to the Manifest Destiny ethos of the American frontier period, and by extension the entire European colonization of the Americas, north and south.

Quaritch says, "You're not in Kansas anymore." He describes the jungle as a place where "Everything that crawls, flies, or squats in the mud wants to kill you and eat your eyes like jujubees." Kansas, of course, is a reference to *The Wizard of Oz*, Cameron's favorite film.

The parallel to *Oz* suggested the mythical elements of Sully's journey. "It's a magical transformation," said Carter. "Going into another land, where one is met with a series of guides along the way that help transform one's awareness. In the second half of *Avatar*, Jake is transformed like in *Apocalypse Now*. When Willard comes out of the water he becomes a killer in a transference of the man he's hunting [renegade Colonel Kurtz]. *Avatar* is quite psychological. Jake goes through a transformation, from a human paraplegic to become another entity, as an avatar, where he can run around 10 feet tall. He goes from being an outsider and a loser to becoming a leader in this new world where he renounces his species. It's a radical transformation and it's done so well that people associate the 'humanity' in the movie more with the Na'vi, rather than the RDA." In *Avatar* it is Jake himself who is seen as "going Kurtz" by the RDA authorities. He's been out in the forest too long, going native. His allegiance becomes

“[Jake] goes from being an outsider and a loser to becoming a leader in this new world…”

Rick Carter, production designer

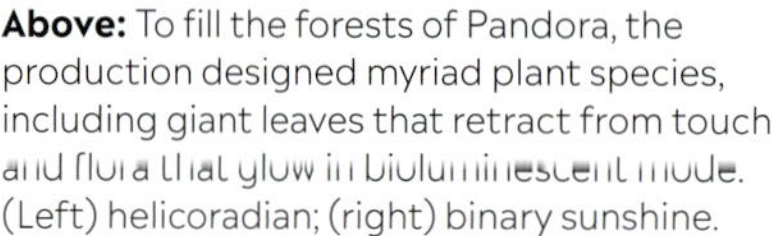

Above: To fill the forests of Pandora, the production designed myriad plant species, including giant leaves that retract from touch and flora that glow in bioluminescent mode. (Left) helicoradian; (right) binary sunshine.

Opposite page: In their Na’vi forms, Jake Sully and Dr. Grace Augustine make a sortie into the rainforest of Pandora. Screenshot by Weta.

questionable. Of course the audience is meant to sympathize with Jake, with their own journey mirroring his as he comes to realize how spiritually superior the Na’vi are to their human invaders.

Carter made use of brutalist design—squat, angular concrete structures to portray the RDA’s industrial compound, called Hell’s Gate. Every piece of human technology was meant to offend the Na’vi sensibility. Instead of their organic curvilinear designs, the humans use massive steel and concrete, squared off and rectilinear. Ugly, brooding and always lit by overcast skies. The base is dominated by industrial processing on a grand scale, inspired by oil refineries with cylindrical cracking towers, hellish sodium lights, and open flames “flaring off” unwanted volatiles. The open pit mine is an utter affront to the Na’vi, a vast scar in the earth, filled with infernal machines—inspired by actual contemporary mining equipment but blown up tenfold in scale. The goal was to look at humanity through the lens of nature, and portray them as a nightmarish invading force.

Silhouettes of arachnids inspired RDA’s menacing air transport and military vehicles. As it says in the treatment, “AT DAWN THE GUNSHIPS fill the sky like bloated death beetles.”

Cameron, a helicopter pilot himself, worked very closely with TyRuben Ellingson on the design of the rotorcraft. The director asked for two types of tilt-rotors, a two-rotor configuration for the smaller craft, like the Scorpion and Samson gunships, and a quad-rotor “four poster” design for the massive Dragon gunship, Quaritch’s command ship. The inspiration for the Scorpion was the Apache attack helicopter, a nimble and narrow-framed aircraft bristling with missiles on its stub-wing weapon pods. The Samson was more like a Vietnam-era Huey helicopter, a general utility heavy-lifter that could transport cargo and troops—dubbed “ass and trash” missions during the Vietnam War. The Samson was wide-bodied, and only lightly armed. The one we get to know best in *Avatar* is piloted by Captain Trudy Chacon (Michelle Rodriguez), who proves loyal to Jake in the final conflict. Both rotorcraft types were meant to look like highly plausible military designs, strongly rooted in contemporary technology, in keeping with overall design themes of using the familiar to ground the exotic otherworldly story in a sense of gritty reality.

Looming menacingly over the other rotorcraft is the Dragon gunship, a behemoth with four massive, ducted rotors. Quaritch conducts his military operations while standing casually on the command deck of the Dragon, coffee cup in hand. These operations include bringing down the Hometree, which has been home to the Omatikaya clan since time immemorial, and his final assault on the Na’vi sacred site, The Tree of Souls, deep in the floating mountains. Quaritch’s gunship is the literal dragon that Jake must slay in the final battle.

Beyond Hell’s Gate, Cameron’s screenplay evoked a landscape of towering rainforests, huge multicolored, six-limbed creatures, majestic winged *ikran*, and magnetically levitated floating mountains. The art department introduced aspects of terrestrial vegetation that were gigantic in stature but recognizable enough to ground the forest in nature. “That allowed the audience to connect in a basic way with this alien world,” Robert Stromberg explained. “Almost every element used to design this world was taken from elements that already exist here on Earth—from the jungles of South America to the mountains of China—and electron microscope imagery. All these Earth-like elements were cross-pollinated in unique ways by using scale, texture, and light to skew and overlay, enlarge, and blend into a new world.”

One fundamental decision to be made was the color of the rainforest itself. Initially Cameron proposed an otherworldly cyan-blue color, as if the Pandoran equivalent of chlorophyll was chemically different. Not only would it remind us we were on an alien world, but there would be a logic to the blue camouflage patterns of the Na’vi skin. But eventually it was decided that, for the day scenes at least, the forest would be good old Earthly green. That color for forest is deeply imprinted into the human soul from primordial times. It would be grounding for the audience and help anchor the sense of photorealism. And the Na’vi skin color looked beautiful against green foliage. The audience would be drawn into a forest that felt familiar in color but alien in scale and detail, with phantasmagorical plant forms and creatures. Then, as day turns to night in the

story, the colors of the bioluminescent forest would emerge to show quite starkly that we are indeed on an alien world.

Avatar Program technology, used to transfer human consciousness into Na'vi avatars, drew parallels between the human neurological system and the planet's biological nervous system that Avatar Program leader Dr. Grace Augustine (Sigourney Weaver) recognizes as a consciousness sacred to the Na'vi—their deity, *Eywa*. In her avatar form, Grace Augustine served as an ambassador to the Na'vi, and through her explanations we come to understand the culture and spiritual belief systems of the indigenous race. "When did she arrive on Pandora? Who was her mentor? How did she wind up inheriting the Avatar Program?" asked James Cameron. "I came up with a backstory around Grace and the guy that she wound up replacing, her mentor, the founder of the Avatar Program, Brantley Giess." Though he ultimately isn't seen in *Avatar*, Giess becomes an important part of the ongoing story, which will be revealed in Avatar 4 and 5. In the spring of 2006, struggling with a script that was too long, Cameron worked with writer Laeta Kalogridis to restructure and simplify. Brantley Giess was removed, and much of his dialogue was merged into the character of Grace. A fun footnote: her name, in the treatment and the first draft screenplay, was Grace Shipley. But when Cameron asked Sigourney Weaver to join the cast, and she readily agreed, he changed her character's name to Augustine, because Shipley was too close to Ripley, the character she played in Cameron's 1986 film *Aliens*.

The art department was tasked with creating the two vastly different cultures—the human world and the Na'vi world. "The left-brain Hell's Gate technical world was one half of Jim's way of looking at the world," said Rick Carter. "That was the militaristic, Quaritch way. And then, there was the world of Pandora, with the Na'vi and *Eywa* mentality. There are dimensions within those: the normal daylight forest, and the nocturnal bioluminescent realm. Jim's script described that as 'phantasmagoric,' which means 'as seen in a dream state.' As we laid out the movie, we tried to understand this on this Jungian iconic level." As Dr. Augustine observes, the bioluminescent patterns in the rainforest resemble a neural network. "The overarching metaphor is that the world of Pandora was created as a direct parallel to our human brain," noted Robert Stromberg. "Just as our neural network is connected to our bodies, the network of root systems on Pandora [is] connected. This Pandora network

"Almost every element used to design Pandora was taken from elements that already exist here on Earth."

Robert Stromberg, production designer

was integrated with the Na'vi clan, they connect to the network with their braids—*kuru*, or "queue"—to connect with *Eywa*. Synapses between the organic neurons represent not only communication but also memory—all their ancestors who have passed on. The [moon] is a living entity."

The filmmakers used light and color to guide emotional response. "When Jake first arrives on Pandora," Stromberg explained, "we are greeted with an ominously gray and rainy sky. He sees a giant mechanical AMP Suit, then a huge truck with arrows sticking out of its tires. As Jake becomes an avatar and is slowly introduced to the world outside of Hell's Gate, we add more light and color. This continues up to the point where he meets Neytiri in a bioluminescent jungle. By transitioning from the gray and rainy environment to the colorful, otherworldly Pandora, psychologically we've changed the viewer's opinion. We now feel as though the humans have lied to us, this place is a beautiful place of peace and unity. We feel compelled to take sides with the Na'vi and see the world of Pandora as paradise."

The character and creature team was not just working in 2D, they were sculpting as well. Expressive, hand-sculpted clay models—"maquettes"—helped define the characters in three dimensions before computer modeling began. One key maquette was artist Jordu Schell's 15-inch-tall clay bust of Neytiri, which captured the regal bearing of her character. Neytiri was starting to come into focus, more human and beautiful than some of the early alien designs, but still decidedly otherworldly, with her long neck, enormous eyes, and catlike ears.

It was time to find the right actress to play her. Whoever she was, this actress would need to master a new language, and move like a Na'vi, with feral strength and grace. *Avatar* casting director Margery Simkin took into account the physicality of the role while searching for Neytiri. It was actually another casting director, Mali Finn, whom Cameron had worked with on *Terminator 2: Judgment Day* and *Titanic*, who first brought Zoe Saldaña to his attention, very early in the production. Zoe was a former classically-trained dancer and theater actor from New York (Queens) with Dominican and Puerto Rican ancestry. Mali

"We feel compelled to take sides with the Na'vi and see the world of Pandora as paradise."

Robert Stromberg, production designer

Left: A bronze maquette Neytiri sculpted by Jordu Schell.

Above left: Cameron confers with the principal cast members for a read-through of the *Avatar* screenplay in Los Angeles, February 2007.

Above right: Dialect coach Carla Meyer (left) reviews script pages with performers (left to right) Zoe Saldaña, Laz Alonso, and Wes Studi, helping to define a uniform accent for scenes where Na'vi characters communicate in English with a unique Na'vi inflection.

Opposite page: In August 2006, Sam Worthington and Zoe Saldaña played their first screen-test together, enacting Jake and Neytiri's love scene beneath the Omatikaya Tree of Voices.

had to leave the project due to illness, and when Margery Simkin took over, she arranged an audition for Saldaña.

The director was instantly impressed with her beauty, grace, and strength of character—especially the absolute ferocity she was able to channel during a videotaped audition. After only short deliberation, Zoe was the first actor signed for *Avatar*. Saldaña's ballet training gave her Neytiri natural poise and power. "Zoe was incredibly lithe, balanced, and graceful," asserted stunt coordinator Garrett Warren. "When she had to do flying scenes on her *ikran*, she was up on the balls of her feet doing all the movements. And when she got off the creature, she spilled off it like water. She just flowed. If she encountered a tree, she became a part of that tree."

Of equal importance was finding their Jake, the male lead. Jake was the storyteller, through whose eyes the audience experiences the entire adventure. Candidates for the role of Jake Sully required searches in the US, UK, Ireland, and Australia. "We found a lot of manly leading men in those places," Margery Simkin told the Los Angeles Times. "But we hadn't yet seen somebody who riveted us." From Australian video submissions came Sam Worthington, a former construction worker from Perth who had recently been making waves in Australian films and television. "Sam just popped. We've all seen movies where favorite actors don't have chemistry with each other, and the movie doesn't work." But Cameron invited Sam to fly over and audition with Zoe Saldaña. He shot with two cameras, and cut the two actors together, as a scene. Simkin recalls, "Once you saw that pairing of him with Zoe, we knew, 'That's it.' There was chemistry."

Cameron and Simkin narrowed it down to three actors, including Worthington, for the role of Jake. Knowing how critical this key casting decision was,

Cameron embarked on a thorough battery of screen tests for all three actors. The tests were shot using the brand new Cameron-Pace Fusion 3D cameras, on cinematically lit sets of both jungle and lab spaces, created just for the screen tests. All three actors had to do five key scenes from the script. Though none were well-known at the time, the two other actors have both gone on to well-deserved stardom, but it was Sam who shone through in one particular scene, which Cameron dubbed the "Saint Crispin's Day speech," referencing Shakespeare's *Henry V*.

This was the scene in which Jake exhorts the Na'vi to rise up en masse against the Sky People, ending with the ringing battle cry "This is our land!" Sam brought such fire to the words that the choice was immediately clear. Said Cameron, "Sam was the guy, out of all the actors I saw, that I would have followed into Hell." And that was the precise quality the character needed, to be believable as the legendary *Toruk Makto*, Rider of Last Shadow, deliverer of the Na'vi People from the Time of Great Sorrow. Worthington also brought a unique sensitivity, even a boy-like emotional vulnerability, to counterbalance his heroic masculinity.

There was only one problem: Sam's thick Australian accent. Cameron imagined the character as having a neutral American accent, but as he recalled, "When I first met him, Sam sounded worse than Crocodile Dundee. I knew he'd have plenty of time to train with an accent coach. But looking back now, it was an enormous leap of faith to cast him. I don't know why, but I just had faith in him."

Unfortunately the top executives at Fox did not share that same faith. They preferred either of the other two actors, and to be fair, their taste has been vindicated by the rise of both of them to household-name status. But Cameron dug in his heels, and insisted on Sam. Finally, to Cameron's relief, the top brass said, "Fine, do it your way." And so Sam, who was at the time sleeping in his car, became the star of what turned out to be the highest-grossing film in history.

Creature design proceeded in parallel with the casting process, including the sculpting of other key animals. One seminal maquette was sculptor Jason Matthews' clay figure of a viperwolf, which was approximately 20 inches long, in a feral six-legged pose. Others soon emerged, for the direhorse, the hammerhead titanothere, and the great leonopteryx— the *toruk*—also known as "Last Shadow" because its shadow as it dove upon you would be the last thing you ever see.

These maquettes stood on the Lightstorm conference-room table when James Cameron met with Richard Taylor, the co-founder of New Zealand's Weta Workshop (a completely separate company from Weta Digital, the VFX house.) This amazing design group had cut their teeth on the Lord of the Rings trilogy and are considered pre-eminent character and prop designers and fabricators, not just in New Zealand, but around the world. Jon Landau invited Taylor to LA for what turned out to be a fateful meeting. "I'm never one to turn down a good project," Taylor recalls, "so I flew out for a day and a night. Jon led me in. Jim was sitting in this room with artwork lining the walls, and this warm, inspiring individual gave me an hour and a half of his time. He explained his vision of the world."

"Jim wanted the audience to feel that they could literally be there in this world," said Taylor. "He wanted viewers to be able to feel a sense of tactility, a beauty and exoticism that was familiar, but foreign. It was Earth-based, but alien. And he explained the digital world that he wanted to create. I asked Jim what role he wanted us to play, and he suggested, 'Well, you guys do a lot of weapons. Why don't you have a go at designing some weapons for the Na'vi as a kickoff?" Buoyed by Cameron's enthusiasm, Taylor returned to Wellington and took an unconventional approach to the design brief. Rather than inviting concepts for Na'vi weaponry, he encouraged the Workshop team to explore the Omatikaya's need for armaments. "I was playing with fire a little bit," Taylor confessed. "You don't ever want to contradict a director, and certainly not one as visionary as Jim. He's a great designer. And I always felt, if Jim had 100 years, he'd train himself in every discipline and make the whole movie himself. But in that first week we didn't design weapons. We designed eating implements."

With some trepidation, on his first video call with Cameron, Taylor explained the thinking behind his design approach. "To define the purpose of a weapon in the cultural setting of an indigenous group," said Taylor, "you have to understand who those people are. Do they want weapons for protection, hunting, violence, or wars? How ceremonial are the weapons? If you define how people eat, then you define what they're eating, and you determine the social structure around their family unit. Therefore, we started to think about what eating bowls the Na'vi would make. How would they communicate? Would they have a written language?" It was decided that the Na'vi would not have a written language, but would use song as a way of remembering the past—like the indigenous peoples of Australia. Every individual would have their own "songcord," a string of beads, each representing a milestone in their life. These would act as mnemonic guides to that person's individual song, to be sung by the one who loved them most, at their funeral.

Weta Workshop became an important collaborator in creating the fabric of the world. "I think Jim saw in us a team of people that were willing to go deep down the rabbit hole of building a culture that had ecological plausibility," commented Taylor. "And that was lovely. As a physical effects team, we typically finish our work around the time that the main unit stops filming, so we don't see anything until years later, when we go to the premiere of the movie. And we threw so much stuff at Jim without knowing what would stick. Seeing the final film was unbelievably uplifting."

Above: Maquettes were realized by hand-shaping clay over a wire-frame armature to capture an expressive pose of a character or creature in motion. Maquettes of Neytiri gesture beside a warlike pose of other warriors, a slinking viperwolf (by Jason Matthews), and a sturmbeest posed in scale reference with a Na'vi.

Weta Workshop physically made many of the Na'vi costumes, jewelry, weapons, and hairstyles. "Jim wanted to build it all physically," Richard Taylor asserted. "His reasoning for that was he wanted the digital effects people not to have to make any assumptions derived from 2D imagery. If we were going to design a feather on Na'vi clothing, Jim wanted the digital artist to be able to touch and feel that feather."

To help bring Na'vi costumes to life, producer Jon Landau invited a trusted collaborator, *Titanic*'s Oscar®-winning costume designer Deborah L. Scott, to join the production team. "Jim was finding his way in the process," Scott recalled of her arrival in New Zealand. "Going into a movie that lives in a virtual reality, the assumption is that we could draw something on paper, paint it, and hand it over, 'Here, you guys, make it.' But, for a couple of different reasons, that wasn't going to fulfill Jim's dreams. As the designs evolved, it became clear that we needed to create realistic samples of material to show how heavy each one was and how it would look in motion."

"Jim was feeling out the landscape that he was planning. Our work needed to be informative to him and to the writers."

Ben Procter, production designer

For the Omatikaya development in *Avatar,* initial concepts were developed with costume designer Mayes Rubeo, including the main Na'vi garments, the loincloths, which were based on the taparrabo used by the indigenous people of Rubeo's native Mexico. This was a simple piece of cloth, laid across the belly from the front, crossing in the back, then wrapped under, pulled up through the front, and draped down over the groin. Simple on a human, but the design needed to be modified with a loop around the base of the Na'vi tail.

Upcoming chapters will explore how the *Avatar* production incorporated these designs with the captured performances of the cast, which were then rendered in fully emotive, completely photoreal CG—something that had never been previously accomplished. In addition, the live-action shooting that would show Jake Sully's human experience will be explored, including the innovative techniques developed to combine the giant Na'vi and avatars with human-scaled sets and action.

Each of these phases—of design, capture, live action, and VFX—will then be explored again, to tell the story of the sequels—*Avatar: The Way of Water* and *Avatar: Fire and Ash.*

As cinema history would prove, the entire production team's passionate dedication to realism in the service of fantasy ultimately paid off. When *Avatar* was released, on December 17, 2009—in deep immersive 3D—audiences felt truly transported to another world that they could never have imagined. It was like "dreaming with your eyes wide open," a motto Cameron had coined when he co-founded Digital Domain with Stan Winston in 1992.

In Cameron's last words to Stan, during a phone call the day before he died, the director said, "We've done it. We made it happen. These characters are real." The next day Cameron rushed over with his laptop to Stan's house, to share with Stan the first fully finished shots of Neytiri—for the scene in which she is first revealed, her golden eyes intense as she stalks Jake in the rainforest. But Cameron's dear friend had gone during the night. It was Stan's vision to see CG become the new way to create fantasy characters, but he didn't live to see it happen.

But the world accepted that new computer-generated reality. Dreaming with their eyes wide open, global audiences propelled *Avatar* to become the highest-grossing film of all time, with a final box office gross of 2.93 billion. Stan's dream had become a reality.

***

In 2010, the 82nd Academy Awards honored *Avatar* with nine nominations, from which it won three Oscars®: Best Art Direction, Best Cinematography, and Best Visual Effects. With the critical and financial success of *Avatar*, 20th Century Fox was very enthusiastic about proceeding to a sequel as soon as possible. But Cameron was uncertain that a sequel made sense. The first *Avatar* was not just the highest-grossing film in history, it was also (at the time) the highest costing film in history. Sequels would cost even more, due to the higher expectations of everyone involved, including the cast and crew who would all, rightfully, want more money to perform the miracle a second time. To say nothing of everyone wanting to raise the bar on scope, scale, and the photorealism of the characters.

> "We've done it. We made it happen. These characters are real."
>
> **James Cameron, director**

Cameron considered it foolhardy, even arrogant, to put a film into production with the knowledge that it would need to be among the highest-grossing films in history to succeed at all. "It was the dumbest business model in history," he often said in interviews.

The director distanced himself from the very idea of *Avatar* sequels for over two years, working on many other projects. He founded the Avatar Alliance Foundation with a multi-million-dollar endowment from his own *Avatar* profits, and absorbed himself with "giving back" to indigenous communities around the world that were under extreme pressure from the toxic and devastating encroachment of industrial development into their traditional lands. This included involvement with indigenous rights groups in the Amazon, struggling to stop the building of massive dams that would flood tribal lands, and lobbying against the oil companies who were poisoning rivers in western Canada through the massive extraction industry at the Athabasca tar sands. In parallel, the filmmaker was completing a project he had started five years earlier: building a submersible of his own design to dive to the deepest place in the Earth's oceans—the Challenger Deep. By mid 2011, this engineering project was absorbing all of his time.

But in the background, discussion with the studio about *Avatar* sequels was ongoing. Instrumental in moving this forward were Jon Landau and Lightstorm's former president, Rae Sanchini, who was brought back in to manage the negotiation. Victoria Rossellini, the CFO of Twentieth Century Fox, was also a staunch advocate of the potential Avatar franchise. A deal in principle was emerging between Fox and Lightstorm.

Ultimately Cameron faced a singular decision point in his life. Continue as a filmmaker, doing Avatar movies. Or commit to being an ocean explorer and conservationist full-time and continue his filmmaking only in the documentary world. This was not the no-brainer decision that the world assumes it was. Cameron was very invested in the indigenous causes, and in his pursuit of deep ocean exploration and science.

What ultimately lured him back to the Avatar universe was not the potential for more money and acclaim, as most would assume. It was the "Avatar Family." Just as Cameron had come to cherish the bonds that emerged between the members of his expedition projects, he also deeply valued the bonds forged between the members of the cast and crew on *Avatar*. They had worked together for years, accomplishing the seemingly impossible, during which time they had become not just respectful colleagues, but friends. They enjoyed working together, sharing the challenges of the exotic new way of filmmaking, and also enjoying the day-to-day repartee. It was an insular group who knew that the world at large couldn't begin to comprehend what they were doing. They had gone down the rabbit hole into a bubble universe of production that outsiders didn't understand. But they all knew what it took, both mentally and physically, to create the magic of *Avatar*. And that connected them in a way that Cameron had never experienced before on any of his prior films.

The end result was that Cameron would make the enormous commitment to do not just one *Avatar* sequel but several together as one massive project. To him it didn't make sense to dump millions of dollars into research and development to improve the methodology, the "pipeline"—which had been a kludged-together prototype on the first film—in order to make just one more film. He and Jon Landau agreed it made more sense to amortize the ambitious R&D across multiple films. A trilogy of sequels would be the goal—a single over-arching production that might span 10 years in total. As Cameron always says, "Go big or go home."

It was a decision not taken lightly. It promised at the outset to dominate the next decade of the filmmaker's life. As it turned out, it would be a decade and a half. And counting...

In fall of 2011, Lightstorm Entertainment struck a deal with Fox Filmed Entertainment to create three untitled *Avatar* sequels. The Hollywood trade paper Variety announced plans for a "threequel" continuation of the saga, with part of the production's profits going to the Avatar Alliance Foundation to support indigenous rights and environmental causes. But first Cameron had to finish his sub and embark on his expedition. On March 26, 2012, Cameron became the first to dive solo at the Challenger Deep, the deepest spot in the Mariana Trench, 170 nautical miles southwest of Guam in the western Pacific. In 1960, USN Captain Don Walsh and French explorer Jacques Piccard had descended in the bathyscaphe *Trieste* to set a world depth record there. They dove in the "west

Above: Cameron on set with Stan Winston Studio's full-scale Na'vi standees.

pond", or western basin, of the Challenger Deep. Cameron chose to dive in the eastern basin, about 40 nautical miles away, which in the intervening 52 years had been shown to be slightly deeper by a dozen meters or so. Scientific consensus now holds that this small basin, about half a mile across and two miles long, is the deepest place on Earth. Cameron's recorded depth was 35,787 feet. He was the first human being to dive in the eastern basin of the Challenger Deep.

When Cameron returned from that historic expedition, he pivoted his focus to the *Avatar* sequels. In late 2012 he sequestered himself at his coastal ranch in Santa Barbara Country, California, to begin the writing process—a solo deep dive into his imagination. He started with notes. Hundreds of pages of notes. Just freely exploring the world of Pandora beyond the narrow spotlight of the first film, including other realms, new creatures, fractal detail on Na'vi culture and their relationship to the global consciousness *Eywa*, and the characters themselves. How were Jake and Neytiri marked by the events of the first story? Where would history and their own relationship take them next? As a "mated pair" would they have children? If so, what would it be like to raise a family who, as Jake's offspring, would be mixed race? What would that mean to the family, to the children themselves, and to the rest of the Na'vi community? What would happen when the Sky People inevitably returned, bent on subjugating and strip-mining paradise? And who, specifically, would be the Sullys' adversary among the human invaders?

Above: Na'vi *ilu* riders pause at a site sacred to the oceangoing Metkayina clan known as the Cove of the Ancestors. Concept art by Steven Messing.

Cameron let his imagination roam far and wide across the exotic world of Pandora. He realized the canvas was vast, more than big enough to easily embrace an epic story on the scale of other towering works of fantasy like the Star Wars universe and J.R.R. Tolkien's The Lord of the Rings trilogy.

In press reports, Cameron described his ambition to create, in each of the sequels, "self-contained stories that also fulfill a greater story arc." To begin exploring that epic arc, Lightstorm assembled an art department at Manhattan Beach Studios, with Dylan Cole and Ben Procter stepping in as production designers. Cole and Procter had previously worked on *Avatar* as concept art directors. In the intervening years, they had gained experience as production designers—Procter on the science-fiction adventure *Ender's Game* (2013) and Cole on Robert Stromberg's directorial debut *Maleficent* (2014). Cameron and Landau invited them to continue the dual design dynamic of *Avatar* by assigning Cole to the creatures, cultures, and environments of Pandora while Procter would design the technological human world: the RDA vehicles, architecture, and weapons. Early topics for the art department meetings were wide-ranging. For the Reef People village, Cameron's first whiteboard sketches for Cole indicated arching, mangrove-like root structures cradling the dwellings of an oceangoing Na'vi clan, the Metkayina. Procter's first task involved a classified concept that won't appear until Avatar 4. "Jim was feeling out the landscape that he was planning," said Procter. "Our work needed to be informative to him and to the writers as to what these major elements would be, so that they could then arrange the puzzle pieces into the story they wanted to tell."

Concurrent with design work, Cameron and Landau scouted for screenwriters to build a collaborative hive-mind writers' room. The new team would include the husband-and-wife team of Rick Jaffa and Amanda Silver, veterans of the recent Planet of the Apes film series (2011–24), who had previously contributed to an unrealized Lightstorm adaptation of the 1966 inner-space adventure *Fantastic Voyage*. Screenwriter Shane Salerno, who had also worked on *Fantastic Voyage*, brought his experience in television and feature science-fiction thrillers, including *Armageddon* (1998) and *Alien vs. Predator* (2004). Another Cameron alumnus, Josh Friedman, was also brought in. Friedman had been the creator and showrunner of *Terminator: The Sarah Connor Chronicles* (2008–9.)

"Jim proposed creating what was essentially a TV writers' room for a series of movies," related Josh Friedman. "It was one of the first times this had been attempted.

Above: Production designers Dylan Cole (far left), Ben Procter, and Lightstorm Lab environments team supervisor Motoki Nishii consult with James Cameron in the Lightstorm art department.

Right: Sea creatures of the Metkayina reef. Early sketches by Daphne Yap.

Overleaf: Metkayina village at sunset. Concept art by Dylan Cole.

He wanted to spend five months breaking down what started as three and then became four movies. Writers' rooms can be collaborative and ideally safe creative spaces. This one definitely was. We didn't know how much time we'd have with Jim—if we'd have him two days a week, or three hours a day. We ended up having him all day, every day, for five months, uninterrupted. That's unheard of. Five months in a room, up to 50 hours a week, with one of the greatest filmmakers of our generation talking about this project that he was so passionate about."

The writers' room was a windowless inner sanctum, with whiteboards on all the walls and a large conference table with a three-and-a-half-foot-high Neytiri statue in the middle. On day one, Cameron handed the writers his notes on the characters, environments, creatures, and broad stroke story concepts: 1,500 pages of notes, bound in black binders, that he had written in the previous year. In addition to this massive homework assignment, the writers were also given DVDs to watch that included rainforest and underwater documentaries and adventure movies, and given access to a massive library of books on the subjects they were expected to immerse themselves in: botany, marine biology, cultural anthropology, interstellar space flight, etc. But to initiate the creative process, Cameron and Landau first invited the writers to re-watch *Avatar* and read reviews, and presented them with an unexpected challenge. "Our first day was like summer camp," said Shane Salerno. "We were ready to start pitching ideas. They said, 'No, we're not doing that.' They wanted us to first do an

autopsy on why *Avatar* worked. They showed us cut scenes that hadn't made the movie in finished and unfinished forms. And then they said, 'Tomorrow, you guys are going to pitch why this was the most successful movie of all time.' Sounds simple, right? 'Cutting-edge visuals, never seen before.' We tried that. Jim looked at us like, 'You guys don't get it.' Whatever we said was just too surface-level and basic. We bombed out."

Jon Landau informed the writers of Cameron's concerns and suggested another screening and review the next day. "I drove home on the freeway," Salerno recalled, "and I was thinking, 'I'm going to be like Pete Best in The Beatles. I was hired, it was amazing, and I got fired.' We came in the next day like forensic detectives. We watched *Avatar* again like scientists. Our conversations weren't about, 'Great visuals.' We talked about the effect the movie had on its audience, and why it played in every country. Why do people in the Brazilian rainforest think it's their story? Why do African Americans who grew up during the civil rights movement think it's their story? There was a universality about the message. We went as deep as you could go. And at the end of the day, Jim said, 'We get started tomorrow.'"

The conclusion, after that rigorous initial-thought exercise, was that *Avatar* operated on three levels. The first and most obvious level was the story itself, Jake Sully's journey, an outsider's quest for belonging, and that journey's final fulfillment, when he becomes fully Na'vi, signaled by his eyes snapping open in the final second of the film. Plot, character, setting, worldbuilding, creature design—all of these are aspects of the surface level.

The second level was thematic: what did it all mean between the lines? Clearly there is an indictment of colonization, in which corporate, government, and military forces were brought to bear against indigenous people, with the latter being decimated and their natural habitats destroyed in the process. The endless war between the takers and the caretakers. There are themes of tribalism—earning one's place among a community of people by striving to live by the standards of their culture. And the theme of the human need to belong, to be accepted, to be SEEN. Thematically, the audience sees good and evil through the eyes of the Na'vi—sees the good that we all have within us, our ability to empathize with each other, and our longing for a sense of connection, not just with other humans but with nature.

The writers realized that the third level was the most important and the hardest to achieve or even describe in words. It was, for want of a better word, the spiritual level. At this level the story, the characters, the culture, and the beauty of the film itself conspire to create a dreamlike feeling of connection to deeper meanings in life. The colors of the rainforest at night, and of the sacred trees—the pastel purples and cyans—suggest a benevolent energy network behind all of nature. Something vaster than us and our dominating human ego. There is a sense that in our civilized world we have lost something, a connection to nature, to a way of being, to a way of seeing that our indigenous wisdom-keepers still understand (though we dismiss and ignore them), but that we in the civilized world no longer remember. The wisdom of the ancestors, that we ignore at our peril. The film also connects us to that atavistic childhood wonder at the things around us, the trees, the animals, that indescribable feeling of being not only in nature, but of nature. The team concluded that the film induced a sense of longing, to be connected to the beauty and power and wisdom of nature, to forces and meanings far beyond the world that we see around us, day to day, in our urban world.

The writers realized they had an enormous challenge before them, to not only tell new stories with new characters and cultures in the Avatar universe, but to always embed, between the lines and within the imagery, that third level of "the numinous," of sacred beauty and connection. Otherwise, no matter how original and action-filled the stories might be, the films would fail.

Sigourney Weaver affirmed her view of Cameron's attitude to science fiction in an interview she gave to *Esquire* magazine in 2009: "James Cameron said, 'Science fiction is the exploration of what it is to be human.'" The quote was resonant of many of *Avatar*'s metaphysical concepts. "The edict that we face as we write science fiction for the screen is the exploration of 'what it is to be

Above: *The Way of Water* shooting script.

Opposite page: Kiri concept art by Joe Pepe. Photoshop collage with digital paint, variant of an earlier design incorporating aspects of a photograph of a young Sigourney Weaver.

"James Cameron said, 'Science fiction is the exploration of what it is to be human.'"

Sigourney Weaver, actor

human,'" Cameron observed. "I extrapolated from that, 'What is it to be in a family?' or 'What is it to be accepted in a clan?' 'What is acceptance, or identity?' After *Avatar*, Jake is physically Na'vi. He breathes Pandora's air and is of that ecosystem, he eats food that a human couldn't eat, but he is still himself."

The writers attacked concepts from high altitude, riffing off ideas that Cameron presented in the 1,500 pages of notes that he had generated during his sojourn as solo writer. "It was hours of unbelievable ideas," remarked Amanda Silver. "We sat there with grins on our faces while Jim was recounting ideas for creatures and characters and storylines. Jim is a brilliant writer. But part of the reason, I think, why he brought us all together was because it was so much material to wrangle that he felt like having many minds in the room would be helpful. We were fresh eyes. It was an extremely collaborative and creative process, with Jim's vision always at the helm."

In a unique arrangement, Cameron developed the designs in parallel with the story, with the art department working on the floor above the writers' room. A synergy sparked between the two creative cells, which would normally have been quite separate on a conventional feature film. "I inhabit both worlds," said Cameron. "I come from a design background. I also come from a writing background. I surround myself with images when I'm writing solo, so when I was putting together the writers' room, I wanted the art team close by. The writing room and art department were a stairwell away—the back fire stairs were the quickest way to get between them. We worked in a virtuous feedback loop."

"Normally our job comes after the writers," noted Dylan Cole. "We'll get the script, interpret scenes, talk to the director. To have feedback from the writers was thrilling. We never had official meetings with them; it was always through Jim. But the fun part was the impromptu meetings when we'd see them in the halls, or at lunch, and we'd have backdoor conversations. Jim would typically come upstairs for a review, and we might not know how that went over. Later, one of the writers might say, 'Oh, he loved that!' Jim might say to us, 'Why don't you concentrate on this now?' And so, we'd know what they were

"It became clear that we were working through, at its core, a family story."

Josh Friedman, screenwriter

Above: The Sully kids and Spider. Concept art by John Park.

Left: Jake tries to resolve an argument between Kiri and Lo'ak. Concept art by John Park.

working on. Other times, Jim would run up and rip prints off the wall, 'Ah, cool, I need these!'"

These artwork hard copies would be put up in the writers' room for constant inspiration. The torrent of artwork emerging from the second floor included renderings of environments, sets, creatures, and characters, created by the likes of Steve Messing, Fausto DeMartini, David Levy, and John Park. Joe Pepe, a veteran of Stan Winston Studio, became Lightstorm's lead in-house character designer, while Weta Workshop and Legacy Effects also contributed to this aspect. The Legacy team were literally continuing the legacy of their former boss and beloved mentor, Stan Winston, who passed away in 2008.

The sequels took into account the 15 years that had passed since Jake's arrival on Pandora, in 2154. His union with Neytiri has now blossomed into a family. The Sully clan includes two teenage sons—proud, athletic Neteyam (Jamie Flatters), and the younger, brooding Lo'ak (Britain Dalton)—as well as their precocious youngest, daughter Tuktirey (Trinity Bliss), who was usually just called Tuk.

The Sullys have adopted teenager Kiri (Sigourney Weaver), a Na'vi-human hybrid girl mysteriously born from the comatose avatar of the deceased Dr. Augustine. Joe Pepe's rendering of Kiri was particularly impactful for writers attempting to visualize Cameron's concept of casting the mature adult Weaver as an adolescent Na'vi. "I remember the first time I saw Sigourney as Kiri," said Shane Salerno. "They had taken a photo of Sigourney when she was a teenager and made her Na'vi. I must have looked at that for 20 minutes."

The family dynamic was central to the saga. "It became clear that we were working through, at its core, a family story," noted Josh Friedman. "Jim has a big, bustling family of kids that he's very involved with. As much as he's a director, he's a parent. I have a 20-year-old son, who was a lot younger when we started. Rick and Amanda have two kids. We all spent a lot of time talking about relationships, about being parents, and those responsibilities, wrestling with obligations of career or leadership and balancing those with your family's welfare and parental anxieties. I see many sides of that in Jim: as well as his strong public persona and his private life as a parent, I still see the 1970s hippie who was playing in streams and sketching. That's a prominent part of his operating system. And he is an emotional filmmaker. In any of Jim's movies, you'll find the primary core of an emotional relationship. Of course, he's a gifted visual storyteller, but that is always married to an emotional point of view. They are not contradictory elements."

Writers' assistant Danny Shelby kept a daily log of writers' room discussions, amounting to hundreds of pages of notes. Ten-hour days ensured complete immersion in the story, which took shape on whiteboards. "The boards were broken up by movie," remarked Shane Salerno, "but it was also fluid. If anyone had a major idea, it had to run through all the movies. It was like a jigsaw puzzle where, if you altered one piece, we had to go back and weave everything through." The process was collaborative. "Jim tasked us with writing outlines for the movies that we don't have screenplay credit on. Everybody cross-pollinated. Jim didn't tell us which movie we were writing until the last day in the room. That was smart because he didn't want us hoarding scenes."

The team referred to each film by shorthand as A2, A3, and so on. Plotting was complex. After introducing Jake and his family sheltering in the Omatikaya's High Camp settlement, in the relative safety of the Hallelujah Mountains, the story introduces the son of Jake's deceased former commanding officer—Miles "Spider" Socorro (Jack Champion). His father was the human Colonel Miles Quaritch, hence his first name. His mother was a gunship pilot, Captain Paz Socorro. It was a clandestine affair, due to the threat of disciplinary action to a senior officer such as Quaritch "fraternizing" with a subordinate in his chain of command. The two never married, so Spider bears his mother's last name. His parent's tempestuous relationship was an open secret in the small world of the human base, light-years from Earth's command authority.

Both of Spider's parents were killed the same day, though separately, in the Battle of the Hallelujah Mountains. When Jake sent the surviving humans packing back to Earth, Spider had to remain behind on Pandora because the cryo-capsules on the starship could not accommodate an infant. So Spider was raised by "the village" of the Avatar Program techs and scientists, now led by Dr. Norm Spellman.

The human boy grows up with the Sully children and spends as much time as he can roaming the forest with them, wearing an "exopack" breathing mask. He begrudgingly spends the rest of his time at Hell's Gate, the human base. Spider's character introduces into the story an important theme of estranged fathers and sons.

Spider has a relationship with Kiri," related Amanda Silver. "He has relationships with her brothers, with Neytiri, with Jake, with *Eywa*, with the guys in the lab at RDA. It was meticulously planned. And that's partly why A2 got so long. We were servicing all these different relationships threading through the movie. It was like writing a piece of music with many different instruments, and they all had to come together in the right way while keeping the audience engaged. It's not by accident that you care about what happens between Spider and Kiri, or with Lo'ak and Payakan," Silver added, referring to another subplot—the close relationship that develops between Jake's youngest son and a massive ocean creature, a *tulkun*. "You care about those things because we've been nurturing those dynamics to keep the audience engaged."

The early scenes had to include a torrent of narrative information—reintroducing Pandora, Jake, and Neytiri, the Omatikaya Clan, the expulsion of the RDA,

Spider and the new members of the Sully family, and finally the devastating return of the RDA that sets the stage for the real start of the story. "The challenge we faced was to get across all of that story within five pages or less," said Rick Jaffa. "But what Jim stated, and was the top priority, was to understand that Neytiri and Jake are warriors who were once unafraid of anything. Now they are parents, they understand fear for the first time. Real fear, being a parent in a crazy, wild world that has now been invaded by the bad guys."

Each writer took passes at different acts in treatment form, and then full treatments were assembled for all three sequels. Finally, after six months of workshopping the stories, from July through December of 2013, Cameron assigned the actual screenplays. Jaffa and Silver were given A2. A3 went to Josh Friedman, and A4 to Shane Salerno. Cameron's role was to be a co-writer on each of the three writing teams. The room then disbanded and the writers separated to work on their assigned drafts.

"Jim knew exactly what we were writing, beat by beat, scene by scene," asserted Amanda Silver. "It was a lot of material, especially in what A2 had to encompass. The first act of A2 became very long, and then the second act had a lot to cover."

Cameron responded to Jaffa and Silver's first pages in a detailed email that kept in mind the saga overview. "We were still getting our sea legs as a group with A2," Rick Jaffa recalled. "What happened when we sent our first 40, 50 pages to Jim, he sent us a beautiful email back, telling us how it was all coming together, except that he was worried it was going to be long. We agreed. But Jim's first decision was to say, 'Keep writing. Don't censor yourself.'"

Realizing that the most difficult part of the whole arc would be act 1 of A2, Cameron took on that challenge himself, sending Rick and Amanda on their own to work out act 2 and 3. Not only did the first act need to call back the important events of the first *Avatar*, after over a decade between films, but it needed to establish the Sully family's new members, account for their growth through the subsequent 15 years of the backstory, efficiently show the return of the human invaders and their absolute victory, then jump one year forward to establish the return of Colonel Quaritch and his special ops team as Recombinant human-Na'vi hybrids. Then, and only then, could the actual story begin—of Quaritch's hunt for public enemy number one, Jake Sully. In the team's original treatment, this first act also included Spider's transformation into the "Airbreather," a plot development critical to the entire saga.

After over a year and literally 12 attempts to craft the first act, Cameron finally admitted it couldn't be done. Then, in fall of 2014, an unexpected inspiration struck. He realized he could take the story of A2 and unzip it into two separate movies, by moving the Airbreather transformation into the second film (which would become A3). He could make it the major plot development of that film's first act. This allowed the still-massive burden of all the backstory and setup in A2 to actually be accomplished within the first hour of the film, a fitting length for the first act of a three-hour epic. Cameron took the second and third acts submitted by Rick and Amanda, and his own first act attempts, threw it all into a mental blender, and restructured the whole thing into two separate scripts, which ultimately would be titled *Avatar: The Way of Water* and *Avatar: Fire and Ash*. In this new configuration, Josh's A3 then became NA4 (New Avatar 4) and Shane's A4 then became NA5.

At first fearful of the expansion of the saga, 20th Century Fox execs came to embrace the new story structure and the massive four-film arc was greenlit for production. As the start of principal capture loomed in 2017, 20th Century Fox was acquired by the Walt Disney Company for 71.3 billion dollars. It is widely assumed that the Avatar franchise was one of the jewels in the crown of that acquisition. Cameron's new bosses at Disney were excited to embark on the epic franchise. The Walt Disney Company had, at that point, already made a massive investment in the Avatar universe by creating its ambitious and highly successful themed "land" in Orlando, Florida... Pandora, the World of Avatar. Disney's top management believed that a virtuous feedback loop could be created between the new films and additional park attractions that would be developed in coming decades, around the world.

> "But Jim's first decision was to say, 'Keep writing. Don't censor yourself.'"
>
> **Rick Jaffa, screenwriter**

With the restructure into four films, the pressure to condense the writing was removed. There would now be more screen time available to focus on family and character development. Jake's fear for his family's safety comes through in his overbearing attitude toward his sons, which creates a father-son rift, especially with Lo'ak. Jake's focus on Neteyam creates resentment in Lo'ak, who feels neglected and persecuted. He seeks solace with the outcast *tulkun* Payakan. A third paternal thread emerges in the return of Colonel Miles Quaritch as part of the RDA's Project Phoenix, in which deceased warfighters with years of experience on Pandora are resurrected through Recombinant

Opposite page: In a key image from *The Way of Water*, Jake Sully's youngest son, Lo'ak, bonds with the outcast *tulkun* Payakan. Screenshot by Weta.

Above: While testing out Pandora's immune response to the Recoms, Recom Quaritch stumbles on the site of his last encounter with Jake and Neytiri—and views the skeletal remains of Colonel Miles Quaritch.

genetic engineering. Their encoded memories are imprinted into the new bodies—which allows Spider's biological father to return as a fierce, 10-foot-tall, blue-skinned "Recom" version of the Colonel. Though Spider carries the burden of shame amongst his Na'vi friends—that he is the son of their presumably deceased mortal enemy—he secretly longs to know more about his father. His longing for family, for a father, for an identity that is acknowledged by some community somewhere, leads him into treacherous waters when this strange version of his father enters his life. Is this his father? His enemy? Or something that is at once both and neither?

The return of Quaritch was an initial surprise to the writing team. "Jim asked us who we thought the villain of the next movie was going to be," recalled Josh Friedman. "Rick, Amanda, Shane, and I spent time working out who was going to be the new antagonist. We knew Quaritch died in *Avatar*. So, who was it going to be? We pitched different ideas. Jim responded, 'Okay, that's interesting. It's Quaritch.'" The writers soon rallied to the possibilities of Quaritch's worldview as a Na'vi. "One of the brilliant things about the first movie is that Jake's mission is what undoes him. It was like a classic undercover cop story, he infiltrates the mob and falls in love with the mobster's daughter, but he has to keep reporting back. And the better he does his job, the more you fear for him, because he's pulling himself apart. He sees how beautiful the forest is, he learns to fly an *ikran*—all those wonderful things. In A2, Quaritch not only has to think like Jake, he has to go through the same arc that Jake has gone through. To conquer the moon, he has to understand Jake. He has to become Na'vi, just like Jake."

Cameron explained the RDA technology where volunteers backed up their consciousness to a "Soul Drive," which facilitated their rebirth as Recombinant "Recom" hybrids in Project Phoenix. "It was interesting," concurred Rick Jaffa. "I wouldn't say we 'pushed back,' but there was a lot of us glancing at each other. 'How's this going to work, exactly?' Part of the reason we questioned Jim was a solid reason, which is there have to be consequences on Pandora. I mean, everybody just can't die and come back. But Jim presented his case, we went with it, and it worked beautifully."

The appearance of the Recom Colonel with gung-ho Corporal Wainfleet (Matt Gerald) personalizes Jake's fears and allows for eerie scenes, including a memorable moment where Quaritch discovers his human remains in the jungle. The giant blue warrior picks up and contemplates his much smaller former skull, in an image inspired by *Hamlet*, then crushes it to fragments. Stephen Lang himself proposed this scene to Cameron, who loved the idea, and wrote it into his act one. It was such a strong visual, symbolizing Quaritch's existential dilemma. Am I this guy? Or someone completely new? Must I play out the destiny of a man who no longer exists? By crushing the skull, he makes a decision to be his own man, and to forge his own destiny. But can he ever truly escape who he was? Is he not still the essence of that man, complete with all his memories and impulses? He is in a deep identity crisis. All of this is further complicated when he is confronted by human Quaritch's son, Spider. At first he rejects any sense of duty to Spider. But as events unfold, he is drawn to Spider as an externalization of his own identity, a son who somehow gives him

“We realized, when it’s fun to write, it’s going to be fun to watch.”

Amanda Silver, screenwriter

meaning. His deepest fear is that he is a construct, an echo—the ghost of a dead man. But his feelings for Spider are both new and real, and seem to give him purpose. In his borrowed memories, he remembers Spider as a baby and how he felt then as a father. How it was shifting all his priorities. Now those feelings are back, and shifting his priorities again.

"When Quaritch wakes up," related Amanda Silver, "He realizes he's blue and he's become the enemy. But the power of being on Pandora in a Na'vi body, the possibility, the danger, and the wish-fulfillment, as Quaritch feels the strength and finds his way around—that was so much fun to write. And we realized, when it's fun to write, it's going to be fun to watch."

While wrestling with themes and character arcs, Cameron and his writers bore in mind the sense of visual majesty that had made *Avatar* so compelling. *The Black Stallion*, Carroll Ballard's 1979 film based on a book by Walter Farley, became a frame of reference in the development of Lo'ak's story. "I remembered seeing *The Black Stallion* as a boy," said Shane Salerno. "There were wordless sequences of wonder with this boy and horse silhouetted against the sun. In sequences where we were talking about the relationship with Lo'ak and Payakan, we were going to have to rely on visual storytelling for large chunks of time. There's an extraordinary sequence where we leave our lead characters to focus on that moment. It was galvanizing in what we were trying to do, and Jim decided to embrace that." Salerno also referred his colleagues to a YouTube video of a woman swimming underwater with a whale. "Jim was mesmerized by that image. Years later, my mom told me her favorite parts of the movie were the quiet moments of the boy and the *tulkun*."

Lo'ak touching Payakan's fin became an integral image of *The Way of Water*. Underwater scenes and images of the Metkayina community living in *marui* habitats above the sapphire-blue ocean immersed the audience in unexpected wonder as Jake and his family find new beauty hundreds of miles from their forest home. "When we get to the reef," said Amanda Silver, "we're suffused with awe at the beauty of the water and the creatures. We paid a lot of attention to moments discovering the physical nature of the beauty of this world. We contrasted that with the ugliness of the RDA and their weapons. And then, character development was the anchor for that."

Character designs continued to take shape as Lightstorm developed concepts for the far-flung clans. The Reef People's physique and skin tone suggested many thousands of years living separately from the forest Na'vi and in symbiosis with the ocean. "We looked to where they lived and to how they had adapted," added Dylan Cole. "The Metkayina have a strong dorsal and ventral coloring, like a dolphin or a shark. They have thicker tails for swimming, and they have strakes"—referring to the cartilaginous fins on the Metkayina forearms and legs.

Pandoran oceangoing creatures continued to exhibit hexapodal anatomy—the six-limbed motif established with megafauna in *Avatar*—including the majestic *tulkun*, the predatory akula, the skimwings (*tsurak* in Na'vi), and the Metkayina's plesiosaur-like mounts, the *ilu*. "The *tulkun* have big pectoral fins," noted Cole, "but then they also have the cephalic [forward] fins, the fin that Lo'ak uses to ride on Payakan. The *ilu* have two larger rear sets of fins and two canard fins on the neck."

While the *ilu* were meant to be playful, social, and communicative, like dolphins, the skimwings are lone-wolf apex predators and quite fierce. The Metkayina consider the latter to be a "warrior's mount" suitable only for adults to ride. The *ilu* are like ponies that anyone can ride, and a large social pod of them live in the shallow waters around the village.

Concurrent with explorations into Pandora's zoology, the art department introduced new RDA technology in the highly fortified walled city of Bridgehead, commanded by General Ardmore (Edie Falco). "We saw the RDA lose in *Avatar*," observed Ben Procter. "The idea is they'll never again allow the Na'vi to catch them by surprise. They now know that the threat is not just the Na'vi, but also the entire planet."

The RDA forces return in an interstellar invasion fleet comprising 10 starships, called ISVs (Interstellar Vehicles). As the ISVs descend into the Pandoran atmosphere, hovering on the mile-long exhaust plumes from their antimatter engines, they incinerate a 10-mile-diameter Kill Zone, a gaping wound in the jungle. On cables they lower "sling-load" Landing Modules. Ben Procter's team modeled the Landing Module as a 40-story-tall triangular block on three piston-like landing legs. Visual effects supervisor David Vickery and his artists at ILM's campus in London, England, were tasked with realizing the scenes of the fleet arriving, the Modules landing, and the deployment of massive bulldozers to clear the remains of the incinerated forest. At the center of the circle of barren, scorched earth, the human invaders build a city for tens of thousands of RDA employees, ringed by a massive defensive wall. This new base of operations is dubbed Bridgehead.

Overleaf: Concept art of Bridgehead at night by Jonathan Berube.

"3D models and 3D layouts are the backbone of everything Avatar."

Ben Procter, production designer

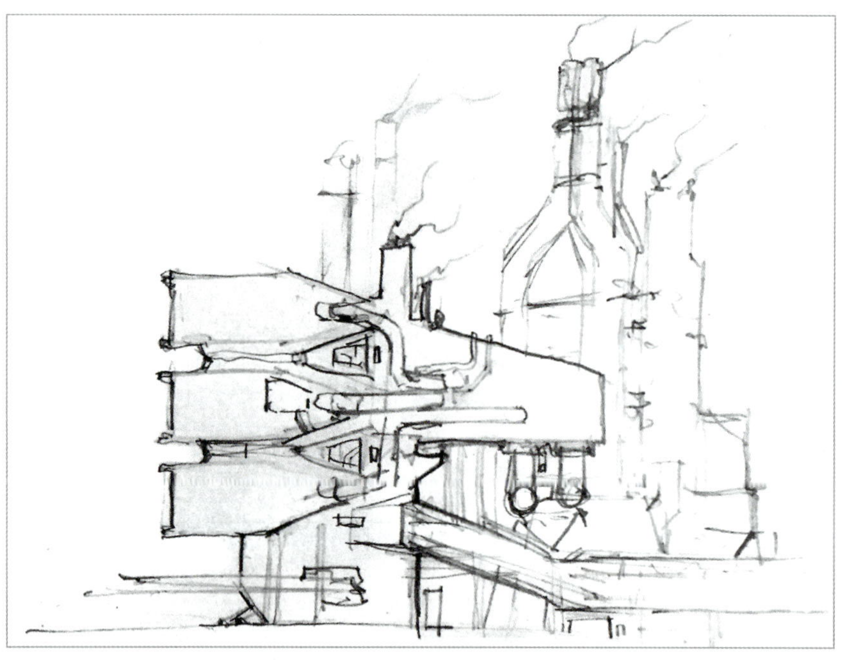

Left: Bridgehead refinery sketch by Ben Procter.

Below: Bridgehead concept art by Fausto De Martini.

The new technology the RDA arrives with includes Skel Suits, powered exoskeletons that can give a human operator the size, strength, and agility of a Na'vi. Unlike the lumbering AMP Suits featured in *Avatar*, which were realized using large-scale practical builds from Legacy Effects, the Skel Suit was an all-digital creation. "The Skel was an opportunity to give RDA more of a fighting chance against Na'vi," said Procter. "We needed a way for Ardmore to have a conversation with Quaritch face-to-face. It was technological world-building." Digital artists used combinations of 3D modeling and 2D texture painting to create conceptual designs, such as the "Skels," that then became assets for the Virtual Art Department. "3D models and 3D layouts are the backbone of everything Avatar," noted Procter. "There's nothing we do that doesn't involve 3D geometry and modeling. In our concept phase, we have a lot of artists who are very experienced in 3D, as well as doing Photoshop painting to solve design problems or to just begin designing. Very often, we work directly in 3D. They'll start with a rough 3D layout and paint-overs. And some artists profoundly embrace 3D—adding textures, lighting, and then rendering to create the concept art." Note that this use of the term 3D refers to volumetric computer modeling, not to be confused with stereoscopic 3D, which is the format in which the film itself is presented in theaters.

"The biggest challenge for me as the hard-surface production designer, was how to keep it fresh," recalls Ben Procter. "As an architectural motif, Bridgehead was military but it's also a construction site. That gave us opportunities to introduce bright colors. It was important to consider how the RDA people think of themselves. There is heroism in what they are doing, and an engineering ambition. To the people of Pandora, they are antagonists. But for the RDA, their everyday job is super exciting. We tried to understand that internal excitement and heroism in our designs."

The RDA soon threatens Jake's sanctuary among the Metkayina, as their exploitation of Pandora expands to its oceans. In A2, a new extraction industry is introduced, in addition to the mining of Unobtanium that drove interstellar commerce in A1. The brains of the *tulkun* contain a gland that secretes "*amrita*," a honey-colored substance that turns out to be the most valuable commodity in the human economy on Earth. A fleet of SeaDragon ships is deployed to hunt the peaceful *tulkun*, under the command of the Cet-Ops Division (Cetacean Operations, pronounced "seh-tops").

Amrita—a Sanskrit word for the elixir of the gods that conveyed immortality in ancient Hindu mythology—is a cure for human aging. Because it is naturally produced in the brains of the great *tulkun*, and cannot be synthesized even in the advanced biolabs of Earth, it is the driving force behind the relentless hunting and harvesting of the *tulkun* by the Cet-Ops fleet.

This concept was based on the 18th- and 19th-century whalers who hunted whale populations almost to extinction in pursuit of ambergris. This was a waxy

Above: Skel Suit concept art by Fausto De Martini.

substance extracted from whales' intestines, used in the manufacture of expensive perfumes. "Ambergris was worth a lot of money," noted Amanda Silver. "Hunters would kill these beautiful, huge whales, for a little bit of this substance. We needed a reason for the *tulkun* to be hunted, so that became an essential part of our story and a natural connection."

Quaritch decides that the best way to flush Jake Sully out of hiding is to provoke the sea-dwelling Na'vi, forcing them to fight, and Jake along with them. To do this he aligns with Captain Mick Scoresby and his whaling operation. He redirects them to the archipelago where Quaritch believes the Sullys have gone to ground. That region's *tulkun* and the Metkayina clan enjoy a merged culture, a cross-species symbiosis that is sacred to both. The Reef People would be quick to defend their *tulkun* Spirit Brothers and Sisters. Complicating this, Lo'ak has befriended the outcast, Payakan, and has become "Brother of Tulkun" in a merging ceremony.

These story threads all converge for *The Way of Water*'s finale, which ends with tragedy and sacrifice. Payakan comes to the Sully family's aid during a confrontation with Quaritch's Recom squad onboard the SeaDragon, but in the skirmish that results, Jake's son Neteyam is shot and dies.

***

The tragic outcome of *The Way of Water* sets the stage for A3—*Avatar: Fire and Ash*—with a new focus on Lo'ak, who becomes that film's narrator. Themes of loss and redemption dominate the third story. In intertwining narrative threads, Lo'ak attempts to atone for the death of Neteyam; Jake faces the RDA to protect his family; and Kiri's deepening relationship with Spider transforms the "pinkskin" boy into what Jake realizes is a new threat to Pandora.

The dramatic arc in A3 is catalyzed by the introduction of new Na'vi cultures, chief among them the Mangkwan, also known as the Ash People, who burst onto the scene as a fearsome clan of raiders who plunder any other clans that cross their path. "Jim felt strongly that it was important to show that there are good Na'vi and bad Na'vi," recalled Amanda Silver. "They are not all noble creatures. The Mangkwan are nihilists. Anything beautiful that the other characters love—about *Eywa*, about Pandora—they want to destroy. In an

"Jim felt strongly that it was important to show that there are good Na'vi and bad Na'vi."

Amanda Silver, scriptwriter

Above: The Ash People's village in the ruins of their incinerated Hometree. Concept art by Steven Messing.

Overleaf: The desolation of the Ash Village took inspiration, in part, from the aftermath of the fall of the Omatikayan Hometree. Concept art by Steven Messing.

Opposite page, above: RDA Cet-Ops sea craft escort a nearly 400-foot SeaDragon *tulkun*-hunting platform. Paul Ozzimo illustration based on Fausto De Martini 3D models.

Opposite page, below: Cet-Ops Matadors and Picadors set out from the SeaDragon. Liam Beck illustration using geometry by Fausto De Martini, Ben Procter, and Alister Baxter.

alliance made in hell, the Ash People connect with Quaritch, and with the human colonizers of the RDA. It was a perfect way of escalating the danger against the moon and the characters."

The script describes the Mangkwan territory as a formerly lush rainforest that was devastated by volcanic eruption—a wasteland buried in gray ash, with the remains of trees poking through like skeletal black hands. The design team proposed that the Ash Village nest in the charred remains of what was once their Hometree. "The burned-out Hometree was an art department idea," said Dylan Cole. "I was in conversation with Jim and Steve Messing, trying to figure out where the Ash People could live. In Mangkwan lore, 15 to 20 years earlier this volcano obliterated their Hometree and so they forsook *Eywa*. But they didn't move on. This was their home, so they decided to stay. The idea is that they weren't incredibly warlike before, but no one liked them. And now, they're full-on assholes, with a culture of dominance and raiding."

To realize the art department's designs, Weta analyzed imagery from volcanic desolation in Papua New Guinea. Cameron gave them reference video he had shot on his 2012 expedition in the town of Rabaul, which had been buried under 30 feet of ash when the nearby Tavurvur volcano exploded in 1994. This event, and his personal involvement with the people of Rabaul, were Cameron's inspiration for the Ash People. In the video, children playing with handmade toys kicked up clouds of gray ash as they ran among the desolate mounds, where the ruins of three-story buildings poked up skeletally. To Cameron it was at once a sad and hopeful image, to see the next generation growing up untraumatized, despite the destruction all around them.

"The terrain was very black and white," said visual-effects supervisor Eric Saindon, "Into that, we added color from the Ash People's set dressings, and we lit that with strong sunlight. It was the opposite of jungle scenes, where we used blue tones to make the Na'vi fit into that world. In the Ash Village, the Mangkwan are mostly white with their ash makeup, and black and red war paint. It's very stark."

The Ash People's aggressive nature is embodied by their ruthless leader, Varang (Oona Chaplin). "We started with an illustration Joe Pepe did with an [early version] of Varang's headdress," said Cole. "It suggested strength and dominance, empowering Varang above all the men who serve her. In Jim's script, when she connects to someone with her *kuru* she shocks and dominates them physically. We went minimal with her costume—just a couple of strings across her breasts and a loincloth—and stark with her body paint and makeup. Her power comes through in her personality." The Mangkwan's fearsome appearance was influenced in part by the pulp fiction of Robert E. Howard, creator of *Conan the Barbarian*. "My joke was I'd put on my Conan hat, adding spikes and tusks, with ornamented skulls. But the Mangkwan are not savages. They are Na'vi, so they are intelligent and talented craftspeople. It's scarier if they're smart."

Costume designer Deborah Scott, along with her teams in Los Angeles and at Richard Taylor's Weta Workshop, took on a huge role in the creation of wardrobe and props for the two new Na'vi clans—the Tlalim Wind Traders and the Ash People—embodying their very different cultures and customs. Working from Lightstorm concepts created by production designer Dylan Cole and his team, Weta Workshop explored Wind Trader designs, including how the Tlalim steer and control their giant airborne gondolas. In *Fire and Ash*, a Wind Trader fleet led by their *olo'eyktan*, Peylak (David Thewlis) arrives at the Metkayina reef village, to much celebration." The Wind Traders' skin is more weathered because they are out in the elements all day," noted Cole. "We differentiated them with wardrobe, culture, and design."

"We thought of them in a nautical way," recalled Josh Friedman. "They are not pirates, but they take the trade winds and move around. I wanted to depict a culture that felt independent of cultural equivalence, and it was also a fun creative exercise. The Tlalim have a ritualized component. They are a mercantile trader culture that is not beholden to anybody, they have their own set of values, and it was important to make sure they remained mysterious in that way."

The Tlalim trade with many clans, including the Metkayina, along global trade routes, carrying their wares in gondolas borne aloft by vast, jellyfish-like medusoids towed by windrays. These flying creatures owe their origins to drawings that James Cameron first made in his twenties, for his unrealized

> "The medusoid [is] like a giant flying Portuguese man o' war, about the size of the biggest blimp that ever existed."
>
> **Dylan Cole, production designer**

Opposite page: The Wind Trader flotilla approaches the Metkayina village. Concept art by Dylan Cole.

Xenogenesis feature, and briefly wrote into the first draft of *Avatar*. "Jim finally got them in," commented Dylan Cole. "The medusoid remained essentially the same idea, but the design evolved. It's like a giant flying Portuguese man o' war, about the size of the biggest blimp that ever existed. The gondola that it carries is like a mini-village, a Na'vi-scale multilevel ship." Windrays and medusoids remain aloft indefinitely, due to their lighter-than-air bodies, filled with biogenically produced hydrogen gas. "They both use a similar system to levitate, with different systems of propulsion. The windray is more like a cuttlefish with a mantle that moves in a sinusoidal way, propelling it forward. The medusoid flows with the breeze, but has big vanes, as we called them, forming a large bowtie-shaped sail that it can direct. It can generate or release gas for lift and descent. And it feeds through tentacles that it lowers into oceans to pull up fish."

Months of work were required to figure out how, exactly, the Wind Traders would sail their ships of the air. Actors and extras require precise direction, specific behaviors. The director wanted a nautical feel, reminiscent of the bygone era of sail on Earth. For a conventional nautical movie you would get experts on how tall ships were crewed, who would then train the actors and extras.

But an aerial ship maneuvers differently. In the ocean, a sailing ship has a keel, which holds the ship firm against the wind. The sails can be angled to generate "lift," the force that propels the ship forward. But an airship drifts with the wind. It has no hull in the water to hold it against the wind and generate lift in a transverse direction. Cameron concluded that the Wind Trader gondolas would need to be actively propelled in order to vector relative to the wind, like sailing ships. But the Na'vi don't have motors and propellers, like those on a blimp or Zeppelin. Thus the windray was introduced—a lighter-than-air creature that could propel itself with powerful thrusts of its fins.

But to take advantage of fair winds, and not just drag the gondolas around using a windray, the Tlalim need to "sail" their medusoids as well. These living balloons have enormous vanes on each side. The idea is that the Na'vi crew can angle these vanes to catch the wind. But since the medusoid has a very primitive nervous system, and can't be controlled by a *kuru* connection like the *ikran*, the crew would need to use rope lines, like on a sailing ship, to furl and unfurl the vanes as needed and to orient them to the wind.

This allowed the director to introduce the nautical vocabulary he was looking for. He worked with the art department and Jonathan Bach along with Cole, to create a detailed rigging plan. And, wearing his writer hat, he wrote up a couple of pages of nautical-flavored commands that Peylak and his officers would use to direct the crew. Starboard and port, conventional Earth nautical terms, were used. The conceit here was that the Na'vi would obviously have words in their native language for the left and right sides of a ship. But since the audience is hearing English but imagining it is all spoken in Na'vi, the director was comfortable using the familiar terms—a recognizable nautical vocabulary, albeit in an alien setting.

Weta Workshop Wind Trader costume concepts took inspiration from mountain-dwelling cultures. "It all had to feel very specifically Na'vi," noted Taylor, "but similar to how people of Tibetan cultures might wear trousers, shirts, hats, and gloves, and those items would be totally different in, for example, South American cultures. We wanted to suggest a similar diversity between Metkayina and the Tlalim. Wind Trader concepts were extensive and elaborate, and we built models of items hanging from their gondolas, showing how they dropped sea anchors into oceans to steer."

The wardrobe department explored Wind Trader costume textures and colors of fabric suited to high-altitude navigation. "Jim's concept was they fly high up in the sky where it's cold," added Deborah Scott. "I worked with artists and designers, some from LA, some from Weta Workshop, who all contributed ideas, and I did a lot of photographic research into colorful garments and plants, until we filled a room with photos and designs that spanned this world. This was such a big project and Jim's time is so precious, we all worked toward making environmental rooms for him to enter to see the world." Wind Trader costumes featured natural fabrics, which Scott's team crafted with looms and other traditional processes. "The Wind Traders are into cloth, with capes and woolen items, like skirts and loincloths, which are very decorative and colorful. And to prevent their hair flying in the winds, we gave them hairstyles that were cut close to their heads."

> "But I believed in Oona for this role. And man, she did not let us down. What a performance she gave! One for the ages."
>
> **James Cameron**

The villains of *Fire and Ash*—the Ash People and their sorceress leader, Varang—especially energized the design crew. Joe Pepe scoured photography of many cultures, including the Nuba, the indigenous people of central Sudan, whom German documentarian Leni Riefenstahl had studied before the Nuba's enforced relocation in the 1970s. "The Nuba would cover themselves in ash," related Pepe. "They used liquefied fat to create lines through the ash that would make their skin shiny in areas. They also did a lot of scarification."

The Mangkwan warriors make their dramatic entrance, swooping down on the caravan of Wind Trader gondolas where Spider and the Sully family are traveling with the Tlalim, high above the Pandoran rainforest. "I told Jim the audience was in for a shock," said Weta's Richard Taylor. "Jim responded that he knew he was taking a big risk, but he wanted to switch it up." Designers equated the Ash People's darker aspects, inflicting pain on themselves with piercings and ritual scarification, to medieval religious practices. "It's like monks whipping themselves with birch branches, the subjugation of oneself, and one's tribe, through suffering. They have horrific keloid scarring, cinching, and self-torturing."

"The Mangkwan are masochistic, they're aggressive, violent," asserted Deborah Scott. "They are all about fire and ash, and they have a very charismatic leader. They have barely any body coverings and are painted all over. Jim was clear that he wanted to use red, white, and black colorations. We did a lot of research into paints. We knew the clan lives in a burned out, volcanic environment, so they use materials that they have on hand."

The Mangkwan leader, Varang, would emerge as the most important new character introduced in *Fire and Ash*. Even before Oona Chaplin was cast to play her, a detailed design was being developed for the character. Joe Pepe generated an early Photoshop study for Varang based on a fashion model headshot. "That was such a fun time for me," noted Pepe. "Jim invited me to his writing office below our second-floor art department. That's where he had his editing suite and private room. He asked me to help him choose between the three actors he was auditioning for Varang. When he showed me images of Oona Chaplin—at the time, I hadn't seen *Game of Thrones*, and I didn't know who Oona was—I immediately knew she was [perfect for] Varang." Cameron asked for renderings of each candidate, and Pepe was inspired. "With Oona, the elements just fit perfectly. She even has this little button under her lip—Oona calls it her 'blip'—that when she smiles is so unique. I showed the concepts to Jim. He had his notes; I finessed them. And then Jon Landau came to me, 'Hey, make sure you push Oona as Varang.' And I told Jon, 'Oh, don't worry. She's my favorite!'"

Cameron pushes back a little on Pepe's recollection, saying, "The selection of Oona was based on her performance at her audition, not anything specific about her appearance. After months of searching and down-selecting, I auditioned three actresses for that role. The other two were movie stars, not character actors... two women that I greatly admire and who had been starring in big films for years. I was a huge admirer of both, and very excited to meet with them and do the audition work with them. On the other hand, Oona hadn't done much at the time, I don't think she'd even done *Game of Thrones* yet, and

Left: Weta Workshop Varang concept art by Rebekah Tisch.

Far left: Varang, *tsahik* of the Mangkwan, embodies her clan's rejection of Na'vi sprituality, and belief in the Gaia-like spirit of *Eywa*, since a volcanic eruption destroyed their Hometree. Designs made use of volcanic materials that suggested Varang's nihilistic expression of the scorched terrain. Maquette by Rebecca Tisch, Weta Workshop.

Above: Bone, leather, and metal materials featured in Varang's necklace, earrings, and other Mangkwan adornments. Weta Workshop concepts.

Above: Texture and color references also informed designs for the fearsome Mangkwan Ash People, including studies of war paint, piercings, scarifications, bone and feather adornments, as worn by Mangkwan villagers and (far right) the warrior Riku. Concepts by Weta Workshop.

Overleaf: Mangkwan villager concepts by (left) Adam Anderson and (right) Iona Brinch at Weta Workshop.

I had actually never heard of her. But her performance at the reading was mesmerizing. She seemed to understand the character so deeply. The ferocity, but also the keen intelligence, and the undercurrent of seduction. Varang is all about power and manipulation. What she can't get by force she will get through her hypnotic charisma, like a cobra hypnotizing its prey."

The audition consisted primarily of the scene in which Quaritch goes to the Ash village and she brings him into her yurt. This puts him out of sight of his overwatch sniper, Wainfleet, and thus in extreme jeopardy. Why does Quaritch put himself at her mercy?

"Her main scene with Quaritch is a double seduction," Cameron explains, "We first think he's in danger, helpless as a field mouse before a rattlesnake. By the end of the scene, we realize it's the other way around. He's been seducing her the entire time. She sees there's another person in her world that can be as powerful as her. And there was a sensual/erotic undercurrent to that seduction." The yurt scene is the longest in the movie, at over six minutes. A challenge for any actor to prepare for, going into an audition.

"Oona was firing on all cylinders of the character that day," Cameron remembers, "She really understood the scene. She understood there was a subtlety in the way Varang wielded power. I wanted to explore the complexity of her trauma, the anger that she feels, the control that she demands that's a result of that, and her vulnerability. I shoot auditions myself, handheld, and work closely with every actor. We had an easy repartee, and I quickly realized that I could work with her. When I played the video back, I couldn't take my eyes off her. She was riveting. It was one of the hardest casting decisions I ever made, to turn away from not one but two really exciting actresses that I had wanted to work with for years, to cast a relative unknown. But I believed in Oona for this role. And man, she did not let us down. What a performance she gave! One for the ages."

Above: Recom Quaritch allies with the Ash People's ruthless leader, Varang. Screenshot by Weta.

Opposite page: Varang meditating while bound with ropes. Concept art by Joe Pepe.

Nevertheless, the character of Varang now needed to be fitted to Oona. "All of our Na'vi characters began from concept art and 3D model turntables," said Weta animator Stuart Adcock. "And then we revised their facial models to help fit the actor to the model, some more than others. Because Varang was new to *Fire and Ash*, we wanted to make sure that Oona was Varang and vice versa, and her facial structure reinforced that."

Joe Pepe's concepts for Varang included an illustration of the Ash sorceress in a trance state, lit by firelight, bound with ropes in front of a giant tree root with her arms tied tightly behind her back. The concept evoked the ancient Japanese practice of kinbaku, a ritualized "tight binding" from the Edo period. Chaplin responded to the power of the image, which reflected her artistic interests in performance art. "That's where the idea for Varang's top [came from]," revealed Pepe. "There was a tribe in Africa where women use twine to bind their breasts. I thought that looked painful, but that's Varang."

Another concept showed her with grisly trophies of her victims. "I did one illustration of Varang standing with a spear of Na'vi heads. Jon Landau saw that and said, 'Oh, I don't think we're going to have severed heads on sticks!' Instead of Na'vi heads, Jim suggested using severed *kurus*—and that's a highly sensitive bundle of nerves." The cutting of a Na'vi's *kuru* is like a neurological castration, an atrocity that leaves them wishing for death. They lose all ability to connect to their creatures, to *Eywa*, to the Spirit World and thus the ancestors. It means that their memories and persona can no longer be uploaded to the Spirit World, and their spirit, after they die, will be incomplete as they walk the afterlife. There is no greater physical insult to a Na'vi than this barbaric act. And so it made sense to the director that Varang, who rules through fear, would be drawn to this ritual mutilation and collect trophies of her conquests, creating a "cloak of many *kurus*" to spread the legend of her ruthlessness and intimidate her enemies. This garment won't appear until Avatar 4, but even for A3 the idea of it helped define Varang's character and the ethos of the Mangkwan.

Varang dresses in corset-like ligatures, consistent with Deborah Scott's theme for her of Japanese ritual binding. With these ideas in mind, Weta Workshop manufacturing team lead by Flo Foxworthy and Lans Hansen fabricated a full-scale maquette of Varang that captured her power. "Varang is provocative," observed Richard Taylor. "She's manipulative, as a lot of tribal leaders need to be. She dances along a knife edge, relying on her matriarchal strength. Iona Brinch and Rebekah Tisch played with that in the 2D concept designs, working under the guidance of Deb to define this very complex character."

Varang's costume designs were further refined after Oona Chaplin's performance-capture sessions. "Jim decided that Varang shouldn't be so minimal," said Deborah Scott. "We went through six or seven variations of her

Above: Lo'ak and Tuk look on in wonder as Kiri's incantations cause life-giving mycelium to grow from the forest floor, encasing Spider. Screenshot by Weta.

wardrobe, becoming more expressive with leather, stone, and bone, to show how she's the head of the clan. The Mangkwan are also the only Na'vi clan that use metal—and their metalwork is crude and messy—but finding those elements tied the clan together through wardrobe design."

The Mangkwan are similar in body type to the Omatikaya and other forest Na'vi, including the Tlalim, whose aerial caravans ply the world's trade routes. Jake and Neytiri's journey with the Wind Traders, flying as outriders to guard the flotilla, ends in disaster as Varang and her Mangkwan raiders swoop down on their painted *ikran* in a ferocious attack. The subsequent air battle separates Jake and Neytiri from each other, and from their children, in hostile jungle territory. Varang's involvement in the story becomes an existential threat to Jake when Quaritch later forms an alliance between the Mangkwan and the RDA. This eventually results in a highly-charged relationship between the Recom Colonel and the Mangkwan leader, fueled by mutual objectives and a growing passionate attraction.

"There's a lot of history around Quaritch's methodology," remarked James Cameron. "There are pressures on him from his command; they don't understand what's happening out in the bush when he goes part-way native. That hearkens back to early American and Canadian history, to the *coureur du bois* French trappers who traded with the First Nations and conscripted tribes to fight on behalf of the French. Later, different tribes were given guns and convinced to fight either on behalf of the British or the Revolutionary forces in the Revolutionary War. The colonial forces played them off against each other. Later, the Green Berets got in trouble with their chain of command when they embedded with the Montagnards in Vietnam. Quaritch is on a fence. He could tip toward Jake's side, being drawn into Na'vi culture. Or, as he says in A3,

“Jake fights on behalf of *Eywa* and all the creatures on Pandora.”

Amanda Silver, screenwriter

he'll remember what side he's playing for. The dime is balanced on its edge and the question is, which way will it fall? We see there's good in him, and there could be a redemptive arc. When Varang comes along, she tips the balance."

Personal grievances added to the equation. "Jake Sully has humiliated Quaritch in the past," noted Amanda Silver. "Jake fights on behalf of *Eywa* and all the creatures on Pandora, who are connected through *Eywa*. Conquering nature and *Eywa* is what the RDA wants to do, to crush Pandora into submission. So, when Quaritch meets Varang, they share a common goal. They both hate *Eywa*. For anyone watching the movie who loves the splendors of Pandora, the audience is on *Eywa*'s side. That leant potency to these nemeses of *Eywa*. The fact that they joined forces was daunting and frightening, and great drama for us."

"It's a dangerous partnership," added Rick Jaffa. "It's like in history, whenever there have been alliances between countries that are 'bad guys,' as in World War Two, there's a feeling that these two could turn on each other at any time. That added another element between Quaritch and Varang, a simmering tension, which made their relationship even hotter. Amanda and I have been living with these characters for so long since we were in the writers' room in 2013. We can't wait for the audience to see those two meet up."

In the director's mind, Quaritch and Varang would become like Mark Antony and Cleopatra, the power couple from hell. They were fascinated by each other, madly in love, and their power fed on itself. Under Cleopatra's thrall, Antony defied Rome, changing the fates of both the Roman and Egyptian empires, the two most powerful civilizations of their time. Their love affair literally changed history.

Varang's attraction to Quaritch begins when they first meet. He holds her at gunpoint to facilitate the escape of the kids, but she turns the tables, subjugating him with her *kuru*. Her ability to use her ponytail-like "neural whip" to send a debilitating blast of energy into another person's brain is unique to Varang. As *tsahìk* of her people, she has trained herself in the dark side of Na'vi shamanic arts. Though she is accustomed to completely dominating any Na'vi with her mental powers, Quaritch is able to resist enough to break the connection. She is fascinated by the unexpectedly strong will of this "Sky Man." "The *kuru* makes a purple electrical spark," said Weta visual effects supervisor Eric Saindon. "You don't see that a lot in earlier *kuru* scenes because most of those happened in daylight."

Varang's *kuru* is revealed in detail when she subdues Quaritch. "When Varang moves her *kuru* toward him," Saindon related, "the tentacles inside her *kuru* aggressively surge forwards, and the other *kuru* pulls back, like a scared dog pulling its tail under. Jim wanted it to feel like her *kuru* was attacking, in a very aggressive maneuver, showing the way she's forcing herself on him. It's a little bit sexual, a little bit aggressive, and a very dominating way of connecting."

Later the dance between these two willful characters will escalate, when Varang leads Quaritch into her yurt in the Ash Village. There she uses her blowpipe to blast hallucinogenic "truth" dust into his nostrils, sending him into an altered state in which he appears to be totally subjugated to her will. However, as the scene progresses, he turns the tables on her—by using his truth-speaking state to lay before her a vision of world domination.

Quaritch's hallucinatory state, seen in POV, would become a plum assignment for Eric Saindon and his Weta artists, as they warped space and color, giving Varang a terrifying demonic aspect. "We took all the geometry close to camera," said Saindon, "and Jim had us give those textures "worms" under the surface, so the objects appeared to move like there were worms inside. Further back, we added streaking camera motion and light effects. It was a very colorful effect; and in stereo, it was really out there."

The scene in Varang's yurt would become Cameron's favorite of the entire film. As the power ebbs and flows between Varang and Quaritch, across the six minutes, the connection is forged between these two willful characters. The scene was a choice assignment for the Weta animation team, as they turned Stephen Lang and Oona Chaplin's performances into stunning photoreality. "Varang has a pretty large chip on her shoulder," commented animation lead, Dan Barrett. "Things have gone badly for her, in the way she believes *Eywa* has treated her people. She finds a partner in crime in Quaritch; or, at least, Quaritch finds a partner in crime in her. To use a Pandoran parlance, they "see" each other. It is an unholy alliance. Quaritch, in his drugged-up state, stands up to her and, at that point, they become lovers. It was a powerful scene with two actors at the peak of their powers, connecting in the Pandoran world. It was electric."

Another absolutely critical scene occurs much earlier in the story. As the Sully kids run through the jungle to escape the Ash, Spider's air supply runs out, and Kiri attempts to save his life by tapping into the network of the forest's roots. She is unsuccessful in getting the Great Mother to help her, and it is revealed later that she somehow has performed this miracle by herself. Her powers over the natural processes of the forest have become greater than those of even the most trained *tsahìk* (shaman).

After their rescue and return to the floating mountains, she connects to the Spirit World at the Omatikaya's most sacred site, the Tree of Souls, to beg the Great Mother for an explanation for how she can do these things. But *Eywa* does not answer her, in fact She actively shuts down Kiri's inquiry, by inducing a seizure. In Norm's scientific parlance, a firewall. There is something *Eywa* clearly does not want Kiri to know, at least not yet. The answer to this enigma does not come until later in the saga, so stay tuned.

"*Eywa* means different things to different people," said Jaffa. "We planted the seeds for Kiri's development all through A2. That continues in a very powerful and beautiful direction. It's a well-laid plan. Nature is the higher power in Pandora. That applies to all things that are open to that connection. Since Jim came up with *Avatar*, it's been scientifically proven that trees communicate with each other, [as do] whales. We did a lot of reading about those beautiful connections. It's out there. All you have to do is to connect to it."

Kiri's act of saving Spider's life—making him the first human able to breathe Pandora's air—puts her world in further jeopardy, potentially opening the floodgates to an influx of colonists from Earth.

Fire and Ash builds to a third-act climax when Quaritch attacks Jake and his family during a major *tulkun* gathering at the Cove of the Ancestors, the Metkayina's most sacred site. The Cove of the Ancestors is framed by a majestic arched geomagnetic formation, and features a dense archipelago of magnetically levitated Floating Islands. It is a design triumph of Cole's art department, seen briefly in *The Way of Water* but back in *Fire and Ash* to host the entire climactic sequence of scenes.

This third act battle sequence was referred to in-house as "The Mother of All Sea Battles," and comprises 37 minutes of screen time, including intense dramatic confrontations between all the characters and even an unforgettable childbirth scene. Pacing the bravura setups, maintaining tension, and charting the emotional pulse of the story was a Cameron masterclass in filmmaking. "The problem with most action sequences in most movies," observed Josh Friedman, "is they don't reveal character or have emotional stakes that we buy, and they don't contain enough sacrifice. After the death of Jake's son in A2, it felt like we'd earned a lot of stakes in the subsequent movies. Anything can happen. But you have to have set that up earlier in the movie and know how to hit those notes for that to land. That's one of the things Jim does maybe better than anyone. I asked Jim how he approached his process. He wasn't being glib but he answered, 'I see the movie in my head, and I write down what I've seen.' The difference for me is I tend to put puzzle pieces together and try to get to a picture. Jim sees a picture, and then writes down the puzzle."

The heart of all three films in the saga to date lies in Jake's responsibility to his loved ones and his conscience as a leader who must lead people into battle, sometimes to their deaths. This duality, and Jake's awakening to *Eywa*, informs his relationships with Neytiri, with his children, and with other Na'vi that he has come to love. And it informs action across the films, leading to a literal cliffhanger at the finale of *Fire and Ash* between Jake and Quaritch. Quaritch's evolution as a character is a descent into darkness. "We saw some humanity in Quaritch in A2 when he stopped the torture of his son," observed Shane Salerno. "A3 ends with a man who has crossed over. Quaritch has embraced darkness. He has embraced hate, embraced revenge, and he is a dark, annihilated soul."

> "I see the movie in my head, and I write down what I've seen."
>
> **James Cameron**

Jake Sully now holds the fate of Pandora in his hands. "Jake is on a mission," noted Amanda Silver. "When we find him in the second movie, he has become *Toruk Makto* (in *Avatar*)—a leader—and united all the clans. But he originated as a human, and that plays with his identity. Jake faces the questions of what it means to be a father, a man, a husband, and a leader. He worries that he's brought war to the reef. And it seems no matter what he does he's up against a wall. He has to decide. Will Jake meet his destiny as *Toruk Makto*, or will he cower to this worry, protecting his family by hiding?"

"We embraced that complexity," added Rick Jaffa. "Jake is in an internal tug of war. He questions himself. He thought he had everything figured out, but he realizes it's not that easy. His relationship with his children is a beautiful mess. You bring kids into the world, and you think they're going to be a certain way, but then they have their agendas and personalities, and how much do you oppose that? Magnify that to include *Toruk Makto*, and you've got some monumental struggles."

Above: At the climax of *Fire and Ash*, Jake Sully clings to Recom Quaritch and Spider above a massive conflagration in the Cove of the Ancestors. Concept art by Steven Messing.

RETURN TO THE WORLD
AVATAR
ON BLU-RAY & DVD
JAMES CAMERON'S
AVATAR
22.1
FOCAL LENGTH
2026B_X0AA002A_0A01A
FON
29.4
FRAMERATE
03193
FRAME
00:02:13:03
SCENE
18:48:03:19
CHARACTER
18:48:03:19
CAMERA
REC
RCAM 01
RCAM 02
RCAM 03

Chapter 2

STRATEGY

Strategy

Essential to Avatar's design and worldbuilding was giving the Na'vi characters the breath of life. James Cameron and Jon Landau knew they would be CG characters, driven by the actors' performances. That had been fundamental to Cameron's vision of the film. In fact, pushing his company, Digital Domain, to develop that technology had been the very reason Cameron wrote *Avatar* in the first place. But how exactly were they going to accomplish that? Early on, the two producers sought the counsel of Richard Baneham, a veteran of the Weta team that had created the creature Gollum for Peter Jackson's *The Lord of the Rings* (2001–2004). Gollum's star turn in Jackson's second *Lord of the Rings* film resoundingly demonstrated the potential that Cameron had been mulling since his Digital Manifesto for performance-driven characters. "There was an epiphany moment where I was watching *The Two Towers*," Cameron recalled. "There is this tour de force scene where Gollum talks to himself in a dissociated state, seen as two different versions of himself arguing. I thought, 'If they can do that, we can do *Avatar*.'"

The time had come.

Weta Digital, the Academy Award®-winning visual-effects house in New Zealand, had realized Gollum by tracking motion of actor Andy Serkis interacting with on-set performers, followed by sessions with Serkis on a motion capture stage. This was later embellished with "keyframe" facial animation, where animators handcrafted the character's key expressive poses frame by frame. However, the challenge to create hundreds of Na'vi across thousands of shots required fidelities of capture far beyond what had previously been achieved. Was Cameron's goal of a true "performance capture" process feasible?

"This all started in 2005 in a room with Jim asking me, 'What do you think of that?'" recalled Baneham, who had joined the Lightstorm brain trust. "We worked alongside Jim's designers, trying to figure out the physical manifestation of these characters. Design for design's sake is dangerous. You need to marry that to the kinematic sense of the character."

"Kinematics"—from the Greek *kinema*, meaning "motion"—in animation terms refers to the dynamic push-and-pull of a character's bones, muscles, skin, and limbs that create illusions of life. To allow human performers to drive the non-human Na'vi characters, performance-capture technical director Vaughn Cato built a 3D skeleton that mapped human proportions to Na'vi physique. "We used an inverse bio-kinematic 'solve,'" Baneham explained. "Vaughn Cato wrote that, and I don't think there's even close to an algorithm out there that's as good at taking surface data and turning it into kinematic skeletal data. The solve works from the inside out. Once we have a skeleton, that skeleton can be parsed into a bone relationship to the taller and slimmer Na'vi. It works really well."

Facial performance capture was even more important than body motion capture, and its solution even more complex. In 1995, when James Cameron first proposed his *Avatar* story at Digital Domain, the big question was how the facial performances would be captured. Body motion capture was in its infancy, but had been demonstrated—in fact Michael Jackson's moonwalk had been successfully captured at Digital Domain by Stan Winston, for a music video. Despite being constantly improved over the years, motion capture, or "mocap," based on body-suit markers, has not fundamentally changed for three decades. But in 1995, facial performance capture had not been done—at all. Cameron did a whiteboard drawing of his crude concept for a "head-rig"—a headband with two short struts, each supporting a tiny video camera aimed at the actor's face—one in front, and one shooting from the side. Cameron was convinced that the solution must be "Image-Based" so that it wouldn't miss even the finest nuances of the actor's performance.

"Design for design's sake is dangerous. You need to marry that to the kinematic sense of the character."

Richard Baneham, VFX supervisor

Previous pages: James Cameron views video playback of Stephen Lang as Recom Quaritch, reviewing imagery of the performer alongside his animated avatar.

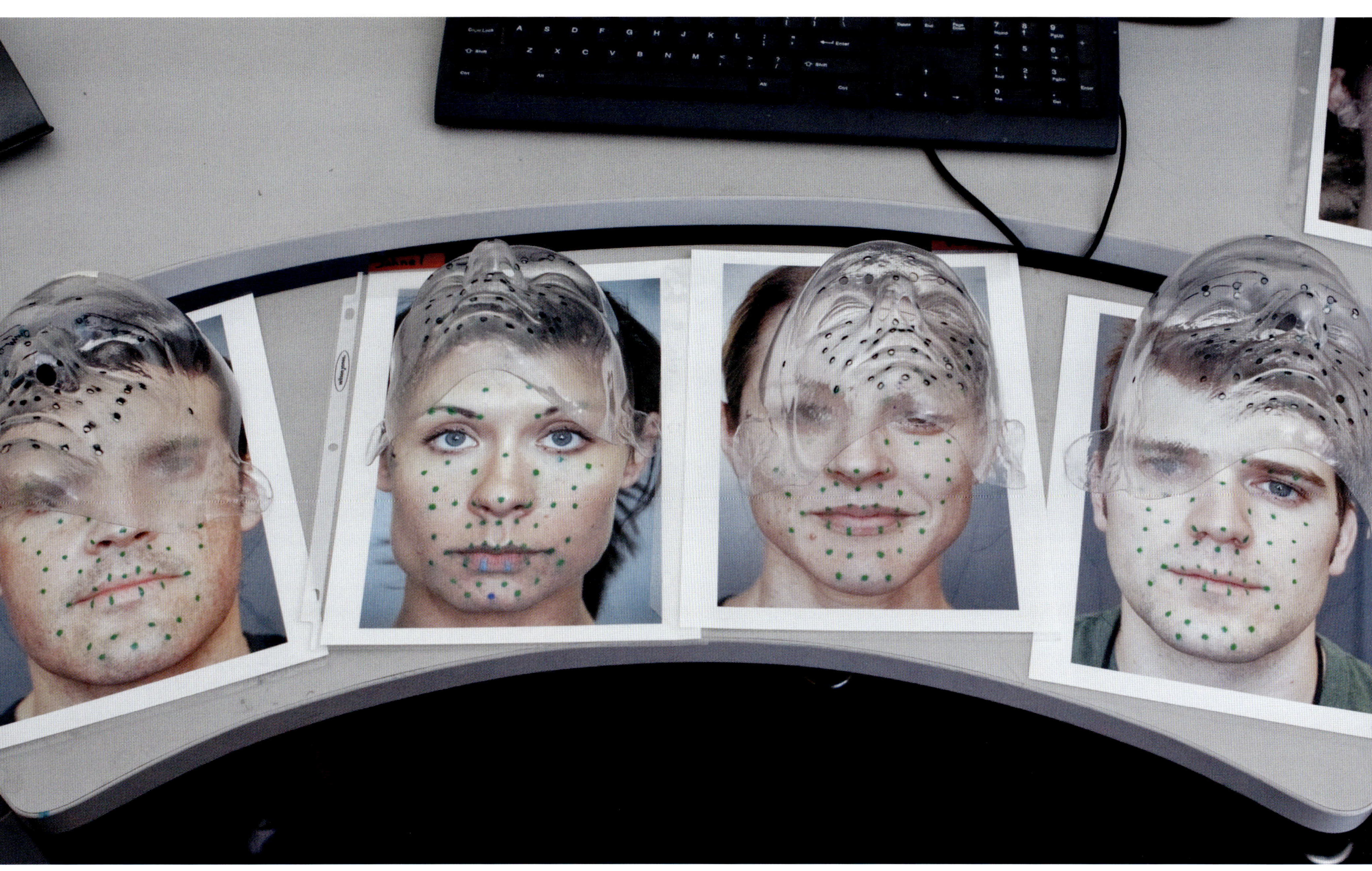

Above: The translation of actors' performances into digital avatars—known as "performance capture"—lay at the heart of Avatar. Each capture session began by applying makeup dots to actors' faces through plastic templates, which helped align facial motion to head-rig cameras. Templates for *Avatar* await troupe performers Woody Schultz, Jahnel Curfman, Julene Renée, and Kevin Dorman.

Left: Performance capture encompassed multiple groups of performers interacting simultaneously, here with Wes Studi (center) as Eytukan, chieftain of the Omatikaya, conferring with (left) Laz Alonso as Tsu'tey and other members of the clan.

The technology was not pursued at that time, because *Avatar* wound up being postponed. When the project was resurrected 10 years later, the director remained utterly convinced that Image-Based was the answer. But even by then, nobody had done it. Facial capture at that time (2005) was being done by gluing 70 or so tiny reflective markers onto the actor's face. It was hideously time-consuming in the makeup chair, and actors hated it. It also produced only a very crude "mesh" of the actor's face, and required enormous amounts of refinement by keyframe animators in post-production. Each one of those invasive refinements took the resulting facial expressions farther and farther from the actor's actual performance in the moment.

Worse yet, the final result had a disturbingly robotic effect. In 2005, CG character creation was still stuck deep in the "uncanny valley." The uncanny valley was a catchy term coined by roboticist Masahiro Mori. His original Japanese phrase was *bukimi no tani*, which translates to "uncanny valley." This refers to a deep saddle in the Y-axis of the curve of a viewer's positive response to a face. On the one end of the curve is the very positive response to a true human face, high on the graph. On the opposite end, the farther a face is from human, such as a cute robot like WALL-E or C-3PO, the better the response is, again plotting high. But in the middle of the curve, where a face seems almost human but there just seems to be something "off" about it—something corpse-like, such as a rubber-skinned robot that looks almost human—the viewer's response plunges. This deep saddle in the curve is the uncanny valley. All previous attempts to create CG characters based on human performance had wound up stuck deeply in that trough of negative response. This was also known as the "dead eye" effect, and a good example from that time is *The Polar Express* which, despite its groundbreaking use of motion capture, never broke free of the curse of the uncanny valley.

Another huge limitation of marker-based facial capture is that the volume needed to be very small, barely a dozen feet across, so the capture cameras could pick up and distinguish those tiny facial markers. They certainly wouldn't be able to do the big crowd scenes and action set-pieces that *Avatar* required. So it was decided to proceed with Cameron's unproven image-based facial-capture approach, even though it had never been done before. The first step was to create a head-rig. Small standard-definition video cameras were readily available. The director decided that a second camera, mounted at 90 degrees to the side as in his original concept, was unnecessary. A young, innovative engineer, Glenn Derry, was brought in to design the head-rig. Long discussions ensued about how to make it light enough, and fit snugly so that it wouldn't shift around as the actor moved, destabilizing the image. Derry figured out how small LEDs could be mounted on it to provide constant lighting so the actor's face was always fully visible, even if the actor looked down, away from the overhead stage lights.

Left and below: Zoe Saldana displays Neytiri's skills with the bow, adopting the Omatikaya's left-handed archery stance. Weta screenshot.

Glenn created a prototype—a form-fitting skullcap made from carbon fiber, based on a scan of the actor's head, with a short boom that supported a video camera aimed at the actor's mouth—looking something like a concert microphone that a pop singer would wear. So that the lights weren't shining in the actor's eyes, the camera was an infrared one, surrounded by infrared LED lights, which were invisible to the actor but lit the face fully in the resulting video.

Cameron was concerned that actors and stunt performers would be running through mock jungles, jumping and fighting, and in the midst of such intense action might accidentally catch the camera boom on some object that could cause a dangerous twist to their neck, resulting in serious injury. Glenn's team worked out a magnetic quick-release so the camera boom would just pop off if over-stressed. Safety first! It was decided that the entire volume would be brightly and evenly lit from above, so that the performers' faces would always be seen clearly. No beautiful cinematic lighting was required—that would all be done later in the CG realm. The stage lighting was as ugly as a supermarket.

Once it was clear how the video of the actors' faces would be captured, this data would be used to drive the performance of their CG characters. This was another technical blank page that needed to be filled in. Enormous leaps of innovation were required to get this facial-performance pipeline working. The raw video feed from the head-rig was a grotesque black-and-white image of the actor's face, distorted by the fisheye lens of the camera. But it gave an incredible amount of detail about the actor's mouth, lips, teeth, and tongue—

and it was the interaction of these rapidly moving structures that created speech and expression. From that video a moving mesh of the face was automatically generated, using facial-recognition tracking software. That mesh was then used to drive a sequence of "blend shapes," individual frames of rigid facial geometry that closely approximated the actor's expressions at any given moment. As these shapes rapidly morphed, or blended, one into another, it created a motion sequence of changing expressions, including speech. The blend shapes were created in advance by scanning each actor while seated in a 360° laser scanner as they performed a pre-set series of expressions, including the specific phonemes used in speech.

"Jeff Unay was the production's facial lead and supervisor of the facial team on all the avatars and Na'vi," noted Andrew Jones, animation supervisor on *Avatar*, who shared duties with David Clayton at Weta and Richie Baneham at Lightstorm. "Jeff was pivotal in coming up with the technique of modeling blend shapes that created the feel of realistic skin movement. Zoe Saldaña's face drove Neytiri's performance, but there was a ton of skill behind the scenes that made that work. When animators moved 'sliders' in the facial rig, they animated combinations of blend shapes, and that made the skin look malleable and elastic. It was very different to what anyone else was doing at the time. And a lot of thought and effort went into figuring out how to do that."

Eye movement was derived from the video using other biometric code specifically written for eye-tracking. Combining that captured eye movement with IK (inverse kinematic) algorithms that determined how eyelids and surrounding skin would deform around it as it moved brought that part of the face to life. This "solve" for the eyes was merged with the blend-shape expressions to create a complete and accurate facial performance, transferred from the actor to their CG character, ideally without any "creative" interpretation by the animators.

Although Cameron demanded that the animators not add any layer of their own interpretation to the character, the system was not perfectly automated, especially in the early days on the first *Avatar*. In practice the animators needed to constantly intervene to make sure that nothing was lost from the actor's performance. They had to constantly check the resulting facial motion against the high-definition reference video that had been shot simultaneously during capture, to make sure nothing was missing. But it was a diametrically opposite ethos from normal animation. Rather than creating a performance from scratch, as animators had historically done, they were fighting to preserve the sanctity of the actor's performance, without their own interpretation. They fought hard to be invisible.

Performance-capture tests began in early 2006, in a 76,000-foot-square stage, the former site of a Howard Hughes experimental aircraft hangar in Playa Vista, California. The stage was called the volume—a space surrounded by 120 video cameras mounted on a big space-frame truss, all looking inward toward the actors from many different angles. Like the head-rig cameras, these saw only invisible infrared light, and each was surrounded by infrared-emitting LEDs. The performers wore capture suits covered in markers made of Scotchlite, the same "retro-reflective" material that makes a stop sign light up in automobile headlights. The mocap cameras were designed to only see the actors' markers, not the rest of the world that was lit by visible light. So each camera only saw a "point cloud" that moved as the actor moved. And each actor's point cloud was unique, based on where the markers were placed on their body-suit. So the system could "see" and distinguish different people at once, and how they were moving in three-dimensional space. The point cloud drove a "skeleton" for each actor. The system incorporated a real-time render-engine based on the Motion Builder game engine. The "mo-bu" engine was used to visualize the corresponding Na'vi or avatar character moving, exactly as the actor was moving, and all in real time.

Because the facial performance was being captured by the head-rig, not by the array of mocap cameras, the volume could be enormous compared to previous mocap movies. On *Avatar* it was 120 feet long, big enough to gallop horses through. This was one of the many revolutionary strides *Avatar* was making.

But how was Cameron supposed to direct his actors within a world that didn't physically exist, and couldn't be seen by the naked eye? What was required was a "Virtual Camera," with which to view the characters and the world of Pandora around them. It would be a window into the unseen world. A virtual camera is not truly a camera in the normal sense—it doesn't have a lens or generate an image optically. It is simply an object fitted with markers—like the markers on the capture suits—that defines its position in space. Then the render-engine is told to render the image from where that object is and from the direction it is pointing. It becomes a camera only in the virtual world. So that the camera operator can see to frame the image and pan to follow the

"Zoe Saldaña's face drove Neytiri's performance."
Andy Jones, animation supervisor

Opposite page, left: James Cameron operates a prototype "Swingcam" virtual camera, lining up a shot on the performance camera stage using a wire-frame model of an airborne *ikran*.

Opposite page, right: A later-model Swingcam, used for the majority of the virtual shot-making process, with lens and scene data overlaying a navigable 3D model of each scene.

> "One of Jim's strokes of genius on *Avatar* was to shoot so much of the film handheld."
>
> **Andy Jones, animation supervisor**

action, that object has a small video monitor mounted on it. The image rendered in the game engine is fed to that monitor, so the operator can pan and tilt to follow the action.

So it's not really a camera at all, because there's no lens, and no light falling onto a film-plane or sensor. Just markers and a video screen. But it allows the director to frame the shot in real time and direct the actors accordingly.

Three critical technologies were converging simultaneously: the mocap system that captured the actors' body motion; the head-rig that recorded their facial performance; and the virtual camera that allowed the director to frame the scene and block the actors.

In addition, the team used a large number of HD video cameras to record "reference" video of the scenes as they were shot. These reference images were critical to the editing process. A dozen or more reference camera operators were asked to get close-ups of every actor within a scene, as well as wider shots, at the moment the capture process was happening. In the cutting room this video was used to create a "performance edit," putting together the actors' best moments from multiple takes into one scene file. On any given day there could be up to 16 reference camera operators, usually working handheld, all scrambling to get the necessary coverage. A torrent of image data flowed into the system. Multiple advances in data networking software were required to manage this vast flow of data and keep it all straight throughout the ensuing years of post-production.

You could say it was cinematography without a movie camera. There was literally no camera. Except the process actually used many cameras, of different types. There was a massive array of motion capture cameras on the overhead grid, cameras mounted to each actor's head, and up to 16 handheld reference-video cameras, plus a virtual camera—a "v-cam"—that wasn't a camera at all. It had no lens.

Four separate data streams, all necessary to the capture of every iota of the actors' performances, poured into the editing room to be turned into cut scenes. These cut scenes, called Templates, were later used by Weta to bring the scenes to life at an unprecedented level of both photorealism and emotional realism. More on those downstream parts of the process later.

The system of Capture would evolve over time, but the very first baby steps

"If you can find a way to have the actor participate and have their choices end up on screen, that's the goal that we're striving for."

Richard Baneham, VFX supervisor

were taken on August 30, 2005. That's when Lightstorm staged a proof-of-concept exercise in its early test volume, with actors Daniel Bess and Yunjin Kim portraying the first meeting of Jake and Neytiri (at the time named "Josh" and "Zuleika," as they were called in the treatment). This was the first time that performance capture specific to the Avatar universe was ever attempted, and the resulting scene, called "The Prototype," would determine the overall viability of the entire project. A flurry of activity followed, including figuring out how to apply the actors' facial expressions to their characters (called the Kabuki; more on that later) and how Cameron would operate the camera in the virtual world, and decide how the editing process would work. The resulting cut sequence was turned over to ILM (Industrial Light and Magic) in San Francisco to turn into a photoreal 3D scene. Cameron went off to his ranch in Santa Barbara County to start turning his treatment into a shooting script, while ILM went to work on The Prototype.

By February 2006, ILM had rendered a 37-second scene from that first Capture session, using very early versions of the character designs for Jake and Neytiri, and placing them in a CG jungle based on the plants being created by the Lightstorm art department. The finished test was viewed in 3D by Cameron and his team to much jubilation. It not only resoundingly demonstrated that the image-based facial capture process worked, but gave a glimpse of the phantasmagorical world of *Avatar* that could be brought to life using the technologies the team was developing. Though crude compared to the finished *Avatar* three years later, it was instrumental in convincing the heads of 20th Century Fox to greenlight the next stage of production, gearing up for full-scale capture and live-action shooting.

Avatar was a go.

The first step was to lock in the VFX house that would do the finishing work. Weta Digital, in Wellington, New Zealand, was selected not only for their pioneering work in facial animation, such as the creation of Gollum in *The Lord of the Rings* trilogy, but for their experience creating photorealistic CG jungles for Universal Studios' *King Kong*, to say nothing of their innovative spirit.

Work on *Avatar* began in earnest. Motion capture specialists Giant Studios equipped the Playa Vista stage with state-of-the-art motion-tracking technology and worked with Weta Digital visual-effects supervisor Stephen Rosenbaum and Lightstorm virtual-production supervisor Glenn Derry to refine the performance-capture system. "The ILM test showed what was possible," observed Ryan Champney, who joined the team with Giant Studios before becoming Lightstorm's virtual production supervisor. "That was two years before we started principal capture. When we started, the reputation was that performance capture was very sterile—you rehearse, clear the stage, close the doors, and then do performance capture. Jim wanted to shoot *Avatar* in a way that was more akin to how he'd shoot on a film set, with crew, props, and sets out there on the stage. The Giant system allowed a more robust approach that we could improve and be flexible. Jim is always pushing technology to the edge until it breaks, and then he'll say, 'Now, fix the part that broke, and let's come back to that.' We kept adding more characters, creatures, props, and stunt rigs in the volume until we realized maybe 10 performers was too much, so we'd pull back to eight. But then we'd figure out why it was slowing down at 10. And behind the scenes, we had people analyzing that data."

A big advantage of Giant's "biometric solver" was that it allowed the characters to be rendered even if an actor was partially blocked by other actors. By interpolating what was biologically "plausible" for the unseen parts of the body, from moment to moment, it allowed the system to fill in the gaps in the data. The algorithm knew that a lower leg, for example, certainly couldn't suddenly be elsewhere across the stage; it still had to be attached at the knee, even if technically the system couldn't see it. The Giant solver was a breakthrough that allowed for more complex setups. Set-pieces in the volume could be much more complex without badly "occluding" the actors. And more actors could be captured together in a scene, up to 20 at a time, even though there was significant occlusion—their figures could still be "seen" by the system. This was revolutionary. Past systems could only capture two or three people at once.

Another big factor: it allowed the reference camera operators to get much closer to the action, thus giving the editors the high-quality close-ups they

Above: To compare action on the performance-capture stage with low-resolution computer-generated renditions of each scene, Cameron viewed arrays of "quad-spilt" monitors, which relayed video feeds from multiple witness cameras that surrounded performers on set.

Left: Ilram Choi and Jahnel Curfman, members of the Lightstorm "troupe" of stunt performers, pose with their virtual Na'vi avatars.

"When we walk into that empty space, which we call the volume, it compels you because there ain't nothing there. We bring things to life. It's acting at its most fundamental."

Stephen Lang, actor

needed to judge performances. The reference team could be very close, even though they might slightly block the action, and the Giant solver would keep the whole thing from crashing.When it did fail, occasionally, the results were comical. The virtual characters would wad up into gelatinous masses of moving arms and legs, like mutant monsters. But over time, as the system was refined, these crashes got rarer and rarer. Giant's software was considered so critical to the work that Jon Landau convinced Fox to allow Lightstorm to buy the company and roll its IP permanently into the system.

Famed science-fiction writer Arthur C. Clarke's Third Law states that "any sufficiently advanced technology is indistinguishable from magic," and to the *Avatar* crew, the virtual production system certainly seemed like magic. Here were these non-human characters speaking and interacting, moving through an alien world, seen by a virtual camera, at the exact moment the actors were creating their dramatic, emotional performances.

The Capture process was truly revolutionary, in that it completely separated acting from cinematography. All the final camera moves, all the choices of lens size, from fish-eye to telephoto, all the cinematic lighting, and all the ways that a camera can be moved through space—handheld, dolly, Steadicam, crane, even drone or helicopter—would all be figured out later. To the actors it was a pure process, unhindered by the normal encumbrances of physical production. More like theater than movie acting. Just a script, a bunch of actors, and a director—and with the most minute nuances of the actors' work being recorded, missing nothing.

The process allowed Cameron to focus completely on performance with the principal cast, before he would embark on a separate shot-creation phase months later. "For the first couple of takes," Cameron explained, "I'd use my virtual camera like a director's viewfinder, to 'block' a scene—we'd get some marks down, tell people where to hit positions, and I'd optimize their positions for their interactions with each other and with the environment. I'd record every take, and then I'd look at the monitors to study reference footage of the actors. After a while, I'd hand the v-cam to another operator and focus my attention as a director on the the actors, not on the virtual image. At its essence, we uncoupled acting from cinematography. That's the quickest way to understand it. Performance capture is a pure acting environment."

Actors loved it for a number of reasons. It was a pure focus on their work, not slowed by the resetting of technical things like lights and camera cranes, or getting hundreds of extras back to their first positions. And because the director wasn't distracted by all those things, the actors had 100 percent of the filmmaker's attention. There was no having to go again for "coverage"—doing a scene over and over from different camera positions. All that would be applied later. There was no having to go again because a shot was out of focus, or a lighting technician missed a cue. There was no having to hurry up because the sun was setting. There was no having to scurry for cover because it started to rain. No having to control traffic on a street so a take could be started. It was just a purely creative flow state.

As Stephen Lang described it, "When we walk into that empty space, which we call the volume, it not only invites you as an actor to use your imagination, it compels you because there ain't nothing there. We bring things to life. It's acting at its most fundamental."

"You have a helmet," said Academy Award®-winner Kate Winslet, "and you also have a helmet camera. And that is how important it is to Jim to really capture every single microscopic movement that the actor's face is making. So it really is the actor who has formed the muscular structure and the emotion within the character." Though Kate wasn't in the cast of *Avatar*, she would spend months in the volume on A2 and A3. Added Sam Worthington, "So anything that you do, anything that you say, anything that you feel, is translated into this system. We did it. There's not one thing that you see us do that is animated. It is all us. It is all true. Acting to me is truth in imaginary circumstance. This is absolute truth in absolute imaginary circumstance."

"It's the purest kind of acting that there is," casting director Margery Simkin said, "It's like being in a rehearsal room. Once you get past the gear, it is just you and the role and the other actor." Jon Landau's son, Jamie, is an actor himself, and was a member of the troupe for years. He remembered, "Some of my favourite moments on set were the times where, right before a scene, the set would practically shut down just so that Jim could sit there with Zoe Saldaña, Sigourney Weaver, Stephen Lang, Sam Worthington... and talk about a scene for 30 minutes. Talk about what their characters had just been through before coming into this scene. It was so important to get those emotional states right."

Above: Cameron rallies cast and crew on the performance-capture stage, formerly the site of a Howard Hughes experimental aircraft hangar in Playa Vista, California.

Capturing the actors' performances in absolute detail was the start, but for the next phase of the process Cameron would return to the volume months or sometimes even years later, armed again with the virtual camera. This time it was to shoot playback of the scene to make the actual shots for the movie. There would be no actors then, or sets. Just the director alone, in the empty volume, crafting his shots in real-time based on those pre-recorded performances. This phase was called simply "Camera." This deceptively obvious term was adopted to distinguish from Capture done with the actors, and from live-action photography, which was a later phase. The term "shooting" might apply to any of these phases, but Camera was very specific. This is when the first actual shots would be made. This is where the rubber would meet the road, in turning all that captured data into actual shots for an actual movie.

After Capture, the Lightstorm editors and the digital Lab assembled the cut scenes into files called "Loads." These were scene files that could be played back during Camera sessions. "When Jim came back into each scene with his virtual camera," Ryan Champney observed, "he concentrated on lensing, camera angles, and focus. That gave him much more control over the final product."

This process lasted many months, during which Cameron performed almost every CG shot in *Avatar* by hand. He would work closely with the "stage op" (stage operator), a kind of digital DJ who would play back the scene files while Cameron operated the "v-cam." The director would first tell the stage op, via a microphone built into the v-cam, what playback speed he wanted. Shots were usually done at a playback of half speed, which allowed the director to crisply follow the action despite the 1/6th of a second lag through the system, caused by the many layers of furious computation. Sometimes, for fast-breaking action or complex flying maneuvers, playback speeds of 1/3rd or even 1/5th speed would be needed. The stage op would say "Half speed, ready," and the director would call out "Playback!" Staring at the v-cam's monitor, Cameron would then perform a sometimes balletic dance to move the camera through space with his subject. He would walk slowly across the stage, often backward, raising his arms to ascend, or bending into a low crab walk to dive the camera, panning and tilting to follow the action. It was as graceful and deliberate as tai chi. Cameron had learned handheld operating from Adam Greenberg, his DP on *The Terminator* and *Terminator 2: Judgment Day*, and decades later he was using Adam's signature sliding cross-step to author a completely different type of movie, in a virtual camera volume.

Above: Stan Winston Studios created Na'vi paint and lighting studies, using human-scale busts with ultraviolet paint and lighting to simulate bioluminescence.

Left: Stan Winston Studio review session, April 2007; (left to right) Maria Battle Campbell, Rick Carter, Reymundo Perez, Scott Patton, Joey Orosco, Joe Pepe, John Rosengrant, Neville Page, James Cameron.

"Cut!" After the take, Cameron would move quickly to a large monitor to watch video playback. A separate video-playback operator would then play out the image recorded from the v-cam.

Though the virtual camera was always handheld, this didn't mean that the finished shot was meant to look "handheld." The team used "smoothing algorithms" so that Cameron's raw handheld moves could be rendered as if they were shot from a dolly, or a Steadicam, or a camera-crane of any size—even from a helicopter. He could shoot as if from any of these platforms by varying the mathematical ratio between the real displacement of the camera as Cameron moved in the volume, and how much it was moving in "worldspace"—the virtual world. For a crane shot, a ratio of 3:1 worked well. If the director raised the camera two feet in his hands, the camera would rise six feet in worldspace, three times the displacement. A ratio of 20:1 allowed Cameron to create "helicopter shots," moving the camera large distances through worldspace just by hand. Sometimes a very low ratio was used, like 0.5:1—half scale. This would allow the v-cam operator to make very small, precise moves, such as subtly tracking in to a character's face in extreme close-up for dramatic emphasis, a move that in real-world cinematography would be done by an experienced dolly grip. To simulate the look of a Steadicam, the team developed a "roll-kill" filter. The system would input the director's handheld move, but filter it to remove all spurious "roll" axis movement, keeping the camera perfectly level. Since a Steadicam eliminates almost all roll from a shot, this made the resulting handheld virtual shots look like they were done by a seasoned Steadicam operator.

But what if the director actually wanted a handheld *cinéma vérité* look to a scene? The trick then became to preserve the bumps, jiggles, and small roll movements of a handheld camera, and not filter them out. For handheld shots Cameron would use a ratio of 1.5:1, essentially making his body the same size as a Na'vi character's; then would operate the shot in a way consistent with the mass of a real handheld cinema camera, as if it were held on the operator's shoulder while following the action. Since he had been operating his own films for over a decade in real-world production, including a number of documentaries, he was highly experienced at handheld camera work. The filmmaker enjoyed the personal touch, giving the shots a "human feel." It became a stylistic motif for *Avatar* and its sequels.

This paid off later, during *Avatar*'s live-action filming, where Cameron was the principal operator of the 3D cinema camera, often handheld. It unified the cinematic style of the film, across the two separate worlds of virtual and live-action production. Cameron felt strongly that the more innately fantastic

Top: Stan Winston Studio resin bust of Neytiri in war paint.

Right: Stan Winston Studio resin bust of Jake's Na'vi avatar.

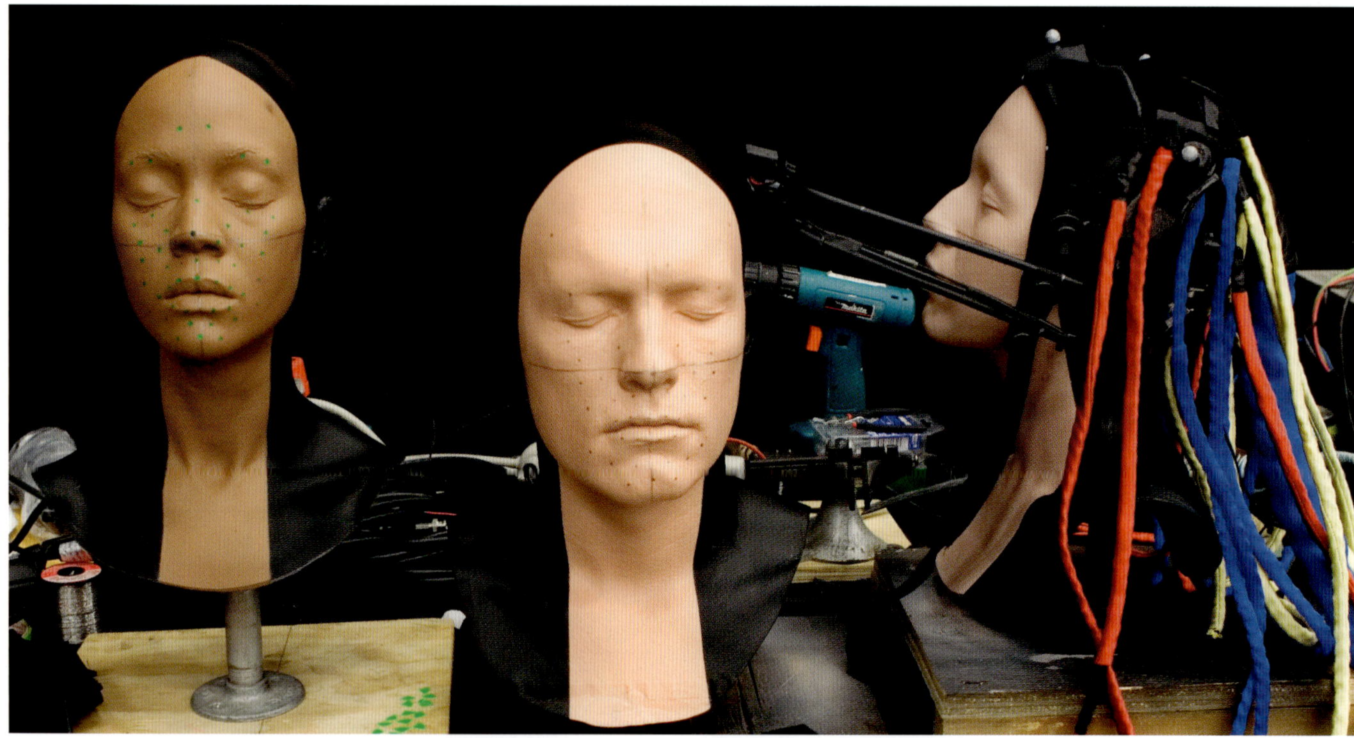

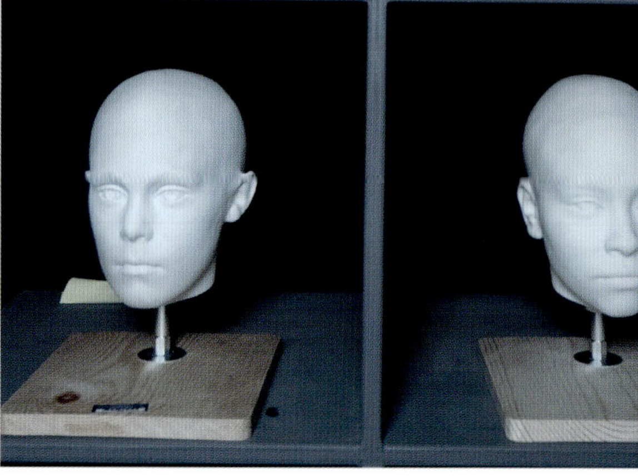

Above left and above: The production used busts of Saldaña, Worthington, and all of the other principal performers to fashion custom Na'vi head-rigs, comprising skullcaps with a tiny reference camera and LED lights angled back at the performer's face.

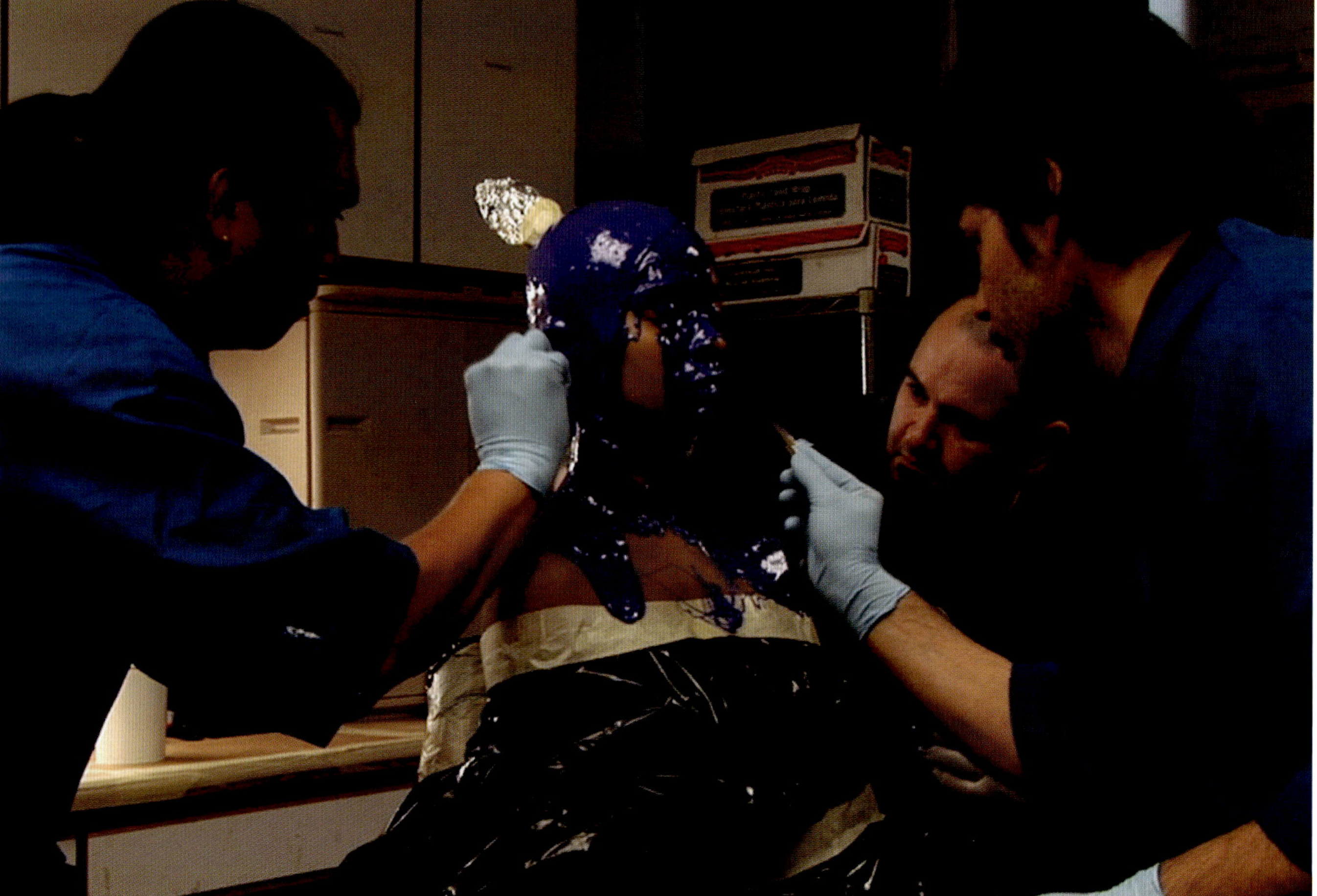

Left: Stan Winston Studio artisans apply alginate impression material to Zoe Saldaña for her life-casting procedure, capturing features of her head and shoulders.

the subject (an alien world, imaginary creatures, non-human characters) the more critical it was to have the photography seem absolutely real, especially for scenes in which it wasn't photography at all, but computer-generated imagery. So the artifacts of real photography needed to be studied, and surgically applied to create the impression of photoreality. This included handheld jiggle but also lens flares, water drops on the lens, and all the other things that might occur using a physical cinema camera.

"One of Jim's strokes of genius on *Avatar* was to shoot so much of the film handheld," noted Weta animation lead Andy Jones, "We were in a completely virtual environment, but because the audience could feel a camera operator walking around the characters, that created a level of realism. I thought that was brilliant."

With the virtual shots in hand, the editors would cut the scenes together and send them to Weta to upgrade to breathtaking photoreality. The Weta animators were the best in the world, and would have had a creative field day with the exotic creatures in the story, but they were asked to do their utmost to preserve the actors' work without interpretation or embellishment. Their work was supervised by Lightstorm's in-house head of animation, Richie Baneham. "It's our job to protect the actor's choices all the way through the pipe," Baneham explains. "The human interaction that happens, the emotional interaction, the intimacy, and the tension that happens between those actors in that moment is everything."

The video close-ups shot by the reference camera team during Capture were critical to the Weta animators. "I've never had more reference in my life for animating anything," declared Andy Jones. "When Zoe was exerting effort as Neytiri running, you could see the subframe jiggle in her skin. That's the kind of detail that if it's missing can make an animated face look 'uncanny.' That was the level of detail we were seeing in the reference as animators."

Despite the goal of complete and unaltered translation of the actors' performances to their CG characters, the facial pipeline was still not perfect. "The blend-shape facial solver for Neytiri featured more than 800 face shapes. But, on the first *Avatar*, it still required animation artistry to exactly match Saldaña's performance," Jones stated. "The solver would get us close, but it wasn't one-to-one. The animators would then adjust the sliders to create the detail we needed."

Plus there were aspects of the Na'vi characters the actors couldn't do themselves. This is where the Weta Digital animators added enormous value, creating expressive Na'vi tail and ear movement corresponding to the character's emotional state—relaxed, curious, anxious, or angry. In the end, it became a delicate equipoise between animation and translating the actors' performances as faithfully as humanly possible.

It's one thing to have truthful performances, but an issue that might keep the characters in the uncanny valley was the believability of the models themselves. On *Avatar*, the process of creating highly detailed character models was still being worked out. Once each actor was cast, Stan Winston Studio took a plaster mold or "lifecast" of their face, a process not for the claustrophobic. From these they sculpted clay busts, blending the actor's actual face shape with their Na'vi character's features. Molds were made of these, and cast in polyester resin. These head-and-shoulder busts were finely painted, and hair was painstakingly "punched in" to the scalp so that it could be styled—plaited and braided to match the artwork. Hairstyles could then be reviewed, and altered, to create the final look. The busts had glass eyes inserted, giving them a highly lifelike appearance.

For the first time, the characters took on a breathtaking level of reality. There was Neytiri, with Zoe's beauty shining through her alien features, and Jake, with Sam's unique strength captured in his avatar form. The other characters emerged one by one: Tsu'tey (Laz Alonso), the proud alpha male of the clan, Eytukan (Wes Studi), the *olo'eyktan*, or chief, of the Omatikaya, and Mo'at (CCH Pounder), the clan's *tsahìk* (spiritual leader). There was Grace Augustine, with Sigourney Weaver's patrician features prominent in her avatar incarnation, and Norm Spellman (Joel David Moore), Jake's avatar sidekick.

But to truly bring the characters to life they needed to be imported into the digital world, with every skin pore and eyelash recreated in their CG models. The baton was now passed to Weta Digital in New Zealand. The Weta Digital artists developed "turntables,"—CG models of each character that could be digitally turned to evaluate the features and pigmentation under different lighting angles. Once the CG models were approved by the director, it was time to give them the spark of life.

Each character would need to have their own "rig", or algorithm, developed to interpret movement and expression. There are more muscles in the human face than the rest of the body combined, and each actor's facial muscles moved differently. So each rig would be unique to the character. The creation of a rig for any given character would take about nine months, coincidentally the same length of time a baby develops in the womb. And as with new beings developing into their true selves, every aspect of a living person needed to be embedded mathematically into each model—the translucency of their ears and fingertips ("subsurface scattering"), the luster of their hair, plus the weight and body that hair would have as it fell across the shoulders, the flexing and relaxation of facial and body muscles, the tension in their neck tendons as they spoke and breathed, the whitening of their nail beds as they gripped an object, the "caustics" inside their corneas as sunlight refracted in from the side, creating golden sparkles in their catlike irises. A thousand subtle details. Hundreds of billions of "vertices" in their mathematically determined models, defining every skin pore, every wrinkle.

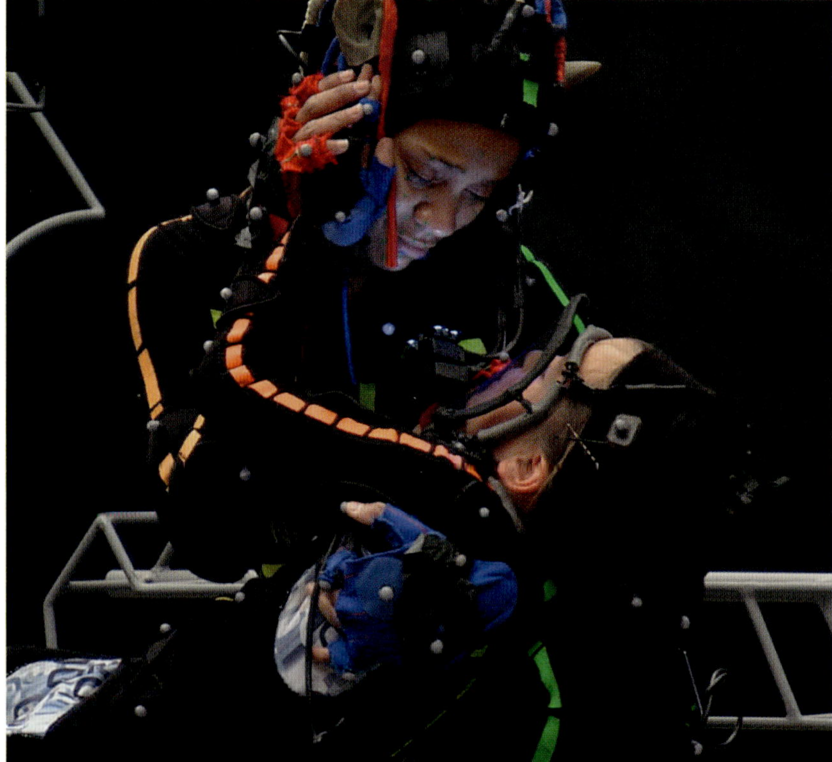

Reference photos were taken of slender human performers in all possible positions, for example kneeling so that the Weta artists could understand how muscle would compress and distort when the leg is folded upon itself and how skin would wrinkle at the knee or elbow. A million details we take for granted and don't think about in daily life, but then added together would create a compelling sense that these CG characters were living, breathing people. It was nothing less than the ultimate VFX challenge—to cross the uncanny valley and emerge out the other side with characters the audience believed were utterly real. Only in that way could an audience be expected to care, and to go with them on their emotional journey.

* * *

It's well and good to have the technology to translate an actor's performance to their Na'vi character, but first the actor must learn to move like a Na'vi, in a not-quite-human way that incorporates animal grace and agility. A team of dancers, gymnasts, and movement specialists was put together to develop that movement style, after which the cast could be trained.

First AD (assistant director) and co-producer Josh McLaglen had introduced Cameron to stunt coordinator Garrett Warren during the production of Robert Zemeckis' 2007 performance-captured fantasy film *Beowulf*. "I wanted a shot at coordinating *Avatar*," stated Warren. "Josh warned me to come prepared." Warren drew on his experience—not only as a stunt coordinator, but also his early training in ballet, jazz, breakdancing, and a variety of martial arts—to develop a video pitch for Cameron. "Josh told me these characters were tall, catlike creatures that could climb like monkeys. They walked on two legs, but when they climbed, they moved like lemurs. I wanted to wow Jim, so I brought in Olympic rhythmic gymnast Stella Angelova. I asked Stella to walk like a two-legged catlike creature but also to move like an Aboriginal or African tribesperson—graceful, but with the relaxed gait that they use to walk long distances. Stella developed a rhythmic stride, walking on the balls of her feet, with her chest pulled forward."

These Na'vi motion tests impressed Cameron and Jon Landau, and Warren joined the production to gather additional stunt performers. These included

Above left: At the climax of *Avatar*, Neytiri cradles the human body of paraplegic Jake Sully. Cameron initiated the scene in performance capture with Zoe Saldaña, who embraced a proportionally-correct body-double of Jake Sully, with troupe performer Kyla Warren in her arms.

Below left: Sam Worthington then performed the live-action portion of the scene before a motion-controlled camera, while two greenscreen performers aligned mock-ups of Neytiri's head and arms.

Opposite page, above: A low-resolution digital composite of Neytiri and Jake guided a Simulcam composition of the scene that Cameron viewed in the Link Shack set.

Opposite page, below: Screenshot of the final Weta composite, which united Jake and Neytiri in a tender embrace.

Left: The New Zealand set of the Hell's Gate Ops Center, overlooking RDA's landing pad and shuttle strip, featured a greenscreen backing beyond the window. A live Simulcam "mix" to monitors on set and the motion-picture camera viewfinder provided perspectives of the vista beyond the protective glass.

> "The production was able to interact a captured 10-foot-tall Na'vi character with a human actor in real time..."
>
> **Ryan Champney, virtual production supervisor**

martial arts expert and stuntman Ilram Choi and dancer, athlete, and stunt specialist Alicia Vela-Bailey, who further explored Na'vi movement. "We first designed how Na'vi were going to climb, squat, and move," Warren explained. "Ilram did that for the men; Alicia did it for the women. Stella and Alicia then continued working through all the films, and Alicia wound up as our main movement person." Later, once the film was cast, Alicia would work closely with Zoe Saldaña, training her in the fluid Na'vi motion.

Later in production, for special sequences of Omatikaya ceremonial gatherings, performance coordinator JoAnn Jansen and choreographer Lula Washington developed rhythmic motions derived from African dance traditions. Dance and cultural references were guiding the principles of Na'vi body language. "We had certain rules for the Na'vi," noted James Cameron. "They never nodded their heads 'Yes.' That's a human gesture, and it's cultural. Certain cultures don't nod for 'yes'; they nod for 'no.' Assent—meaning, 'I agree with you'—from a Na'vi has the head going back with a click of the tongue in the roof of the mouth. Or, if they close their eyes for a second, that's a solemn agreement, like a contract. Some of those rules fell by the wayside much later, because the dramatic demands of the scene ultimately were more important. And when an actor was in the moment of a feeling, I didn't want to interpose too much on that."

A major part of what makes the Na'vi alien is their size. It took everyone on the film a while to get their minds around the sheer scale of the Na'vi characters, and the ramifications of that scale to how the film would be made. The Winston team created full-scale, 10-foot-tall Na'vi puppets that could be posed and even performed, using *bunraku* (Japanese puppetry) techniques, to give the actors playing the human roles something to react to.

The scale differential between the giant Na'vi, played by normal sized actors, and the human characters, also played by normal-sized actors, would account for a great deal of the production's energy during both Capture and live-action phases. As plans for Capture took shape, the production focused on the problem scenes that required human and Na'vi-scale interactions. A good example was the scene where Jake wakes up for the first time in his avatar body, then stands up among the human med-techs, swishing his tail around and knocking things over. Another key scale-interaction was the climactic scene where Neytiri for the first time encounters the true human form of Jake Sully, the man she loves, and cradles him in her arms. The script contained a number of scenes requiring characters of different scales to interact closely with each other, and that would prove daunting. To solve it, new technology would be required.

Live-action scenes for *Avatar* would be shot at Stone Street Studios in Wellington, New Zealand in 2008. But years earlier, in anticipation of the live action, the team created another unprecedented new tool: Simulcam. Cameron knew there would be scenes combining 10-foot-tall Na'vi or avatars with human characters on live-action sets. But how would he see both sets of characters at once, to be able to compose his shots?

Ryan Champney recalled, "Jim asked us, since we could track our virtual camera, why couldn't we throw markers on a live-action camera and then mimic what that camera was doing in the CG world? That way, we'd have a one-to-one correlation of those images mirroring each other that we could view." So a down-and-dirty prototype was made using a home video camera, and within a couple of days the production was able to interact a captured 10-foot-tall Na'vi character with a human actor in real time. It required literally years of refinement, but the Simulcam system was used extensively on *Avatar* and has subsequently evolved into the primary working system on the live-action set of *The Way of Water* and *Fire and Ash*.

Simulcam was yet another layer of unprecedented and unproven technology added to an already insanely complex production. It was used to put CG characters into the live sets and also to add CG set extensions, allowing the art department to build less physically. The camera operator (usually Cameron himself) could see the CG world and the physical set in his eyepiece, combined in real time. "Jim was often operating," Champney recalled. "The only time Jim didn't operate was if it was a Steadicam shot. Our first Simulcam had a six-frame delay (1/4 of a second). The playback lagged."

Which meant that if the actor moved too quickly in their pre-recorded performance, they might dash right out of frame before the operator could catch up. A quarter of a second is a long time when a character is moving fast. "In those instances," Champney continued, "we used Simulcam to spot-check lineups in rehearsals, and then Jim operated to a clean plate. But the majority of Simulcam shots on *Avatar* were slow-moving, and so Jim operated most of those with Simulcam directly to his eyepiece."

"Looking back to Simulcam on *Avatar*," commented Richie Baneham, "it was in some ways crude. But it was a huge breakthrough. What we were really doing was a dance between the live-action character, the CG character, and the camera, telling the story with a camera based on what we could see on set. That was incredibly empowering."

***

The quest to create a detailed Na'vi culture of course had to include their language. Long passages of Cameron's screenplay called for scenes to play in subtitled native Na'vi, hammering home Jake Sully's initial feelings of alienation, and later—as he learns their tongue—his gradual immersion into the "Na'vi Way."

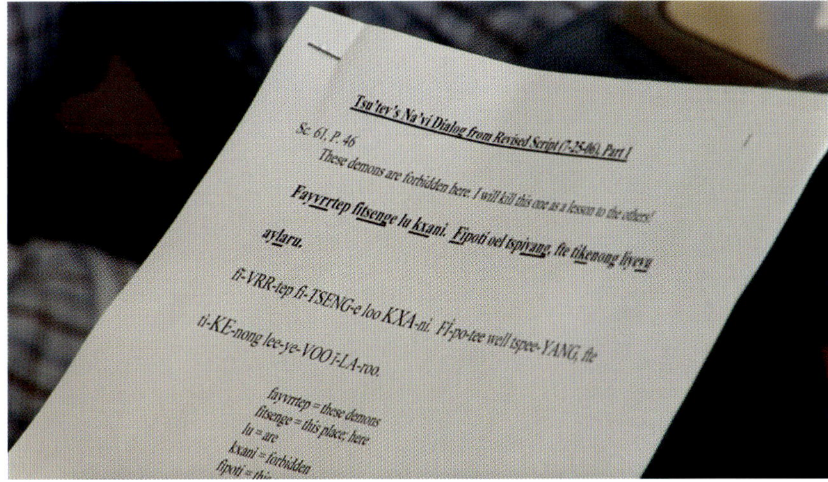

Top: To ensure authenticity in scenes set among the Na'vi, the filmmakers created an extensive vocabulary for the indigenous clans of Pandora.

Above: Linguistics specialist Professor Paul Frommer (right) consults with Zoe Saldaña and dialect coach Carla Meyer (left), discussing Na'vi meter and articulation.

Above: Professor Frommer assists Bailey Bass in her delivery of Na'vi dialogue as Tsireya of the Metkayina clan.

Na'vi names already mentioned in the script were clues for Professor Paul Frommer, a linguistics specialist from the University of Southern California, whom Cameron conscripted to develop a vocabulary, amounting to approximately 1,000 words, that served the needs of the script. "Jim's script had names of characters and animals as Na'vi words," noted Professor Frommer. "For example, Tsu'tey, Eytukan, and the great beast *palulukan* (the thanator). Those gave me a sense of the sounds Jim had in mind. When we first met, Jim had recently returned from New Zealand, and the words he invented sounded somewhat Māori. I incorporated that into the phonology of [Na'vi] and expanded on it."

For inspiration in constructing the sound and grammar of Na'vi, Frommer drew from diverse international languages, ancient and modern. "I learned my first foreign language when I was 6 years old in Hebrew school," Frommer recalled. "Through high school, I had Latin and French, and later some German in college. In the mid-1960s, I was in the United States Peace Corps and wound up teaching in a Malaysian high school, so I had Malay. Later, I had some Chinese, a little bit of Arabic, and my dissertation was on Persian syntax. That wide range of languages was very useful in constructing Na'vi, although we wanted to avoid having anyone thinking that Na'vi sounded like any specific language. Phonology was the first thing I had to define. Na'vi has some familiar sounds—*muh*, *nuh*, *luh*—but I wanted to make it interesting, given the fact that this was a language spoken 4.37 light-years away, so I introduced less-familiar 'ejective' sounds. These are found in some human languages, and they sound like *p-ah*, *t-ooh*, *k-eh*—popping sounds. I indicated those in written Na'vi with an *x*—where *px*, *tx*, and *kx* are the ejectives *p-*, *t-*, and *k-*." Paul's written Na'vi also used apostrophes to represent additional consonants, indicating a glottal stop, as heard in English "uh-oh." The glottal stop shows up even in the word Na'vi itself, and in names like Mo'at and Tsu'tey. These sounds would give the actors plenty of fun detail to work with in preparing for their characters.

"I was very fortunate in that I had a chance to work directly with the actors."

Professor Paul Frommer, linguistic consultant

Casting director Margery Simkin would learn to pronounce Na'vi herself, so she could run auditioning actors through the sounds, to see if they had a good enough "ear" to learn Na'vi. This included the "ejectives" and the "glottal stops."

Cameron invited Frommer to participate in Na'vi tutorials, introducing cast members to the Na'vi language. "I was very fortunate in that I had a chance to work directly with the actors," Frommer recalled. "Often, as a language constructor, you make recordings, and then a dialect coach on set will work with the actors. I met with Sigourney Weaver, Zoe Saldaña, and the other actors who spoke Na'vi in the film. We had language exercises to help them pronounce the more difficult sounds and words. I'd start with an English screenplay sentence, translate that into Na'vi, and present that to them. It's a pretty transparent writing system and quite phonetic, so you can almost always pronounce what you read. One difficulty was learning when to stress syllables in Na'vi words, which is not always predictable. When I presented the actors with written materials, under each Na'vi word I had its meaning. In addition, I gave them easily comprehensible quasi-English phonetic transcriptions. And then, most crucially, I provided mp3 recordings. The actors could put those on their phones, to listen while they were working out."

While the performers focused on memorizing scripted Na'vi dialogue, Frommer guided the meter of their speech to help clarify meaning. "Nobody signed up to learn to speak Na'vi," added Frommer. "It was more important for the actors to understand how words were pronounced and sentences contoured. It worked well. Everybody was very serious about convincingly reproducing the language."

***

The tale of the production of *Avatar* will continue in later chapters, including live-action shooting, VFX, and post-production. But it's helpful here to see how the radical new technologies developed for Capture and virtual production continued to evolve for the even more ambitious sequels. When Lightstorm regrouped in 2012 to tackle a continuation of the saga, Cameron gathered his team to analyze what they had already done; what worked, and what was nightmarish and cumbersome. *Avatar* was the prototype. Now they needed to make the whole process user-friendly and more efficient. Not only had the first film nearly killed them, but the new films were going to be far more ambitious. On *Avatar*, Cameron designed the script so that at least a third of the film could be filmed conventionally on live-action sets, as the story follows Jake's human reality between Link sessions. This would reduce the budget impact of creating photoreal CG characters.

By the time of the new stories Jake's human life has ended and he is fully Na'vi. Grace, his human mentor, is dead. Quaritch is dead. All of the significant characters in the sequels would now be fully CG. Instead of a third of the film taking place in the human world, it might be more like 10 percent. And even then, those human-centric scenes would still include CG main characters, such as a Recom Quaritch at the RDA base, the Sully kids with Spider at High Camp, or characters in the forest or on the SeaDragon. Which meant that basically 100 percent of the movie now required CG characters. In addition, the new films were going to be significantly longer, targeting three hours. These factors combined meant that CG character shots jumped from 2,600 in the first film to over 3,500 for each sequel—7,000 new shots in all. Adding to this, Cameron also hoped that the emotional reality of the characters, and the photoreality of the scenes, could be significantly improved.

It was a triple threat of increased difficulty—more shots, more characters, better quality. Add to that the need to perfect simulated water (the highest level of difficulty there is in CG shots) and it was clear that the challenges of the sequels were a multiple of what the team had done before. So enormous improvements in the efficiency and capability of the pipeline would be needed. They needed a mass-production machine; one that would not sacrifice quality, and in fact would increase it. These were ambitious goals, but they had the time. And the success of the first film ensured that they had the resources to do it.

"There was a five-year period," said James Cameron, "where we were not only writing the scripts and designing the worlds for A2, 3, 4, and A5, but we were

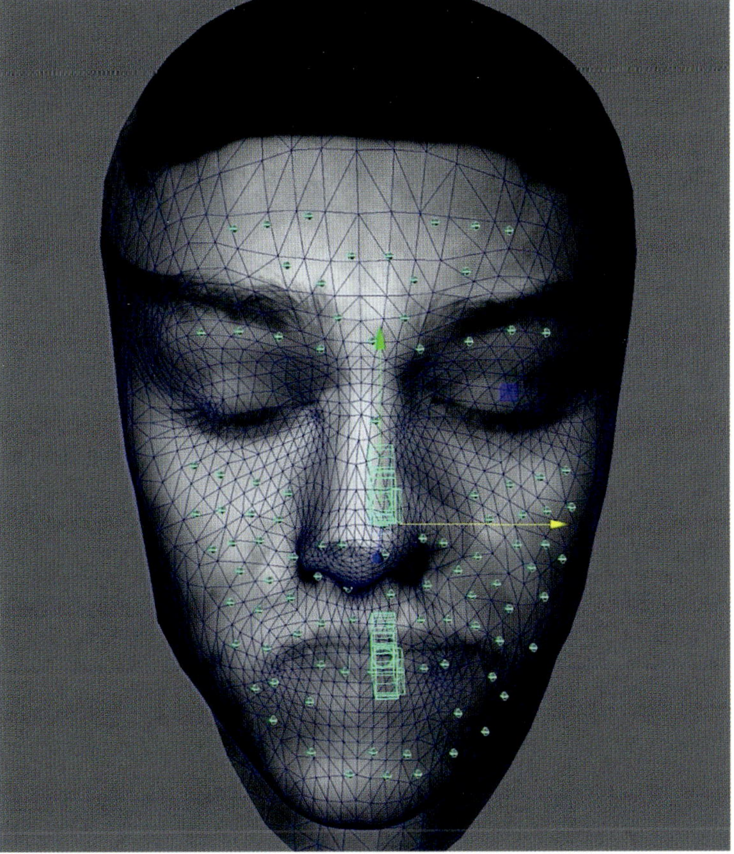

Top: While gearing up for the sequels, almost a decade after *Avatar*, Weta proposed a new paradigm in its approach to facial animation. The "Anatomically Plausible Facial System" (APFS) was based on analysis of muscle motions, here featuring Jamie Flatters.

Right: Weta used data from Jamie Flatters' head-rig imagery to conform a three-dimensional mesh to markers on the performer's face. Weta artists then used colored markers on the mesh to help align facial data with the digital model.

Right: APFS tracking marker layout on Lo'ak performer Britain Dalton.

Below right: The new APFS animation process was based on studies of facial muscles— resembling a *Grey's Anatomy*-style model—and measurements of muscle behavior. As the performer emoted, networks of "strain curves" affected the structure of the face.

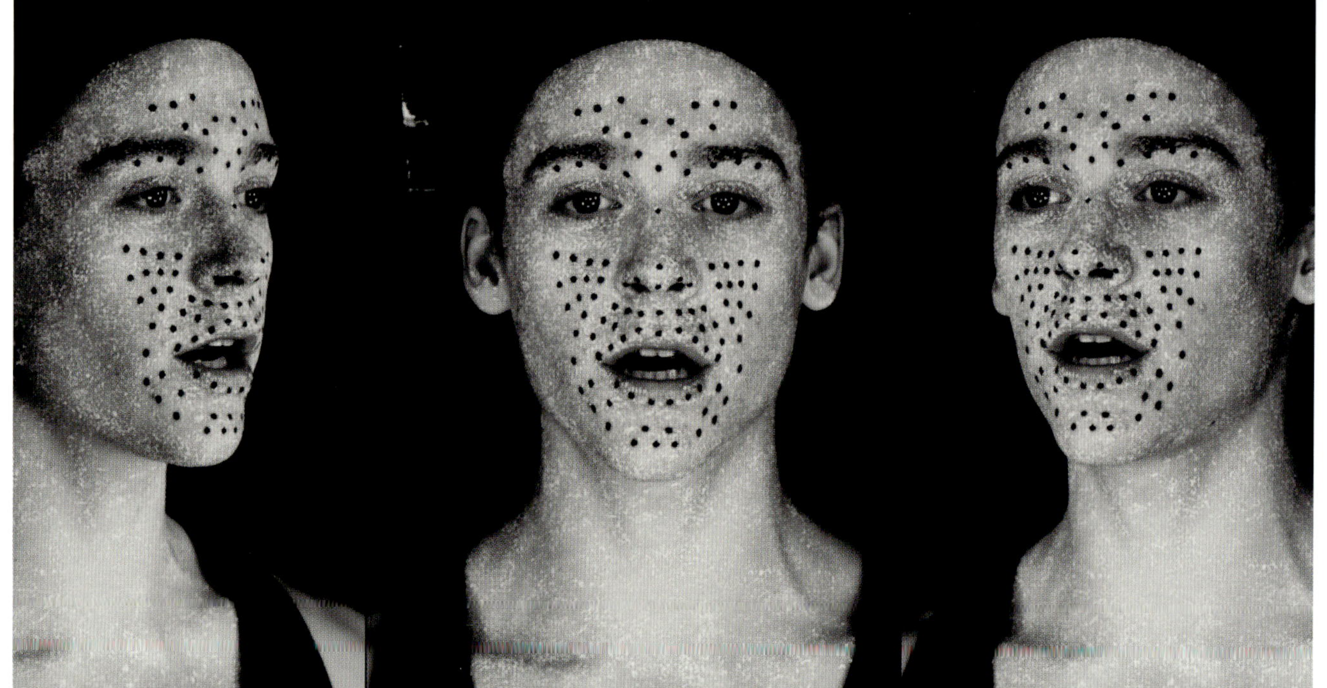

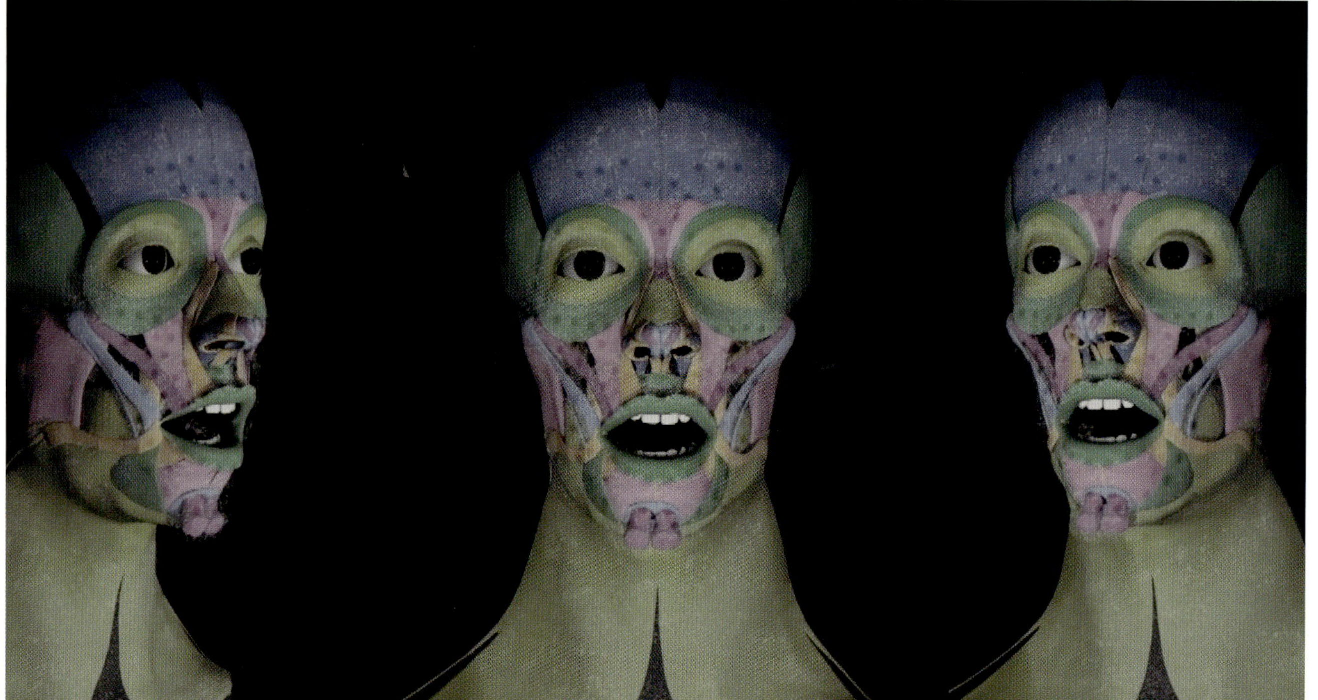

"We started to look for better ways to understand how, when a muscle moves on a face, all the other muscles move relative to it."

Joe Letteri, VFX supervisor

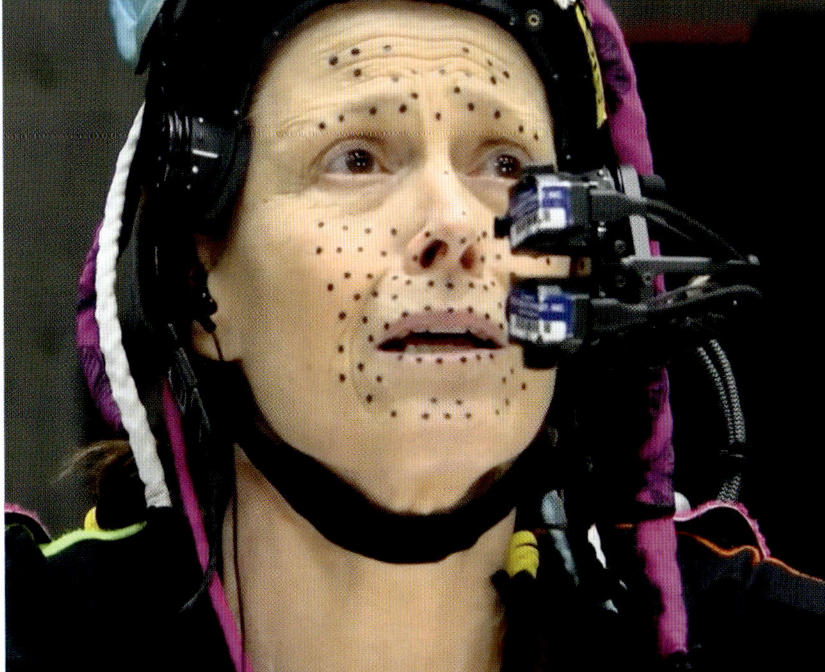

Above: Technology improvements also allowed more fidelity in performer head-rigs, which featured two cameras that captured three-dimensional depth in faces. Sigourney Weaver wears a dual-camera head-rig, while performing as Kiri, who gives thanks to the Na'vi deity of *Eywa* after rescuing Tuktirey and Neytiri from the sinking of the SeaDragon.

also spending significant amounts of money on R&D. That was to improve every aspect of the pipeline, to create more efficiency, to make it more user-friendly for the artists up and down the chain, and to give a higher sense of veracity in characters' performances."

For visual effects supervisor Joe Letteri, the back-to-back productions of the sequels—*Avatar: The Way of the Water* and *Avatar: Fire and Ash*—presented an opportunity for his team in New Zealand to implement major technical advancements. These included addressing the entire facial performance pipeline—not with a tune-up, but with a whole new engine under the hood. New innovations to the facial system were tested out on Lightstorm's *Alita: Battle Angel* (2019), to bring the cyborg character of Alita to life with absolute photorealism. "It was when we were doing *Alita* that I started to feel the limitations of FACS (Facial Action Coding System)," Joe Letteri recalled, referring to Weta's legacy facial pipeline. "That was essentially a pose-to-pose system. That worked, but it was also difficult to express complex behaviors. The face is nothing if not a complex system. We started to look for better ways to understand how when a muscle moves on a face, all the other muscles move relative to it. I mapped that out. As I was drawing my diagram, I realized I was drawing a neural network—and I thought, why not write a neural network that allows us to control all these behaviors? That's what we did."

"The advantage to that is, when we're solving a face, all the muscles come into play at the same time," Letteri explained. "That's what actors do. This system allowed us to take all those forces and figure out relatively how they all balance... and it helped us to get deeper into the emotions of the characters." Adding to the improved facial capabilities, the production re-engineered head-rigs and face-cams worn by the actors. "When we did the first film," recalled Letteri, "we opted for a single camera to make that as non-intrusive and lightweight as possible for the performers. Fast forward to A2, new camera designs brought down the weight, and we realized that we could get two cameras for the same weight ratio as one. We presented that to Jim, and he saw it was no worse than what we had before, and the actors were used to that, so we did that. What we got from that was a stereo field of the camera."

The stereoscopic face-cam allowed Weta to create 3D facial models directly from head-rig footage. The higher-fidelity data of the performers' faces fed into Weta's new facial system. "It was Joe's great leap of faith," commented Weta's Daniel Barrett, who served as animation supervisor for the sequels. "We were moving into this huge production, dispensing with a facial animation system that had delivered a pretty great film (*Avatar*). But Joe had become convinced over the years that there was a better way, and with nerves of absolute steel he brought that to where it needed to be."

Facial-motion lead Stuart Adcock joined Weta on the cusp of this massive upgrade. "I arrived at Weta thinking they had the best facial system in the

09:22
12:11

business," Adcock concurred. "Joe met me and says, 'Welcome aboard, Stu. We're just about to go into a meeting about how we're going to completely tear up the existing facial system and do something completely new.' I thought, 'Crikey!' But I was super excited to join them on this journey, revolutionizing their approach to facial animation."

A scene of Neytiri and Jake in their High Camp home served as a test case. Stuart Adcock recalled that "Joe didn't want to show him anything too early, because he wanted to get the technology in a good place. But you could see, as the months went by, Jim was getting a bit nervous. There was a lot riding on this, and we hadn't shown him too much. We worked on this scene with Jake and Neytiri where she's anxious. Jake is explaining why they need to leave the Omatikaya village. There were so many subtleties, and Zoe had so many 'inner monologue' moments where you could feel her emotion. We got the scene into a good place and showed it to Jim."

Cameron's positive response gave Weta the go-ahead to roll out the facial system to all the characters. "We stepped it up a notch," said Adcock. "Suddenly, Jim was loving the fact that he was seeing more resolution in all the frequencies of the face... It had more depth; it had more resolution; it had more everything."

"Fidelity and efficiency were incredibly important," said animation supervisor Dan Barrett. "The solver also helped us keep the characters 'on model'—retaining the structure of the Na'vi face and honoring the actor's expressions. It was a huge breakthrough for the team."

Preparing for the sequels' expanded scope, the production required more space for larger capture volumes. In 2011, Jon Landau signed a five-year lease at Manhattan Beach Studios, that offered a studio office complex and two large soundstages containing a shooting area of 115,000 square feet. The new studio would also accommodate one of the saga's boldest propositions—a performance-capture water tank. A very large water tank. This would be used for shooting the water scenes in Pandora's ocean "wet for wet," meaning the cast would actually be captured in and under the water.

Cameron's affinity for underwater shooting was well-known since his 1989 science-fiction thriller *The Abyss*, which had filmed on sets built inside an abandoned nuclear power station in South Carolina. A 7-million-gallon filming tank was created, using the unfinished reactor containment building (the reactor had never been installed). The filmmaker also shot portions of *Titanic* (1997) using Russian Mir submersibles at the actual wreck of the famous ocean liner, 12,500 feet down in the North Atlantic. He returned to deep water for his documentaries *Ghosts of the Abyss* (2001), *Expedition Bismark* (2002), *Aliens of the Deep* (2004), *Last Mysteries of Titanic* (2005), and *James Cameron's Deepsea Challenge 3D* (2014)—the latter chronicling his 2012 expedition to dive seven miles down to the deepest place in the world's oceans. As expedition leader and the co-designer of the Deepsea Challenger sub, Cameron mandated to his engineering team a keen respect for the physics of extreme ocean depth and a rigorous approach to safety.

There was historical precedent to argue against shooting any film in water. Steven Spielberg's *Jaws* (1975), and *Waterworld* (1995), among many others, were infamous for going way over schedule and budget due to open-water filming. In addition, *Avatar* itself had proven that a "dry-for-wet" approach could work, as in the sequence where Jake Sully evades a thanator by diving into a pool at the base of a large waterfall. This was achieved on the Playa Vista stage with Sam Worthington supported by a rolling office chair and pantomiming swimming to shore.

"When we did dry-for-wet on *Avatar*," said Richie Baneham, "we struggled with that in animation to make Jake feel like he was underwater. That was manageable as a small-scale process. But scaling that up, to where 30 percent of a movie was underwater, became a whole other challenge. The main thing is that pantomime is the enemy in this process, as it is in all animation. I've spent a lifetime trying to elevate the importance of looking for truth in performance, both from an emotional standpoint, but also from a physical standpoint."

Cameron never, from the day he started writing *The Way of Water*, believed they would do it dry-for-wet. "You need that resistance," he explains. "You need how the human body interacts with a medium that's 800 times denser than air." He knew what he was getting them all into, but it still required convincing the rest of the production, especially first assistant director Maria Battle Campbell, who dreaded the impact that real water would have on budget and schedule. Cameron and Maria agreed to shoot a side-by-side test—the same action captured on a flying rig, and also underwater in a small test tank Ryan

Opposite page: After their traumatic encounter with the RDA, surviving members of the Sully family reunite beside the burning wreckage of the SeaDragon. Performance capture in a giant water tank at Manhattan Beach Studios allowed Cameron to capture physically accurate interactions of performers in water. Weta then recreated the scene with atmospheric lighting and digital water simulations.

Above: Underwater performance capture required a huge leap of faith for the production, as no technology existed to allow the realism that *The Way of Water* demanded. Early testing included work in a test tank on Stage 28 at Manhattan Beach Studios. The smaller tank later housed overflow for a much larger water volume.

Champney had cobbled together. The result: there was no comparison. Even Maria grudgingly agreed the underwater capture looked much more real. The curse of Avatar is the never-ending quest for authenticity. As Cameron glumly mused, "It's a stick for your own back."

"It's Jim to a tee," said Richie Baneham, "You get to a point where you finally finish a movie where we feel like we've climbed the mountain. And then Jim goes, 'Well, what if we did it underwater?'"

"The second you decide to make a movie in and under water," said Cameron, "You just opened up a gigantic can of whoop-ass on yourself. Because nothing about water is ever easy." Maria Campbell braced herself for the can of whoop-ass that was heading her way. The only answer was to build a big tank and do it in the studio, using some kind of marker-based system—an underwater version of the dry capture volume. But first they had to prove that marker-based underwater capture was even possible at all.

Ryan Champney described that investigation, "It started with Babak Beheshti, who builds all our performance-capture cameras and a lot of our custom video hardware. Babek built these Jacques Cousteau-style housings—a box with a window in front, a big thick tube going out. We put a motion capture camera inside, put the lens up against the glass. We ran the hose up to the surface and fed all the cables through that. Then, it was a lot of trial and error."
Infrared light, as used on the dry mocap cameras, would not transmit through water, so the capture team switched to ultraviolet (UV) light. Champney explained, "We had to find a frequency of UV light that transmitted through water, that the camera sensor could see, and was readily available as LEDs on the market. Those were the customizations we did for the camera. And a lot of that we started in Jon Landau's swimming pool." They placed two UV cameras at one end of Landau's pool. Champney submerged a piece of pipe with LED markers into the far end to test visibility. Additional tests involved a performer in a markered wetsuit, acting out a range of movements underwater.

"Nobody had ever done performance capture in water before," said Jon Landau, "And not just below the water, but at the water surface, which was even more complicated." The problem was that characters would need to enter the water, dive down to the bottom, swim around, return to the surface, ride on creatures at the surface, and climb back out. There would be moments when they were in an upper "air" volume, and a lower "water" volume simultaneously. The two volumes would need to be merged seamlessly into one, in the computer.

"We basically put one of our performers, Kevin Dorman, treading water at the surface," explained Champney, "So we had an infrared volume above and ultraviolet volume below with the water as a medium in between." With some software tweaks they were able to see Kevin's character as a whole person, bridging the two worlds. Tests expanded to include multiple performers at Tank One, an above-ground water tank facility in Long Beach, which gave the production confidence to proceed with tank construction at Manhattan Beach. "After the Tank One test," said Champney, "we were pretty sure this was going to work. We now had to make it production-ready so that we could put a film crew in the tank and still have the motion capture system behave."

Tests revealed a potentially insurmountable issue: the UV mocap cameras became confused by reflections from the water surface. "If you're underwater and you look up at any water surface, you'll see a silver metallic reflection that looks like mercury," noted Champney. "We're seeing a reflection of everything. So instead of one performer or one marker, you would see ten performers, ten markers."

To eliminate reflections, Cameron recommended a technique they had used on *The Abyss* when they had a similar problem—seeing the surface when they were supposed to be 1,000 feet underwater. On that film they poured tons of black polyethylene beads, normally used for injection molding, onto the tank's surface. The beads floated, but just deep enough to completely black out the surface reflection from the underwater cameras. But it was pointed out that for performance capture they would need a lot of light pouring down from above, to illuminate the actors' faces for the underwater head-rigs. The black beads would have blocked the light. So a brilliant variation on the plastic beads idea was proposed.

As Ryan Champney recalled, "I suggested covering the surface of the water with semi-translucent white balls that would allow light to go through in a nice diffuse lighting. And they would safely allow the performers to get out." The director was thrilled by the solution.

Construction of the water tank on Stage 18 at Manhattan Beach Studios was one of the production's most daunting engineering feats. Lightstorm entrusted this assignment to J.D. Schwalm, a second-generation special effects supervisor who embraced the challenge. "This was all about water," said Schwalm. "Jim surrounded himself with brilliant people. As well as his team of camera wizards figuring out how to get the ultraviolet to work underwater, he was talking to scientists about materials we could put in the water, what metals would or wouldn't work because of electrolysis, and what paints to use. After that, we engineered the tank for him to fit on the stage. And that ramped into the way the water was going to move. Jim had some pretty strict criteria as to what he wanted the water to do. He had scenes where he wanted waves crashing on a beach, and scenes where he wanted it to look like characters were in the open ocean. And then, for A3 it was about making current in the rivers."

Many hours were spent at the whiteboard with Cameron, Schwalm, and the capture team bringing the tank concept into focus. It would be built above the stage floor out of steel, almost filling Stage 18. The height of the permanent lighting grid limited the wall height, and thus the water depth, to about 20 feet.

> "I've spent a lifetime trying to elevate the importance of looking for truth in performance."
>
> **Richie Baneham, VFX supervisor**

Above: For a scene where the *tulkun* Payakan helps Jake and Lo'ak escape the sinking SeaDragon, special props and a surface covering of white translucent spheres helped define water surfaces in the performance-capture tank.

Cameron said "not deep enough." So he asked for a pit—a deep end—like they had done on his stage sets for *The Abyss*. The production had to get permission from Manhattan Beach Studios to jackhammer out a 30-foot-square hole in the stage's slab floor so they could excavate and pour the concrete for the pit, which gave an extra 10 feet of depth at one end of the tank. Cameron wanted the natural movement of ocean swells. So he requested a wave machine—a very large wave machine. Schwalm's engineering team proposed a number of techniques that would be able to displace enough water to get the big oceanic swells that the director wanted.

"Jim had a very specific wave that he was trying to create, J.D. Schwalm recalled, "It was a swell... for the actors to be floating in the middle of the tank and a large roller to come through, and them to be able to bob up and down four to six feet."

They also needed enough space to run the "creatures"—water-jet powered vehicles that could be ridden like an *ilu* or a skimwing. Cameron suggested making an "underwater wind tunnel"—not moving the creatures through their little ocean, but moving the ocean past the creatures. This would allow fixed camera positions to get good reference close-ups of the actors while they were riding at high speed. So the idea of massive propellers driving water around the tank in a big loop was incorporated into the design—an additional layer of technology that was an engineering feat in itself. Schwalm explained, "Early on Jim had a dream, a vision I should say, of putting in giant, like really giant, boat propellers inside the tank and using those to create the current."

It got worse. There was a scene in A3 where the kids were shooting down dangerous river rapids. Cameron said, "Hey, now that we've got this 10-knot current generator. Let's build our own rapids." This was where first assistant director Maria Battle Campbell gave that scowl which told everyone he'd gone too far this time. It was like "If you give a mouse a cookie." But the art department found an off-the-shelf system of polymer blocks that was actually designed to create man-made rapids for kayak training. So it was decided the tank would have "rapids mode" as well.

The director also asked for a raisable platform that would cover the entire tank floor. He recounted how much time was lost on *The Abyss* putting in and removing set-pieces, all of which had to be done by SCUBA divers. He proposed a platform that could be raised to the surface so that pre-fab sets and set-pieces could be quickly bolted to it, then lowered into place underwater, allowing multiple scenes to be shot in a single day. The platform would be raised and lowered by chain motors from a robust overhead truss system. It could be angled to create a beach that waves could break onto, and even be moved vertically during a take, to simulate the deck of the sinking SeaDragon.

After big engineering projects, like sinking the whole front half of the *Titanic*, Cameron and Landau were not particularly put off by any of this. But there were a lot of glances around the table during the whiteboard sessions. People were getting really nervous about the many layers of technology required, which all had to fit into the one design. Someone remarked that it was becoming the "Swiss army knife" of filming tanks. It could do it all: mid ocean swells, coral reefs, waves breaking on rocky shores, submerging ship decks, waves on a beach, fast creature riding, and even river rapids.

Schwalm's team drew up schematics for a 90 x 40 x 20-foot structure, the biggest that Stage 18 could handle and still have the necessary fire lanes around it. The tank would have two levels of windows in its walls, for reference cameras to shoot the action within. The "pit" would allow breath-hold dives to a depth of 30 feet, a skill the cast would need to master. The deep end also housed an enormous manifold containing two 6-foot-diameter bronze ship propellers, each powered by a 1,000-horsepower electric motor. These would push water around the tank in a fast recirculating flow, once an oval center island had been temporarily installed. This was known as racetrack mode, and would be used primarily to create the "wind tunnel" for creature riding. Also at the deep end, above the manifold, were the monstrous black steel wedges of the wave-maker. Schwalm shared the parameters of the water tank design with Cameron, who approved of Schwalm's disciplined engineering methodology. "We came up with multiple ways of making waves move from one side of the tank and absorb the waves when they hit the other side," related Schwalm. "The way we pushed the waves had to work with the water at various levels in the tank. We couldn't build the wave-maker at a fixed level, because the level of the water was changing constantly. We had to be able to raise and lower that whole device."

Schwalm selected a hydraulic control system for its versatility and tested cube, cylindrical, and sphere-shaped blocks for plunging into the water. "Jim suggested that we build giant wedge shapes, with a flat side up against the back wall of the tank and an angled front that drove into the water. We designed that wedge and figured out the size. Weta has a really good water simulation setup. My team drew the tank from scratch, incorporated our wave-maker wedge, and sent Weta the CAD drawing with specs for the speeds that we could achieve with our hydraulics. They ran digital simulations of what that wedge would do in the water and the waves it created."

Each wave-maker blade suspended above the tank weighed approximately 2,000 pounds. Four computer-controlled hydraulic cylinders controlled the wave-makers' vertical motion as they slammed down into the water at approximately six feet per second. Ultimately it was found that the wave-maker

Right: Manhattan Beach Studios, Stage 18, housed the main underwater performance-capture water tank, an enormous structure built to Lightstorm's specifications.

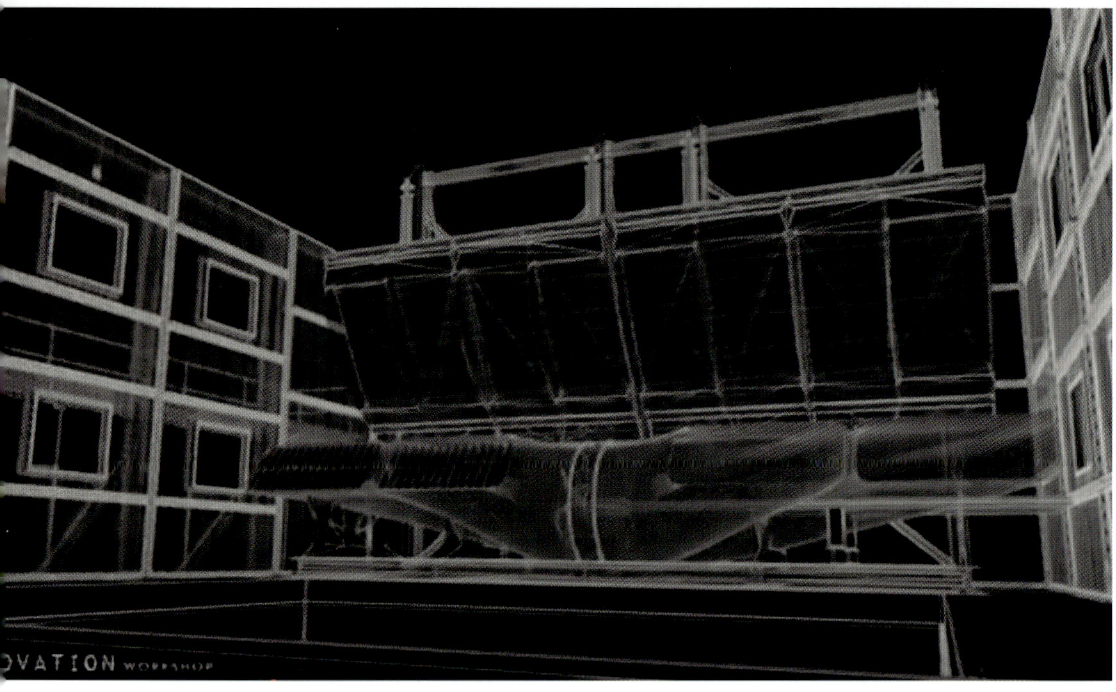

Above: Computer models laid out the configuration of a giant wave-making machine and twin turbines that propelled water around the tank.

could generate an impressive 7-foot swell in the middle of the tank, a bigger wave than any other wave-making system ever created for a film.

"It was a lot of engineering," noted Schwalm. "The wave-maker wedges could push down with 20 tons of force, so the columns that held those in place were trying to rip out of the ground with the same amount of force. We had to sink 20 x 8 x 8-foot blocks of concrete in the ground to anchor all of that."

When the "dry" performance capture required even larger volumes, Stages 26 and 27 had a central door that, when opened, joined the two stages into one volume. Recalled Ryan Champney, "In some cases, we'd combine the two stages to make one mega-stage if we needed it, for instance for the performance capture of horses running across two stages. The scale of that amount of data acquisition required a great deal more automation."

Before Capture could begin, both dry and wet, the virtual sets had to be designed, and the physical proxy sets built and fitted to them. The v-cam became an invaluable tool for "scouting" the Pandoran environments as they emerged from the art department, similar to the live-action process of filmmakers doing location scouts. Instead of a director looking around a location with a viewfinder or video camera, Cameron could "scout" locations on Pandora with his virtual camera. A team of performers—known as the "troupe"—served as stand-ins for the actors during the scouts.

The troupe consisted of actors and stunt people, most with some aspect of dance, movement, or gymnastic background. Each troupe member would play

Right: The base of the Stage 18 tank contained a mechanically operated floor that could be raised or lowered to accommodate set-dressing, and included a removable central island. Portholes in the tank sides facilitated "witness cameras" access to capture reference of submerged performers.

scores of different characters over the course of multiple Avatar movies, both Na'vi and human—whatever the scenes required. An individual troupe player might be an old Na'vi woman one day, a child the next, and an RDA Skel trooper the day after that. They were like radio theater actors of the 30's, ready to take on a new character at the drop of a hat. On the sequels, many of the troupe were veterans of *Avatar* and had lived within the culture of the world for years, confident in Na'vi movement, dance, chant, ceremony, creature riding, and weapons technique.

The troupe players were invaluable at multiple stages of the process. As soon as the art department had a rough layout of the set for any given scene, everyone would go into the volume to do a scout. Cameron would direct the troupe players through a rough blocking of the scene, just to make sure the environment worked the way he imagined. Troupe members would be assigned the roles of Jake, Neytiri etc., and act out the scenes just to see how it was all working. These performances were not definitive, and later the principal actors would be free to do it in whatever way they chose, but it was a starting point for pre-visualizing the scene.

Regarding Cameron's "pre-viz process," Ben Procter added, "Sometimes he'll do scouts raw with no actors. Other times, he'll use our troupe who he can pose, or have them moving around, grabbing onto things as he's blocking out his shots. Scouting allows Jim to figure out whether he likes the set, or which part of a set he wants to use for different functions. That lets us know what we call the 'Extent of Build'—'EOB' is a term we throw around a lot. Once we know the EOB of a sequence, we can dress the set to look its best in the hero zone, and prepare for the real performance capture."

It's important to keep in mind that for every virtual set, whether a jungle path or the deck of an RDA ship, there needed to be a physical set that exactly matched the virtual terrain. Actors can't climb on pixels. These sets consisted of dull gray ramps, risers, and platforms configured to exactly match the contours of the virtual terrain—jungle paths, horizontal tree limbs, rocky cliffs, or perhaps the multiple deck levels of a SeaDragon ship. During this scouting stage, changes to the virtual lighting would be explored, including deciding if the scene played better under a moody gray sky, or in bright sun, or at dusk, or at night by torchlight or moonlight.

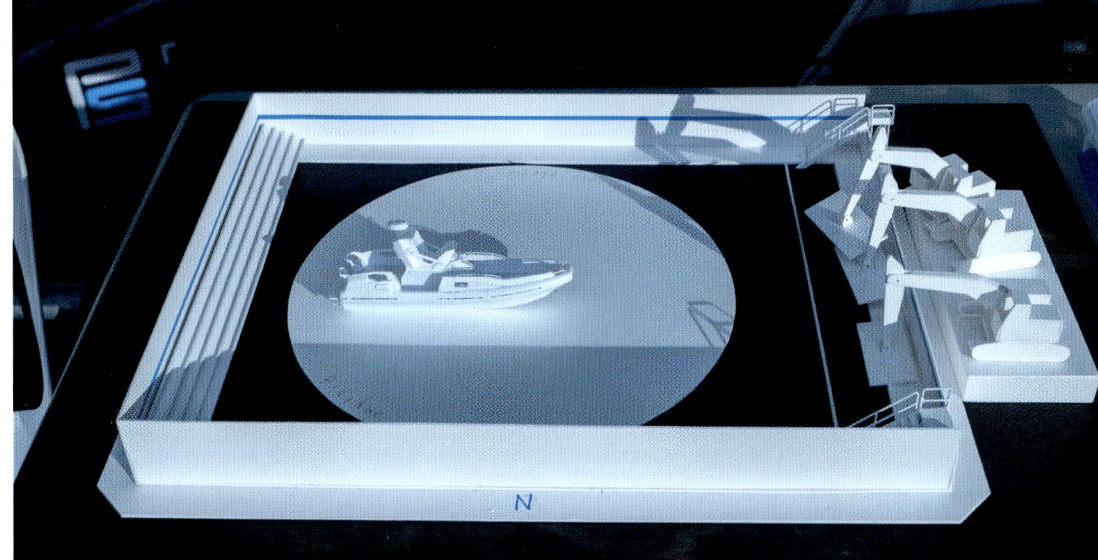

Top: For scenes of RDA vessels interacting with Metkayina oceans, New Zealand special effects supervisor Steve Ingram also designed water tanks for a Kumeū Film Studios shoot in Auckland. Technicians seated a full-scale, fully powered *tulkun*-hunting Picador craft on swivel mechanisms beneath the waterline.

Center and bottom: The New Zealand special-effects team then fitted 14.5-foot mechanical diggers with 13 x 8.5-foot strengthened steel plates, which they used as "wave paddles" to agitate the water surface.

Above: The New Zealand water tank served the sinking of the SeaDragon, when Spider pulls the bedraggled Recom Quaritch from the ocean. Cameron directs Jack Champion and blue-suited Kevin Dorman of the stunt troupe.

Top right: The deep water tank at Kumeū Film Studios, Auckland, New Zealand.

Below right: The SeaDragon breaches its hull on a rocky outcrop, which causes the giant vessel's engine rooms to flood. The New Zealand special effects team built a floodable set rigged with two 17,435-gallon dump tanks that released water into the engine room on the backlot at Stone Street Studios, Wellington.

"We do our scout with the troupe," said Baneham. "That informs the build-out of the environment. It also informs the camera language that we're going to employ to tell the story. From the inception of a scene, we start to understand cinematography, or how we tell the story in a cinematic way. After that, we go to the Capture process."

On both *Avatar* and the sequels, once the scouting was done, Capture with the principal actors could begin. "Once Jim started the performance capture process," explained production designer Dylan Cole, "we'd be on set all day, prepping the next set, making sure virtual sets were ready, making sure the practical proxy sets were working."

During this phase, once the principal cast had arrived the troupe players would shift from doubling the main characters to taking on other roles. They would play background characters, such as other members of the clans, or additional techs or troopers in the RDA scenes. They gave a lot of energy to the scenes, which enormously helped the principal actors to be in the moment. Often troupe and stunt performers would rehearse and capture complex motion, such as creature riding, so it could be worked out before the actors were asked to try it for themselves.

For crowd scenes the troupe players would play multiple characters within a given scene, being captured a number of times, in groups of a dozen or so, in different places around the set. These "crowd tiles" were then assembled together into large crowds. A crowd of a hundred might consist or eight or more tiles, meaning that each troupe player appears in the final scene as eight different people.

After a scene was captured, the director would sit with the editors to make "selects"—choosing the best takes for each actor. From these selects, the editors would assemble a Performance Cut. This was a complex process, using picture-in-picture multi-screen effects to layer in bits from different takes into one composite scene. Once the Performance Cut was approved by the director, it went to the Lab to be turned into what were called Loads. These scene files included the actors' and troupe players' performances, put into the environment of the scene, carefully edited to fit together in the right timing and positions, and with all the props, creature animation, lighting and "effects" (fire, smoke, explosions, waves, water splashes, etc.) added. Creating the camera Loads could take weeks, or even months, of effort by a large team of Lab artists. All this needed to be done before Cameron could even start doing the virtual camera moves—the actual shots themselves.

As Cameron was fond of explaining, "It was an insane way to make a film. Everything was shot twice and edited twice. We'd "shoot" the actors, by capturing them in the volume, then edit those performances together to create the camera Loads. Then we'd do the actual cinematography, with the actors no longer around, creating, for the first time, actual shots for the movie. Then we'd edit those shots into the final scenes."

On the first *Avatar*, the complexity and scale of the editorial process had been grossly underestimated. Cameron, confident in his editing skills from being one of the three Academy Award®-winning editors on *Titanic*, and having solo-edited several documentaries, believed he would edit *Avatar* himself. It quickly became apparent, shortly after principal capture began in April 2007, that he was being buried by the demands of both directing the film and trying to do the performance cuts. He brought in a second editor, Stephen E. Rivkin (*The Pirates of the Caribbean* films, *Alita: Battle Angel*, *My Cousin Vinny*), who had done a number of huge, and very successful, visual effects films. Despite being

"It was an insane way to make a film. Everything was shot twice and edited twice."

James Cameron

a seasoned editor with extensive VFX experience, Rivkin required months to fully master the complexities of performance editing.

It was a whole new editing paradigm… uncharted waters. It was counter-intuitive for an experienced picture editor to have to cut without actual shots. Every moment of performance, as seen in the reference-video footage, contained an infinity of "potential shots," but was not yet any specific shot. Any given moment of capture could later be turned into a wide shot, a dolly shot, an extreme close-up, an insert of a hand on a bow, or a helicopter shot from far above. It was like closing your eyes and using The Force to presage what shots might later be created, all the while having to make precise decisions about performance—but without knowing where the final cuts from shot to shot would be. It was a brain-twisting mental exercise. Cameron and Rivkin worked closely together, with a lot of trial and error, to develop and master the hideously complex process.

Eventually, due to the scope of work and the painstaking nature of the process, they decided that a third editor was required to meet the crushing deadlines, and John Refoua (*Transformers: The Last Knight*, *Magnificent Seven*) was brought in to help divide the load. Refoua was a Cameron alumnus from the *Dark Angel* series (2000-2001). But despite his deep experience with VFX, he too required months to come up to speed. Cameron recalled telling Refoua, upon hiring him, "You won't be any good to us for three months." Undaunted, Refoua plunged in and learned the mind-bending system, bringing his own unique swerve to the process.

It was one of the great miscalculations of the first *Avatar* that the editing would be straightforward. It was not only the complete opposite, but was in fact a wholly new process that had to be created from scratch, on the fly, in the middle of production.

Another miscalculation was the amount of time it would take Cameron to perform the virtual cameras for all the scenes. It quickly became clear that this was a far more arduous process than they had foreseen, largely because the whole thing was a big, kludged-together prototype system that threatened to collapse under the weight of its own complexity every single day. It was a slow process, because they were learning as they went, overcoming obstacle after obstacle in the camera volume. The "Brain Bar" of brilliant technical artists that supported the Camera process like mission control were struggling every day to develop new code, new tools, to deal with all the challenges of virtual lighting, set layout, and motion editing. To say nothing of trying to get the complex scenes to run fast enough for the real-time camera process. As the number of elements in a scene grew, the ability of the system to render in real time would degrade, until the frame rate went down to a stuttering crawl, and it became impossible to shoot.

As Cameron grew increasingly frustrated, brilliant coders were scrambling to figure out how to "optimize" scenes so that they could even be played back. Many hacks and tricks were developed, on a daily basis, to get the scenes to run. It sometimes seemed that they were building an airplane while already in flight.

On this phase of the first *Avatar*, it quickly became clear to Cameron that he was the bottleneck of the entire production. Every shot flowed through his hands, and there were only so many hours in a day. Despite constant and ingenious upgrades to the system, they were falling farther and farther behind. Late in 2008, with deadlines looming, a second-unit camera stage was created, by walling off a portion of the volume with a black duvatyne curtain. Richie Baneham was tapped to do cameras on the second-unit stage.

This was the origin of what later became known as the RCP process: the Rough Camera Pass. It turned out that many of the glitches that Cameron was experiencing could be anticipated and solved in advance on the second-unit stage. The virtual second unit was a perfect solution that allowed the production to (barely) make the deadlines on *Avatar*, just slipping the final turnovers to Weta under the wire, with no time to spare.

As a result of that successful approach, by Avatar 2 and 3 the RCP stage was an integral part of the overall workflow. Every scene went through a Rough Camera Pass before it was handed over to Cameron, with either Richie Baneham or talented animator A.J. Briones doing v-cams first to fine-tune the lighting, fix all the problems, and make sure all the Loads ran smoothly.

On the sequels, the editors were soon taking these RCP shots and doing rough assemblies for review with Cameron before he even got to his own virtual camera stage. This proved enormously helpful. By the time Cameron got to any given scene, he had a clear idea of how he might shoot it, based on Richie Baneham's RCP assemblies. If Cameron saw problems in advance, there was plenty of time to fix them before he even picked up the v-cam. This really sped things up, and gave him more time to focus on creative matters versus trudging along problem-solving and patching holes.

"In the world of performance capture, Jim sees his backgrounds, he sees his characters, and he can be creative like a director on a live-action set."

Richard Hollander, VFX supervisor

Now there was much more time for high quality cinematic lighting to be applied to the scenes before they reached Cameron's hands. Richie and the virtual "lighters," working closely with the designers, Ben Procter and Dylan Cole, were able to give a gorgeous cinematic look to every scene before it reached the director's camera stage. A lot of time and money had been spent improving the suite of virtual lighting tools between *Avatar* and the sequels.

On the first film they literally had only 8 lights. Now they had hundreds, and much more user-friendly tools for deploying and adjusting them. What used to take hours, and still look rudimentary, now took minutes and looked spectacular.

The director now didn't have to fight hard to get to a basic look, but could spend his energy polishing the scene and adding his own specific narrative insights. These improvements to the workflow really shone through in the depth and splendor of the imagery in *Avatar: The Way of Water* and *Avatar: Fire and Ash*, which set a cinematic bar much higher than the original *Avatar*.

As Richie explained, "We shoot our cameras and fill them into a live edit as we go, two or two-and-a-half minutes after we shoot a camera. We can then start to understand the language of the scene and that empowers the environment artists, lighters, and animators to take a detailed pass. By the time we get all that to Jim, we'll have a cut sequence that rolls off the RCP stage."

The purpose of all this virtual production at Lightstorm was to do one thing: to create "the Template." The Template was the final cut scene which was then turned over to be finished, to a level of absolute photoreality, by the VFX houses—Weta in New Zealand and ILM in San Francisco. The Template was not a "pre-viz," but an absolute blueprint to be closely followed by the VFX houses: the final cut, to the frame, of the scene as it would appear in the movie. Every shot in it consisted of the final smoothed and refined camera move, plus the main characters with all their precise body and facial performance data, all the background characters, the creatures (roughly animated), and the entire layout, including every tree, vine, flower, and cloud in the sky, and also low-res proxies for all the effects like waves, fire, smoke, and so on. In addition, the cinematic lighting design was highly developed, though it would be refined by the VFX houses later.

The purpose of the Template was to contain all the data that Weta or ILM would need to bring the shots to a level of photoreality, in stereoscopic 3D. Template scenes included not just wholly CG capture scenes, as previously described, but also live-action scenes as well. The live-action photography required a great deal of CG enhancement, including the addition of capture characters (Na'vi, Recoms, and avatars) and also CG set extensions, creatures, vehicles, and effects (fire, explosions, water). In addition to its many other duties, the Lab was tasked with fine tuning the Template for each scene, after the final cut was approved by Cameron. Once completed, the resulting Template scene was called a "Turnover," and delivered to the VFX house for finishing.

The object of all this furious activity at Lightstorm was to get every turnover submitted to Weta or ILM by the contractual deadline for each scene. This ensured that the VFX houses would have time for the vast undertaking of finishing the over 3,500 shots for each sequel. The finished shots would require the work of literally thousands of artists, working for literally years, using techniques and tools that, following Clarke's Third Law, are best described as magic.

Producer Jon Landau invited Richard Hollander, who had recently served as senior visual effects supervisor on *Alita: Battle Angel*, to oversee operations at the Lightstorm Lab—the company's in-house army of digital artists. "There is something that the Lab does in general that's inherently different from most other pictures," Hollander observed. "For virtual production, the Lab creates a Template. That Template is not just a visual representation of the movie. Along with the visual representation of every scene, it contains links to performance capture, a rough idea of lighting, references to props, environments, and data. All of that informs a tremendous amount of information that then goes to Weta. The main point is that, within the structure of the Lab, Jim can participate in all phases of production. He can structure, shape, and redo many things in many ways. In the world of performance capture, Jim sees his backgrounds, he sees his characters, and he can be creative like a director on a live-action set."

A critical component of the director's creative process during Camera is the Kabuki. This is an interim form of facial expression that appears on the characters during Camera, editing, and in the final Template. Kabuki starts with the head-rig video recordings of the actors' faces. These videos are made to feed into Weta's facial pipeline, in order to render the character's expressions in almost molecular detail. But that only happens after the scenes are turned over to Weta. So how does the Lightstorm team see the facial performances in the meantime, so they can even cut the movie together?

Top: During performance capture of Metkayina village scenes, Cameron operates the latest model Swingcam. Small, porcupine-like sticks protruding from the camera body serve as tracking markers to help track camera motion relative to the virtual scene.

Above: The Swingcam monitor displays rough digital renders of Na'vi in their environment, while Cameron composes his "A-camera" blocking as a first-pass overview of the scene.

Above: New RDA technology included robotic Skel Suits that elevate humans to Na'vi height. To help human characters maintain eye contact with Na'vi characters, the production devised a new on-set visualization tool—Eyeline—that flew a small video screen through sets displaying Nav'i facial animation. Here, Courtney Rosemont stands in as General Ardmore in Skel gear alongside Kevin Dorman as Recom Quaritch for a camera test. The Eyeline system is being used as a pacing tool to enable the performers to maintain the correct walking pace to match Stephen Lang's captured performance.

Right: James Cameron uses a proxy object of a Na'vi weapon—a representation of a Mangkwan X-bow—on the performance-capture stage.

Far right: To demonstrate human height in proportion to a Na'vi Recom officer, Cameron interacts with troupe performer Jamie Landau, who wields a full-scale Na'vi prop.

In the earliest stage of development on *Avatar*, in September of 2005, Cameron suggested a way to see the actors' expressions in virtual scenes. He remembered the woman in the crystal ball at the Haunted Mansion attraction at Disneyland, a compelling illusion in which 16mm film of an actress talking is projected onto a bust whose features are blank. As a result, the head appears to the naked eye to be talking. Cameron asked his technical team if they could create a blank white face for a character, and then "projection-map" the video from the head-rig onto the face, in sync with the body motion, to create the illusion of the character's eyes and mouth moving. This innocent question set in motion a 20-year process of the Kabuki facial pipeline that is used to this day.

The first Kabuki test was done right after Yunjin Kim and Daniel Bess were captured for the Prototype test. A blank-faced version of each character's model was created and the facial video was mapped onto it. When played back with the sound track, it created a powerful illusion that the characters were talking and looking around naturally, with nuances of emotion coming clearly through. Because initially the blank face area was white, the characters looked like they were in the white-faced make-up of ancient Japanese Kabuki theater, so the technique was nicknamed Kabuki. That name has stuck, for 20 years. In that time, the process has been significantly refined. Now color is applied so the Kabuki mouth and eye areas blend perfectly with the rest of the character's face. So the original inspiration for the name no longer applies.

"When a CG character is talking, Jim wants to see the mouth and eyes overlaid onto the CG character."

Richard Hollander, VFX supervisor

"When a CG character is talking, Jim wants to see the mouth and eyes overlaid onto the CG character," Hollander explained. "That helps him get the right eyeline or the right pacing on a cut when the character states a line."

When it became time on the sequels to transition from Capture mode to live-action photography, there were many new problems to solve. Both *The Way of Water* and *Fire and Ash* called for far more direct interaction of human and Na'vi characters than the first *Avatar*. Of course, all were played by human actors, but their characters were in two very different scales to each other, and the final blend had to be seamless. A major subplot of *The Way of Water* features Quaritch's teenage son Spider (Jack Champion) interacting with Jake and Neytiri's family, and dramatic scenes of Spider confronting his father, Recom Quaritch. Since Champion, playing a human character, was to be shot during live-action photography, while Quaritch and the others were previously captured in the volume, these interactions required next-level Simulcam technology.

"On our first Simulcam system," noted Ryan Champney, "the actors couldn't see our playback. That was frustrating for Jim because the assistant director guiding actor eyelines—using a tennis ball on a stick—was sometimes not getting the marker where it needed to be. So we introduced the Eyeline system."

Eyeline brought the performance of a virtual character into live-action filming. An iPad displaying the actor's face was mounted on a moving rig at the height of a Na'vi. Robotically controlled winches maneuvered the tablet around the live-action set, programmed with the exact movement of the captured character. This gave Jack Champion and the other actors a clear idea of where the Na'vi or Recom character was at all times. A small speaker, mounted to the tablet, played back the character's dialogue, adding directional sound to the sense of presence.

Cable-flown camera technology, such as Skycam, was introduced in the 1980s to shoot swooping aerial perspectives at sporting events. The rigs used a cat's cradle of cables to winch a camera around a stadium. "We miniaturized that," said Champney. "We wanted to make this nimble and mobile." Casey Schatz, Lightstorm's "tech-viz" guru, mapped and plotted each Eyeline scene in advance, using CG models of the live sets.

As always, it all started with Capture. In the volume in LA, plain gray proxy sets were built that precisely matched the live-action sets which would later be built in New Zealand, except they were 2/3 scale. Stephen Lang and the other actors playing Na'vi-sized characters were captured in these sub-scale sets, so they would be forced to duck under low ceilings and around lighting fixtures and furniture. A little person, four-foot-tall Kacie Borrowman, would often stand in for Spider or other human characters, such as Ardmore or Selfridge. This ensured that Lang's eyeline would be suitably low enough. Sometimes young Jack Champion would do the scene himself, kneeling so he was the right height. This gave Lang, or Sam Worthington, or Sigourney Weaver the actual presence of Jack to play to, so the emotional truth of the scene would be easier for them. A year later, on the live set Lang's recorded performance was used to drive the Eyeline system, so that Jack and the others could see where Quaritch was. Lang's captured motion was also played into the Simulcam system, so that Quaritch appeared in Cameron's eyepiece and the director could operate to follow him. Meanwhile Stephen Lang himself was off making another movie, somewhere else in the world.

The same process was used to film Jack interacting with Jake and Neytiri, and with Kiri, Lo'ak, Tuk, and the other Na'vi characters. For over a year of live-action shooting, Jack Champion (now 15 years old) would interact with these

Above: Recom Quaritch later returns Spider to RDA's Biolab at Bridgehead to consult with General Ardmore (Edie Falco). The production built an open-topped set backed with bluescreen, which allowed the Eyeline screen to maneuver playback of Quaritch's Na'vi face around the lab based on Stephen Lang's performance-capture data.

ghostly giants. He would have to adjust his movement and timing to them, because their performances were captured a year or so earlier, and never changed from take to take. Jack took this all breezily in stride, because it was his first movie and he didn't know that this was not how all movies were made.

The system proved itself dramatically in a pivotal scene where Spider is locked in a medical holding cell as the 10-foot-tall Quaritch looms over him, talking about their relationship. Stephen Lang first acted Quaritch wearing a head-rig and mocap suit in a scaled-down version of the room, playing to a 13-year-old Jack Champion. Two years later, Lang's recorded motions drove the Eyeline system on the live-action set. His face on the tablet glided around the set, just as it would if Quaritch were really there. It gave a powerful illusion to Jack that he was actually talking to his Recom father.

***

Long before live-action production in New Zealand, before principal capture, before any production on the sequels could begin, all the new characters and environments needed to be created by the design teams under Dylan Cole and Ben Procter.

Former Stan Winston Studio veteran Joe Pepe became Lightstorm's first hire as lead character designer on the sequels. "I was a one-person team at the start of work in Manhattan Beach," Pepe recalled. "This time I got to work at the production facility under Dylan and Ben. One of the first things they said to me was that they wanted to better integrate characters and environments. On *Avatar*, when I was working with Chris Swift at Stan Winston Studio in Van Nuys, we were isolated from the rest of the production's art department. Ben and Dylan wanted to participate more in the character design process. I was all for that, and they had tons of input."

Pepe began with the basics—the natural aging effects of the passing years on the two central characters, Jake and Neytiri. "Jim wanted the characters to age as much as the performers had in real life," noted Pepe. "I started with photos that I had of Sam and Zoe from the time when I was with Stan Winston Studio. We lined those up to study whatever age lines had developed, and I worked those in Photoshop onto the models of Jake and Neytiri. Weta then finessed my concepts using scans of the actors."

Younger members of the Sully family blended aspects of their parents' genetics. Lo'ak, played by Britain Dalton, inherited his five-digit hand from Jake's part-human avatar. Jake and Neytiri's adopted daughter, Kiri (Sigourney Weaver) inherited her "extra" digit from her biological mother, Grace's avatar. "The Metkayina make fun of them because they are not true Na'vi," Pepe observed. However Neteyam, played by Jamie Flatters, and little sister Tuk (Trinity Bliss) both favor their mother, with typical Na'vi four-digit hands.

Lo'ak's hands, revealing his human genes, add tension to the dramatic scene in which Recom Quaritch captures the Sully children in the forest and is able to quickly identify Jake's son. This detail also comes into play as a relationship develops between Lo'ak and the Metkayina chief's daughter, Tsireya (Bailey Bass). She tenderly touches his "extra" finger, as she says "I see you." This

"Jim wanted the characters to age as much as the performers had in real life."

Joe Pepe, lead character designer

Right: The Eyeline camera assisted a dramatic scene where Recom Quaritch interrogates Spider, his human predecessor's son. Jack Champion emoted to a small video screen bearing Stephen Lang's Na'vi facial performance, which lowered into the scene and moved around above a blue-suited troupe performer (Kevin Dorman).

Below: Weta then integrated the 10-foot Recom Colonel into the scene with Spider, including reflections and digital extensions of the interrogation room ceiling.

expression has great meaning to the Na'vi. In Na'vi, it is "*oel ngati kameie.*" It can be a simple greeting, meaning no more than "hello". "I see you in front of me." Or it can be a realization "I see you for who you are," as if understanding that person for the first time, seeing into them, seeing their soul. It can be an assurance—"I know who you are, the real you that others don't see." It can even mean "I love you." Sometimes it means several of these things at the same time. The way Bailey Bass says it, as Tsireya, it is an earnest assurance that not only does she love Lo'ak, but she does so for exactly who he is, including for his "alien" uniqueness, symbolized by his extra digit.

Joe Pepe stated, "That metaphor was strongly established by Jim in the first film. Humans are the aliens here, versus the people that are native to the land. On A2, we leaned further into that idea with Lo'ak and Tsireya. Jim wanted Tsireya to appear more alien than the Omatikaya Na'vi, to show that contrast in her relationship with Lo'ak."

Designs for Kiri, the girl mysteriously born from Grace's brain-dead avatar, required the artists to revisit one of *Avatar*'s most challenging character creations. "None of our Na'vi design methods had worked with Grace's avatar," asserted Pepe. "We added the triangular feline nose and made everything from the philtrum (upper lip) down to the chin one-to-one with the performer. We added larger eyes, spread further apart. But we struggled to get that methodology to work with Grace's avatar. Neytiri took about a month and a half to get right, around 60 versions. Most other characters were approved in a week or less. With Grace, it just kept going. Jim concluded that the amounts of Na'vi and human DNA varied in each avatar. And so, with Grace's avatar, there was more Sigourney DNA than Na'vi, so she didn't look as 'alien.'"

Left: Lo'ak concept art by Joe Pepe.

Opposite page: The Sully family at the Metkayina reef. Concept art by Steven Messing.

"The Metkayina make fun of them because they are not true Na'vi."

Joe Pepe, lead character designer

To blend Weaver's features into a gamine teen Na'vi, Pepe began with a Photoshop rendering based on photo reference. The Internet yielded a black-and-white headshot of Weaver, age 17, from the Ethel Walker High School 1967 yearbook—with the motto, "Please, God, don't let me be normal!" Weaver provided higher-resolution family photographs and referred Pepe to footage of her, age 14, attending a Beatles concert at The Hollywood Bowl in 1964. Cameron was pleased with the 2D Kiri mock-up, but the character remained elusive as she took 3D form. John Rosengrant, one of the co-founders of Legacy Effects, (formed by the alumni of Stan Winston Studios, after Stan's death), assisted the character's evolution. "After my initial artwork," related Pepe, "Glenn Hans at Legacy Effects did more work on a 3D scan. They sent that model back, we made printouts, and Jim drew on those to indicate points he wanted us to shift."

Revisions continued at Weta. Reference was key to defining Kiri's facial model, including studies of Weaver's feature film debut, at age 29. "Jim referred us to the shape of Sigourney's lips and her jawline in *Alien* (1979)" said Stuart Adcock, "He wanted to see some of that in Kiri."

Weaver added insights into Kiri's character in a visit to Weta with her co-star Stephen Lang. "Sigourney had already done quite a bit of work on set as Kiri by that point,"Adcock recalled. "She shared with us what Kiri meant to her, and how she'd been channeling her daughter, little moments that she recalled of her growing up, doing eye rolls, or giving her the cold shoulder. That helped her imagine Kiri as a troubled teenager. When Stephen Lang walked in to meet us, he was in character as Quaritch. He was stern and intimidating, playing his character pretty much the whole way through. He scared us all!"

"Sigourney completely embodied Kiri," declared Dan Barrett. "She's one of the great actors of our time. Her performance was spot-on as a 15-year-old, she performed every one of Kiri's scenes."

To develop the animals introduced in the sequel scripts, Zachary Berger was asked to join the team as creature designer (later creature-design lead). Working under Dylan Cole's purview, he began with the inhabitants of the Pandoran ocean. The most ferocious reef marine predator, the akula, was an early design assignment that embodied attributes of a great white shark writ large—70 feet long in its final iteration—a design meant to show the perils of the primordial ocean beyond the safety of the Metkayina's barrier reef. Cole and Berger pitched Cameron on akula predatory behavior. "Jim wanted a claustrophobic scene of Lo'ak swimming through coral where the creature ripped through that coral," Berger recalled. "The shock of that surprise had to

Left: Cameron invited Sigourney Weaver to return to play the Sully family's adopted daughter, Kiri. He encouraged his long-time collaborator to bring her great charm and depth to the teenage offspring of Dr. Grace Augustine.

“[Kiri’s design] was complex, but it was worth spending all that time on her. She’s one of my favorite designs.”

Joe Pepe, lead character designer

Top: Kiri facial studies, Legacy Effects.

Above: Kiri observes Grace Augustine’s unconscious avatar in the High Camp Biolab

Overleaf: Kiri reclines in the Omatikayan rainforest. Concept art by Saiful Haque..

scare the audience. Dylan and I landed on a trifurcated look (for the jaws) and we pitched Jim on that design, gesturing with our hands and making sound effects in the meeting room."

All the Pandoran creatures, whether in the forest or ocean, had thematic similarities that were quite different from Earth's fauna. "Most have six limbs, two pairs of eyes, and black teeth," added Berger, "A lot have armor flush with their shape, with crazy patterning. And they breathe through opercula, which resemble nostrils in weird places on their body. Jim requested that we carry through those design motifs into the second film, and those became our rules."

Multiple artists contributed to creature designs, especially to that of Payakan, the outcast *tulkun* who befriends Lo'ak and forms a bond with Jake's lonely son. Weta Workshop and Legacy Effects designer Scott Patton contributed *tulkun* designs. Lightstorm conceptual designer Constantine Sekeris then created a breakthrough design that seemed to give Payakan personality, a strong lower jaw with impudent, almost human-like "lips."

Cameron himself went into seclusion for a couple of days and returned with a sheaf of pencil drawings showing his vision for the *tulkun*. There was a prawn-like, multi-finned tail that could spread out and thrust vertically like a whale's flukes, or fold into a shape more like a fish's tail so it could swim with a horizontal sinusoidal motion, like a whale-shark. It was imagined that when cruising just below the surface they would use the "fish-swim," and for deep diving and rapid power strokes, a tulkun would use the vertical "whale swim," thrusting its flukes up and down. It could also add a strong flapping motion of

"Jim's go-to ethos guiding creature designs was that they are not monsters; they are animals."

Zachary Berger, lead creature designer

Opposite page and above: Lo'ak launches skyward as a ferocious marine predator—the akula—explosively attacks, its trifurcate jaws engulfing the young Na'vi warrior's ride, a defenseless *ilu*. Concept art by Dylan Cole.

Left: Akula jaw mechanics. Concept art by Zachary Berger.

Top: Lo'ak uses sign language to communicate with Payakan. Concept art by Zachary Berger.

Left: Lo'ak attempts a more direct sensory input with Payakan by swimming into the *tulkun*'s immense luminescent gullet. Concept art by Steven Messing.

Opposite page: Payakan's *kuru*. Concept art by Steven Messing.

its wing-like pectoral fins for maximum power, such as when hurtling upward before a vertical breach out of the water.

Cameron also drew a segmented aft-body, like the chitinous bands of a shrimp's tail but with lateral strakes like a great-white shark. His drawings detailed a pronounced arched jawline, reminiscent of a bowhead whale or right whale, and a flexible neck section forward of its massive armored shoulders so that Payakan's rostrum (head) could articulate for more emotional interaction. Several drawings detailed multiple approaches to the *tulkun* "sensor crest" which became a signature feature of Payakan—the silhouette of his head becoming like a hammerhead shark. Cameron's drawings suggested ways in which the sensor crest could have sensitive acoustic organs, resembling gills, on the ventral side. Lightstorm artists later developed this idea into the detailed reactive "ears" of the *tulkun*, as seen in the film when the *tulkun*-hunters are herding the mother using sound cannons.

Other artists would develop designs differentiating the crests of male and female *tulkun*—the males more splayed out and rectangular, while the females are more sloped and streamlined. Cameron also contributed a series of postural drawings to show some of the arched balletic positions he wanted the *tulkun* to be able to achieve in their social play and ceremonial dances. He was saying to the design team, "yes they are heavily armored but they are also very graceful and beautiful."

The design of Payakan (and by extension the entire *tulkun* species) suddenly snapped into focus. But Cameron's sketches were gestural, and there were still many specific details of color, texture, biolume patterns, and the structure and interaction of the creature's armored plates to be worked out. Some design elements went through many revisions. Payakan's eye, for instance, was featured in important scenes where Payakan had to be able to emote when interacting with Lo'ak.

"The shot where Lo'ak first wakes up on Payakan's shoulder and thinks the *tulkun* is a rock was a gag that Jim really wanted in the film," said Berger.

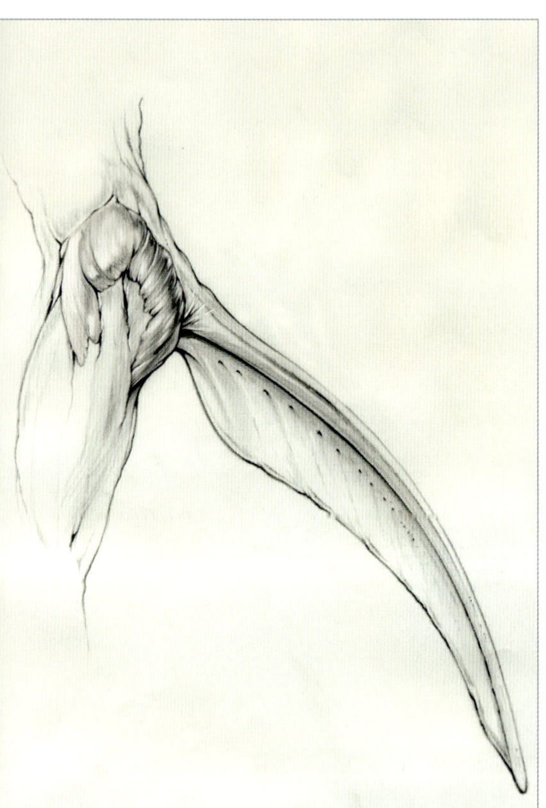

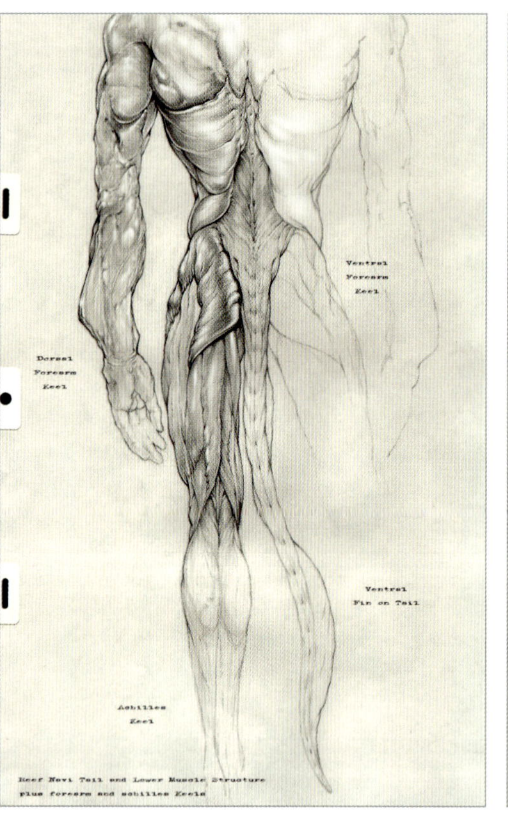

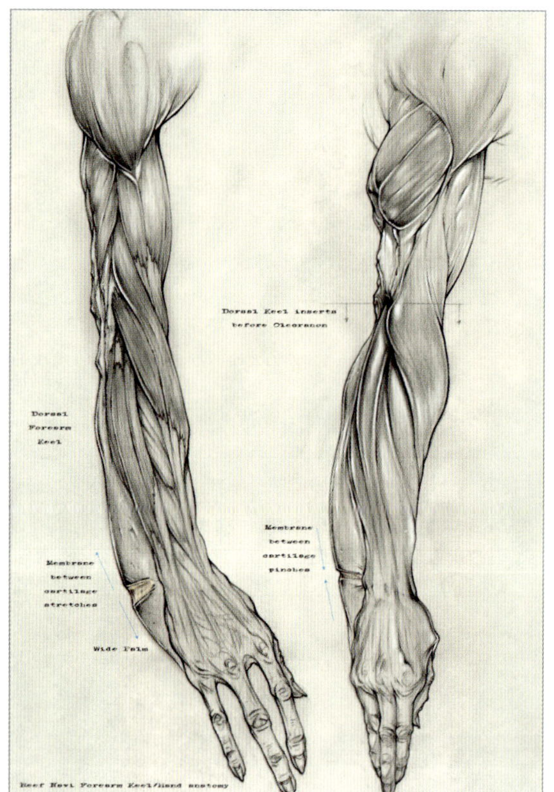

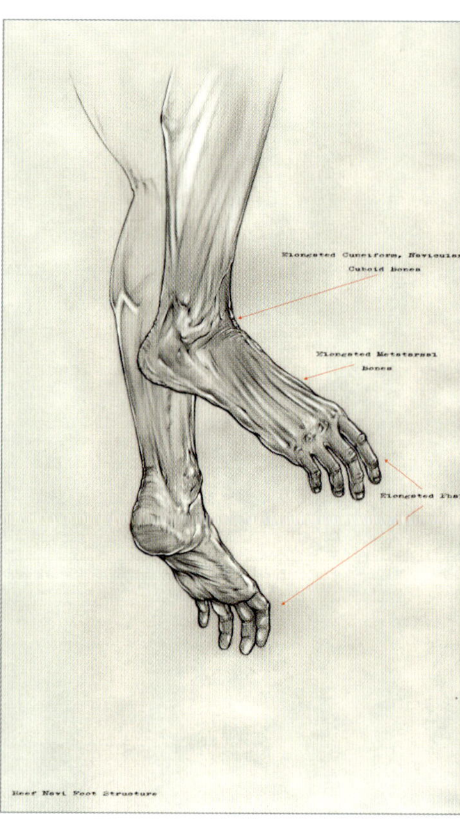

Above: Metkayina anatomy studies by Joe Pepe.

Left: Tsireya, daughter of Tonowari and Ronal. Concept art by Ian Joyner.

Right: Early *ilu* concept art by Dylan Cole.

"Dylan and I had ideas for tropical fish patterning. But Jim didn't want to mess up his rock gag." So Payakan's coloration remained muted—dark grayish greens, with some tan shades in the grooves between the armor plates.

To underline the diversity of reef culture—and to provide a strong contrast with the forest world of the Omatikaya—the production designed the Metkayina with a physique that could have evolved from generations living in symbiosis with the ocean. "In my early notes," James Cameron explained, "I called them the 'littoral' Na'vi, meaning they were a near-shore species. I evolved to calling them the 'Reef People,' because they were a shore-based ocean culture. They weren't living pelagically [in open water]. They don't have gills, they can't breathe water, they're not fish people. They're air breathers. They were a land-based, ocean-adapted species, like sea lions or seals. But I didn't want to make them like The Creature from the Black Lagoon, with big webbed hands and feet, which I felt we've seen a million times. They are an artisanal culture. Their habitats are woven, so they needed dexterous hands to weave. Physiologically, they are very different from the forest Na'vi, almost to the extent of being a subspecies that diverged in their evolutionary path."

Legacy Effects artist Scott Patton created Metkayina anatomy studies, indicating muscular development derived from a powerful swimming style. He recalled, "Jim sketched his perception of how the Metkayina swam. He didn't want webbing in between their fingers because that had been done before. We talked about how alligators and crocodiles swim with their limbs at their sides, with their tail doing a side-to-side swish, and how powerful that was. That translated into meetings with Legacy Effects, discussing how the Metkayina's erector muscles connect in their back and tail. We figured out all that anatomy, and collectively how that could function."

Legacy Effects also created designs for the Metkayina's oceangoing mount—the *ilu*—that combined the elongated neck of Mesozoic marine reptiles like the plesiosaur with the playful nature of a terrestrial dolphin, providing a pleasing contrast to *Avatar*'s more aggressive airborne *ikran*. "Jim wanted the audience to feel like they wanted to take a ride on the *ilu*," said Zach Berger. "Legacy's design was very successful. Dylan and I did bioluminescence patterning and colorations in abstract, butterfly-like blacks and yellows."

The Metkayina's warrior mount, the skimwing, is a ferocious apex predator. Riding it was meant to be not for the faint of heart, as Jake learns the hard way.

"Jim wanted the audience to feel like they wanted to take a ride on the *ilu*."

Zachary Berger, lead creature designer

"The skimwing was gigantic and badass," noted Berger. "It didn't deviate much from the concept of a flying fish, but the head shape went through several iterations. We pitched Jim on a longer snout, something like a needlefish. Jim liked that idea, and then he came to the next meeting with a three-foot-long plastic replica of a gharial skull. He plopped that on the table, and said, 'Let's do the long snout, but make it meatier and more powerful.' I still have that skull in my office. I don't know if he wants it back!"

The reef environment was conceived as a wonderland of crystal clear water teeming with life. "Jim wanted it to feel like snorkeling in the Maldives and life all around," Berger recalled. "Dylan, Constantine, Daphne Yap, and I came up with hundreds of designs for potential Pandoran fish. We pinned them to our

Above: Skimwing concept art by Zachary Berger.

Above right: Skimwing concept art by Zachary Berger.

> "Jim wanted it to feel like snorkeling in the Maldives and life all around."
> **Zachary Berger, lead creature designer**

meeting room wall. Jim took a look and we could tell that he was not feeling it, so our hearts sank a little. But we always kept Sharpie pens and paper on the table for Jim, and he proceeded to sketch, in five or 10 minutes, a dozen or so thumbnail sketches of fish. They were rough, but so communicative. That gave us just enough information to communicate the direction that he wanted, with room to interpret and add flavor to the designs. A lot of our hero fish came from those sketches."

Featured reef creatures included a small predator with a staring dotted eye derived from seven Sharpie strokes. Cameron's sketch inspired the pincer fish, a tapered cylindrical body with a rainbow-hued, fan-like tail and two bony tusks for snipping. The chandelier fish evolved from a Simon Webber Legacy Effects design, which Berger developed into a string of four translucent diamond shapes trailing gelatinous tendrils.

***

Fire and Ash introduced larger creatures inhabiting the skies of Pandora, including one derived from Cameron's unmade screenplay *Xenogenesis*. "The aerocoelenterate was an airborne jellyfish," Cameron explained, referring to his creature from *Xenogenesis*, painted in 1978. "It was a big gas bag, maybe 100 feet in diameter, with tentacles hanging down, purple-striped, that floated around. In *Xenogenesis*, there was a planet with toxic gases down below, and tall mesas with habitats above the clouds, and these creatures preyed on the tops of the mesas. There [was] another species that I called the 'air sharks,' and they eventually evolved into the banshee, or the *ikran* in the first *Avatar*."

The aerocoelenterate conceptually evolved into the gargantuan, gas-filled medusoid in designs that Weta Workshop initiated and Lightstorm refined. "Weta figured out the broad strokes of the medusoid," said Berger. "It was always blimp-meets-jellyfish. It was the biggest aerial creature that we've done, and very abstract. We pitched the idea that it had visual sensory organs, not a

Right: Coral concept art by Annis Naeem.

Far right: Coral fan concept art by Jonathan Bach.

Below: An idlyllic view of Metkayina reef life. Concept art by Steve Messing.

traditional face or eyes. And we gave it a nervous system, like CT scans of brains with all these little nerves, implying internal organs. The initial thrust of that idea came from Jim's early paintings."

The windray, which tows the gondola slung beneath the medusoid, was inspired by a cuttlefish, mixed with another exotic creature from the ancient past. "Jim compared the windray to a prehistoric aquatic animal called the anomalocaris," noted Berger, referring to a Cambrian sea-dweller that vaguely resembled a giant shrimp. "That had a series of segmented fins. And so, at one point, the windray had clusters of tiny little fins. It ended up more like a gas-filled cuttlefish, with a ray-like sinusoidal action. There are fleets of medusoids pulled by windrays. A medusoid is difficult to steer, so the windray is like a tugboat."

Concepts for the people who tame these aerial creatures, the Tlalim Wind Traders, were informed by producer Jon Landau's desire to show the diversity of Na'vi clans. Physiologically, the Tlalim were identical to the Omatikaya and other forest Na'vi, but the clan's activity navigating high-altitude air currents led to comparisons with the complexions of Mongolian nomadic peoples. "I found images of Mongolian tribespeople with very rosy cheeks and skin that was very weathered and sometimes peeling," observed Joe Pepe.

"We knew the Wind Traders live in the sky. They're always up in the high winds, so that affected the colors of their skin, with abrasions from cold temperatures. Jon suggested they should be thinner than the Omatikaya. We reasoned that if Tsu'tey (Laz Alonso) had represented an alpha male of the Omatikaya clan,

Top left: Early windray concept art by Weta Workshop.

Above: Windray concept art by Zachary Berger.

Above right: Early medusoid concept by Wayne Barlowe.

Opposite page, above left: 2005 medusoid concept art by Wayne Barlowe.

Opposite page, below left: Medusoid and windray concept art by Weta Workshop.

Opposite page, right: Early medusoid and windray concepts by Weta Workshop.

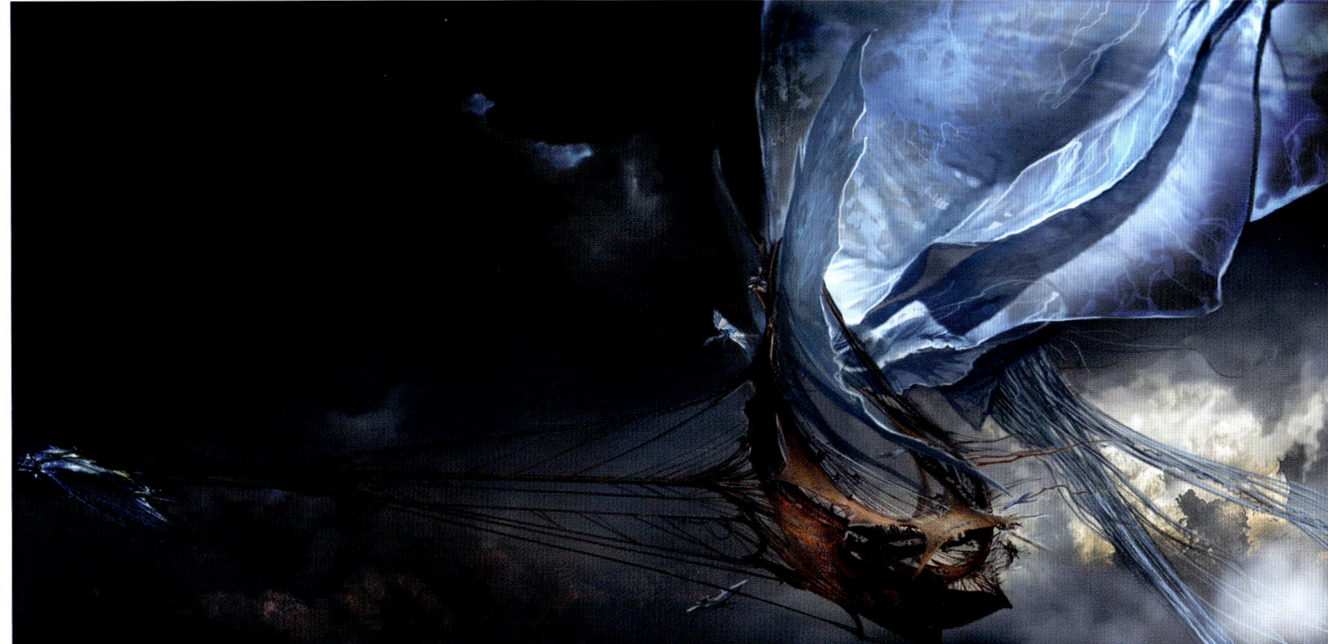

CORAL
Medusi_Rev_07_Texture_B_01
WW
4757

“Legacy Effects created a 3D model and thinned out [David Thewlis’] face to push that gaunt look.”

Joe Pepe, lead character designer

Left: Peylak hi-res model render by Weta.

Opposite page, top: Peylak model based on David Thewlis' likeness by Legacy Effects.

Opposite page, bottom: Mangkwan *ikran* war-paint patterning. Concept art by Zachary Berger.

LEGACY EFFECTS

V005 with warpaint and feathers removed.
Nose lines brought back,
slightly accentuated

the Wind Traders should all be a little thinner than Tsu'tey."

The casting of actor David Thewlis as Tlalim leader Pey'lak impacted the Wind Traders physiology. "I only did one illustration of David as Pey'lak," recalled Pepe, "but it's funny. I sized his eyes accurately to the Na'vi, but Jim wanted them a little larger. I scaled them up in my 2D art. And then Legacy Effects created a 3D model and thinned out his face to push that gaunt look."

The Mangkwan ride into battle on *ikran* daubed in black, red, and white—the colors of charcoal, blood, and ash. However, to signify Varang's dominance as leader of her clan, Cameron suggested she needed a more impressive flying creature, singular to her. "Jim and Jon decided we need a new creature for Varang," stated Zach Berger. "She got a badass new creature, another flying creature that, initially, did not have a Pandoran name. We referred to her among our crew as 'Ashley'—because she's part of the Ash People. We gave

her feather-like dragonfly wings, similar to the *ikran*, but Ashley is like a peacock, so she had a whole bunch more of those. We also gave her a big horn, like the beak of a hornbill bird, that she can use in battle. Her coloration is natively black, red, and white."

Cameron recalls "Somebody said 'Ashley' and I laughed my ass off. The incongruity between the Valley Girl name and the absolute ferocity of this creature. From that moment on she was Ashley. Of course, much later we had to come up with a more suitable name, and somebody suggested Nightwraith, which sounded appropriately badass."

The design team suggested Mangkwan ash makeup and clothing to symbolize Quaritch's mindset at the close of *Fire and Ash*, evoking literary and cinematic themes that had influenced Avatar. "I did some illustrations of Recom Quaritch like Colonel Kurtz from *Apocalypse Now* blended with *Conan the Barbarian*," said Joe Pepe. "In one illustration, I sat Quaritch on a throne made of a whale skull. I didn't even think about it at the time, but that resembled a young *tulkun* skull."

As principal capture on the sequels loomed in 2017, designs continued to pour out of the Costumes and Art Departments for creatures, costumes, and props, driving the fabrication of both physical and virtual assets in California and New Zealand. There was a flurry of activity as everyone prepared for the next phase of production on the sequels—performance capture.

Chapter 3

PERFORMANCE

Performance

By the time performance capture began on the as yet untitled Avatar 2 and 3, in September of 2017, it was not only a mature technology, refined over the four years of Avatar, it had been significantly improved in the intervening years by extensive R&D.

But to understand the evolution of performance capture for the sequels, it's helpful to consider the origins of the process on *Avatar* itself. It started in 2005: a few miles north of Los Angeles Airport, where egrets stalked the pampas grass of the Ballona Wetlands, two hulking gray buildings stood side by side in a nondescript industrial park. The former site of Howard Hughes' 1930s aircraft facility had become Playa Vista Studios, where Lightstorm's *Avatar* production made its home in 2006. Empty factory bays became revolutionary performance capture stages. All of the film's capture work was done there from early 2006 through October 2007, followed by two years of virtual camera sessions and post production, through the film's final delivery in November, 2009. Even some live action photography was done in the adjacent building, the vast hangar for Hughes' "Spruce Goose," the infamous boondoggle aircraft, officially known as Hercules.

Inside the warehouse-sized stage, the newly assembled capture team installed an extensive aluminum truss with an array of hundreds of mocap cameras, and an overhead lighting grid that flooded the stage with diffuse light to fill the actors faces from any angle. It would become the largest capture volume ever created, by a factor of 10, far beyond anything that had been done before. Capture tests began using simple wooden ramps to create the contours of tree limbs, so that Jake and Neytiri doubles could run through the high canopy of Pandora's enormous trees. It quickly became apparent that a comprehensive modular set-construction system was needed, so that actors could move physically through the complex virtual world created by Rob Stromberg's virtual art department. Early production had to be paused while the group sat down—in the middle of a production day—to quickly design a system of modular platforms and ramps that could fit together, like a child's building-block set, to create specific terrain that would underly virtual jungle environments. Each ramp and platform carried an alpha-numeric ID, so the art department could quickly reconfigure the modules to support a variety of Pandoran environments. The physical modules could quickly be wheeled into the empty stage, and the set for any given scene in the film could be assembled in just a few hours. Then the virtual version of the environment was "snapped" to the physical version, precisely aligning the two worlds. Smaller objects like rocks (molded in fiberglass), or cylinders representing logs or tree-trunks, were then brought in, and snapped to their virtual counterparts. Fairly quickly a set could be assembled so that actors and stunt players could run through the jungle, vaulting over roots and logs, pushing off of vertical trunks—physically supported by and contacting the otherwise insubstantial world that existed only in the computer. Everything was painted a flat gray, so it wouldn't reflect the light from the mocap camera's LED arrays, and confuse the system with "noise."

What appeared then, from this drab stage where people in black marker-suits ran around on dull gray platforms, was a virtual image of the Na'vi interacting in a natural way with their vibrant, colorful world.

It was necessary to physically build only that which the performers would touch, or walk on, or climb upon. The rest of the world—vast canopies of trees, distant waterfalls, steep cliffs, and floating mountains—all the wondrous landscapes of Pandora—needed only to exist in the rendered image. The set construction edict was clear: only build what you physically touch.

Cameron, in his signature motocross racing jersey, would use the handheld v-cam to view his characters in their world. His camera displayed images of an alien jungle, through which Na'vi characters moved, driven by the motion of the actors. While he might be seeing, with the naked eye, performers in black marker-suits leaping from a wooden platform onto padded mats, the real-time render would display an Omatikaya hunting party moving through the Pandoran

> "We first designed how Na'vi were going to climb, squat, and move."
>
> **Garrett Warren, 2nd unit director/stunt coordinator**

Previous pages: Varang (Oona Chaplin) and Neytiri (Zoe Saldaña) confront each other.

Opposite page: Eytukan (Wes Studi), *olo'eyktan* of the Omatikaya, welcomes Jake Sully (Sam Worthington) as a son of the clan while Neytiri (Zoe Saldaña) and other members of the clan press forward to connect with Jake in a living mandala. Every Na'vi character was derived from human performance. Screenshot by Weta.

rainforest—a simultaneous image of the scene. The director could request changes to the action, and see the actors adjust moments later, on the next take. No days or weeks of animation required. The process combined the real-time responsiveness of live production, with the fantastic imagery of animation. To a filmmaker like James Cameron, striving to get the worlds that existed only in his imagination out into the world and on film, it was intoxicating. Unlike anything he'd ever done before.

***

The stunt department used combinations of wire-rig "flying" harnesses and other mechanical devices to assist characters' movement in spectacular leaps and falls. The capture system couldn't "see" any of this rigging, so tricks were possible that couldn't be done in live-action shooting. Garrett was infamous for his "kill stick", a massive foam padded brick-bat that he would wield like Conan's battle axe to slam the stunt players sideways, simulating the impact of a creature or the shock wave from an explosion. One of the joys of capture was that such devices remained invisible to the mocap cameras, though the effect was quite visible on the characters. In fact, if you wanted to see a gun or bow in the rendered image, it had to be a "markered prop" or it wouldn't show up in the scene. There were many such props, such as cast-rubber guns and bows made from PVC pipe, that property master Andrew Siegel and his team created to simulate RDA and Na'vi tools and weapons.

For one of Jake Sully's early encounters with Pandoran creatures—fending off a pack of voracious viperwolves—Warren's team used weighted foam puppets and kill sticks to provide visceral impacts. Stunt performer Nito Larioza had the unique ability to run on all fours like a dog. He provided the feral intensity of the lead viperwolf's snarling attack, which in turn elicited natural reactions from Sam as he was chased and attempted to fight back. "In any interspecies relationship," observed Richie Baneham, "—whether it was Na'vi to human, creature to Na'vi, or creature to human—the single most important moment for us was the imparted force. When one character hits another, if the strike on the live-action character and the animated character feels aligned, we can mimic those behaviors in our animation."

One of *Avatar*'s most ingenious stunt set-ups was designed for the scene where Jake's avatar attempts to follow Neytiri in a free-fall plunge down through the forest canopy, during which she arrests her fall by deftly cascading from one massive leaf to another. The stunt required a special stage which the filmmakers constructed in a former Hughes Aircraft Company engine testing tunnel. "Jake and Neytiri had to jump off a high branch, and hit the leaves as they fell," Warren explained. "We needed height, so we built what Jim called the world's tallest motion capture stage. Next to Howard Hughes' office [we assembled] what we called the "elevator shaft." It was 85 feet high. We took six-inch-thick PVC pipes and added pads on top of each pipe to represent monstrous leaves.

We fixed bungee cords to each pad to give some resistance, so as the stunt performer hit the leaf it would bend down. We stuck those out from a truss in the shaft. The stunt people started up high and jumped. As they fell, they hit each leaf, which would bend, and then they'd fall to the one below. That's how we captured Jake and Neytiri falling through the leaves. We did that for real."

Other large-scale capture included horses fitted with glued-on mocap markers, playing the six-legged direhorses, which the Na'vi ride for hunting and, when necessary, in battle. To control their mounts, the Na'vi connect to them with their *kuru*, a "neural-whip." The *kuru* is an extension of the Na'vi's nervous system, emerging from their brain at the base of the skull. It is covered with thickly braided hair for protection from the rough and tumble of daily life in the rainforest. They connect their *kuru* to their creature's kuru, thus joining their two nervous systems. The rider then commands the animal through mental commands.

The point here is that there could be no reins, as you'd have with an Earthly horse. The solution: the horses were led through the action by trainers running on foot, using lunge-leads. Since the trainers were un-markered, they didn't appear in the virtual world at all. This method allowed tight control of the

Overleaf: Neytiri guides Jake Sully through the nocturnal Pandora forest, which glows with bioluminescence. *Avatar* screenshot by Weta.

Above: Reflective markers on horses' bodies and bridles allowed Lightstorm to record animal motion simultaneously to their Na'vi riders, here portrayed by stunt performers on the Playa Vista stage.

Above: Akwey (Peter Mensah, left) and Tsu'tey (Laz Alonso) astride their direhorses. Weta screenshot.

skittish animals in the confines of a sound-stage, and gave the illusion that the Na'vi riders were controlling them mentally. This left the riders' hands free for weapons, such as bows and arrows. But the stunt riders had to have excellent balance to actually pull this off, and once in while they'd wind up flying off the horse when it turned sharply.

But how can a four-legged Earthly horse provide the right motion for a six-legged direhorse? Early on in the creature design phase, tests of walk-cycles and run-cycles were done on the six-limbed Pandoran creatures, to figure out their gait. Testing on the viperwolf model showed that when the animal was walking, its pairs of legs oppose each other. The creature team called this the "ant walk", because as it walks, its three pairs of legs move in opposition. When an ant runs, it just moves its legs in a more furious version of that same cycle. But this scurrying motion would look unnatural in a larger-scaled mammal. For the viperwolf's run, the animators tried coupling the foreleg and the mid-leg on the same side, as if they articulated from a common shoulder joint. In the model, they gave the skeleton a common scapula for the foreleg and mid-leg, and as the creature ran in a galloping motion, those two legs swept forward together. This gave a naturalistic effect for a mammalian run. Then the principle was scaled up to the direhorse. At a full gallop its fore and mid-legs moved in a coupled motion, preserving a powerful and graceful stride, like an Earth horse. So captured motion from real horses mapped very well to the six-legged direhorse. And since the rider's motion was captured simultaneously, the rider flowed well with the movement of their mount.

For the riding of flying creatures, Cameron wanted the same fluid integration of rider and mount. The script called for the Na'vi to expertly ride their pterodactyl-like *ikran*, which the humans call banshees, through the forests and floating mountains of Pandora. Neytiri is one of the clan's best riders, and she sets the challenge to Jake to pass the test of learning to ride. Through this trial, called *iknimaya*, Jake earns his place among the clan, and as it turns out, in Neytiri's heart. Riding the *ikran* was clearly a critical part of the storytelling. But when the production began, nobody had the slightest idea how it was going to be done. A whole new set of techniques had to be developed from scratch. The first step was to figure out what *ikran* flight dynamics would look like. Little bent-wire models of the *ikran* were made, with which Richie Baneham and Jim Cameron would create "flight paths." Like two boys running around dog-fighting with toy airplanes, Richie and Jim would hand-pilot their wire *ikran* around the Volume, banking and diving. They were figuring out the dynamics of how the creatures would interact with mountain terrain, and with each other—swerving around giant "beanstalk" vine formations made out of gray-painted wooden posts, or diving down sheer cliff faces that were nothing more than platforms hauled out from the scene-dock.

With some experience as a helicopter pilot, Cameron has a good sense of aerodynamics, and was striving for highly realistic aerobatic motion. The rigid *ikran* models looked like airplanes flying around Pandora, but later the animators would use classic "keyframe" techniques to bring the creatures to life with wing flaps, tail movement and head turns.

The team then needed to work out how such a creature could be piloted by a humanoid rider. The stunt team first experimented with cowboy rodeo training barrels and stunt pads. Then they progressed to more accurate representations of the creatures' bodies. Stan Winston Studio hand-carved human-scale *ikran* body forms out of urethane foam cast over rigid steel structures, which were then coated with fiberglass. "We fabricated those forms to make them strong but tried to keep them as lightweight as possible," noted Winston character design supervisor John Rosengrant.

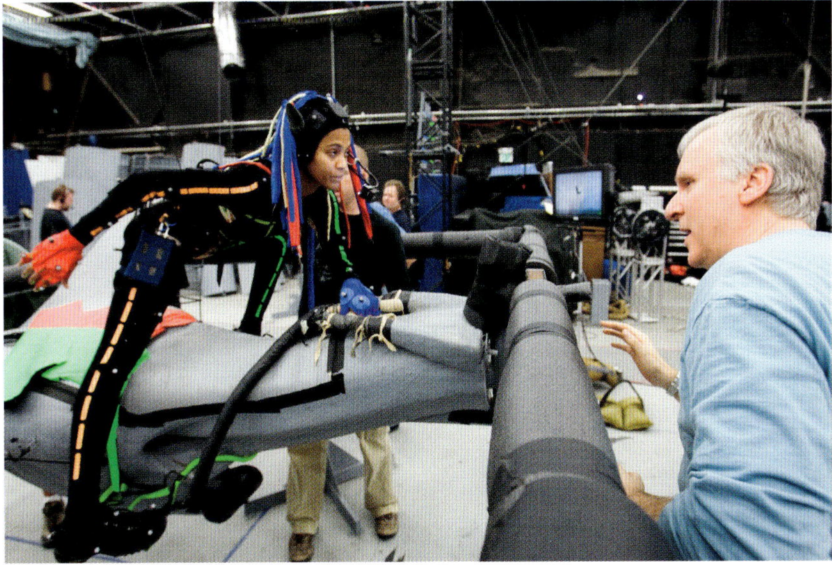

Top: Cameron directs Zoe Saldaña on an *ikran* gimbal rig.

Center: Cameron indicates *ikran* motion, and Sam Worthington uses a stepladder to provide an approximation of his character's eyeline from an adjacent flying creature, while Zoe Saldaña flies her *ikran*.

Bottom: For Jake Sully's first *ikran* flight, Sam Worthington wore a hip-mounted stunt harness that held him aloft, helping him depict Sully clinging precariously to his *ikran*'s bridle as the fierce creature soared through the Hallelujah Mountains, trying to shake its inexperienced rider.

The rigid body form—or "buck"—was designed to be ridden by stunt performers first, to figure out the riding technique, and later by the actors themselves. But first the creative team needed to figure out exactly how one would ride an *ikran*.

To support the flying rigs, the production erected a stunt gantry from I-beams set up inside the Volume. The stunt team then suspended the *ikran* buck, on cables and pulleys, in a way that allowed performers to interact with the flight dynamics. It had been proposed that a motion control system be used, moving hydraulically to match the creature's animated flight dynamics. Cameron rejected that idea. It wouldn't look right for an actor to be tossed around, like riding a mechanical bull, when the character was supposed to be in charge and commanding the creature. Cameron wanted an actor-driven riding system. So the buck was moved by stunt riggers, by hand, assisting in the banking and diving maneuvers that were initiated by the actor's own weight-shifts. The actor could initiate any maneuver, and the riggers, feeling the start of a bank or dive, would react quickly to increase the tilt or roll appropriately. This required a lot of rehearsal and split-second timing, but the result was a naturalistic and highly athletic riding style.

"We started with the idea that they could ride like jockeys," said Garrett Warren. "So we laid pads on the ground and tried hanging the buck on wires. That was hard to balance. We then came up with an idea to mount the buck in a metal frame. Jim suggested we put the creature on a spindle, and he sketched the box configuration, so we could tilt the creature in different directions." Cameron himself jumped on the rig, to get a feel for what it would be like for the actors. He never likes to ask an actor to do something he hasn't tried himself. As an experienced motorcycle rider, the director had imagined that the rider would lean into the turns as you would on a bike. That turned out to be a disaster. By leaning into a turn, and having the creature follow suit into a steep bank-angle, the rider immediately fell off headfirst. Cameron quickly realized that you had to move opposite the creature's roll angle, pushing your weight aggressively to the uphill side. This allowed the rider to stay upright as the creature banked sharply. It was more like skiing on steep terrain than riding a bike.

Top: Cameron shows playback of the *ikran* flight to Worthington on the Playa Vista stage.

Above: Witness cameras record closeups of Sam Worthington's facial performance as stunt team members pitch the *ikran* rig skyward. At the same time the wire-rig hauls Worthington toward the ceiling of the performance-capture stage.

It turned out that the rider could never rest their weight in the saddle, but needed to keep the weight on the balls of the feet, like a jockey. To bank rapidly left and right required the rider to make aggressive weight shifts from side to side, all while leaning far forward into the "windstream", torso horizontal, jockey-style. Also keeping the weight in the legs versus the seat of the pants allowed the legs to absorb the rhythmic up and down motion imparted by the flapping wings, like posting on a horse. This posture put serious strain on the quads and glutes. After a day of riding the performers were limping around in pain.

"Riding those creatures was very taxing for the actors," noted Warren. "(they) were riding on the balls of their feet, so their leg muscles were burning constantly. Within 30 minutes, your legs felt like they were on fire. Jim called it the 'Banshee Buns of Steel Workout.'"

In case they fell off in the aggressive maneuvering, the performers wore a stunt harness that fitted around their hips, with a safety line attached to the overhead gantry. Warren kept a grip on the safety line "pick-point" in the small of the performer's back, helping to maintain the center of gravity. Four stunt riggers then manipulated creature motion by hand. "It was hard," admitted Warren. "On the sequels, we decided we were going to change the flying rig to be more like a marionette, hung by wires."

The design of the *ikran* saddle and "stirrups" became a critical factor. To make the correct position for a steep bank, the actor needed firm footing, especially on the downhill leg. A steel bar with foot-pegs on either side was added to the buck, and soon the performers were developing a very athletic and plausible riding style, that looked great in the virtual images when mounted on the animated creatures. These footpegs were incorporated into the design of the "tack" the Na'vi strap onto their creatures, as seen in the final CG shots.

But the script also called for Jake to tame and ride a wild *ikran*—flying bareback. So how do you ride with no tack—no foot pegs? To solve this, the design of the *ikran* itself was modified. *Ikran* breathe through large forward-facing nostrils in their chests, called opercula, inspired by the air intakes on a jet fighter. Each operculum is nested in the hollow between the neck muscles and creature's clavicle. By thickening and lengthening the *ikran*'s clavicles, it was possible to design in a ledge that Jake could just barely hook his foot into, to act as a natural footpeg. So the urethane *ikran* buck was given enlarged fiberglass clavicles that the Sam could hook his heels onto. In Avatar, during Jake's first ride, you see him clinging on tightly, with his foot occasionally slipping off the clavicle.

The *ikran* buck was also used for other moments besides flying. By adding a foam rubber head with operable jaws, it served as a big puppet for interaction with the characters while it was perched on the ground, as seen when Neytiri introduces her *ikran* 'Seze' to Jake. "The banshee pushes Neytiri like a horse because it wants her to feed it," noted James Cameron. "That was Garrett Warren with an *ikran* head—Garrett ended up doing a fair bit of *ikran* acting. He'd vocalize, Zoe would pat the puppet, it would push against her. That was all performed, and then the animators took their cues from that, backing into how Zoe moved. When Jake first wrestles his banshee, that was a big, jointed *ikran* rig, made from cloth, PVC pipe and foam rubber, puppeteered by five or six people. We called it the 'rubber chicken.' Sam wrestled that, grabbed its neck, bent it down in a [wrestling] figure-four chokehold, wrapped his legs around the neck, and trapped the head, and then he got his hand free so that he could make his *kuru* connection. It was full-on MMA! During production, Garrett and I sometimes train together, early in the moring, in kick-boxing and kali. For that scene we worked out the moves together, down on the floor, wrestling that rubber chicken. Everything was physically based."

***

The basics of creature riding were worked out on *Avatar*. But for the sequels, there would be a lot more riding of creatures, on land, sea and air, and the production planned accordingly. In 2015 the riggers equipped the new Volume with an even larger stunt gantry, with more dexterous controls designed to simulate airborne motion for multiple riders. "We mounted four posts around the stage to support a 3D cable-winch system," said Warren. "That allowed us to fly creatures all around this football-field-sized stage. We built a T-bar rig, where the back part of the 'T' was positioned behind the creature's wings. A long pole went down to the nose of the creature. That was counter-balanced, so it always stayed flat, hanging on a single wire, so a rider could sit on the rig and it would move." Stunt players and actors could control the creature, while riggers on the ground assisted the maneuvers. " We'd have one person in the front and one or two in the back," Warren explained. "They would amplify the motion as the actor was 'talking' to the creature. The rider had to think, 'Go right,' and then it would go right. We'd lightly touch the creature, and when the rider pushed their feet down, we'd keep it going forward. The new rigs gave us a much greater range of motion. They took far fewer people to maneuver, and we were able to do so much more." The overhead gantry supported three flying rig tracks, which allowed multiple airborne riders to be captured simultaneously, flying in formation, even landing together. "We could put a creature on each track. We could position them beside each other, push them forward, pull them back, fly them around the stage. We could take them as high or low as we wanted and change the angle mid-flight. It was incredibly valuable to have that fluidity."

Before the RDA's expeditionary force returns to Pandora, Jake and Neytiri enjoy an idyllic evening soaring on *ikran* around the Hallelujah Mountains. The stunt team's flying rigs worked perfectly for the scene—informally-known as "Date Night"—allowing Worthington and Saldaña to interact in mid-air.

Above: Sam Worthington performs on an *ikran* rig on the Manhattan Beach stage. Jake, on aerial reconnaissance, has learned from his youngest son that the Sully siblings have stumbled across an RDA Recom team. Performance capture and Weta screenshot.

> "Riding those creatures was very taxing for the actors... Within 30 minutes, your legs felt like they were on fire..."
>
> **Garrett Warren, 2nd unit director/stunt coordinator**

JPARK

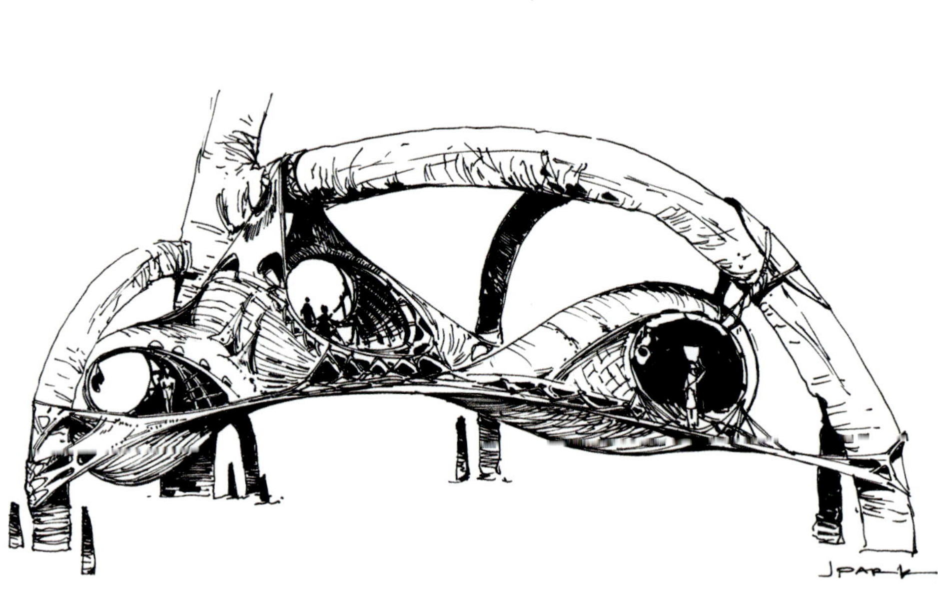

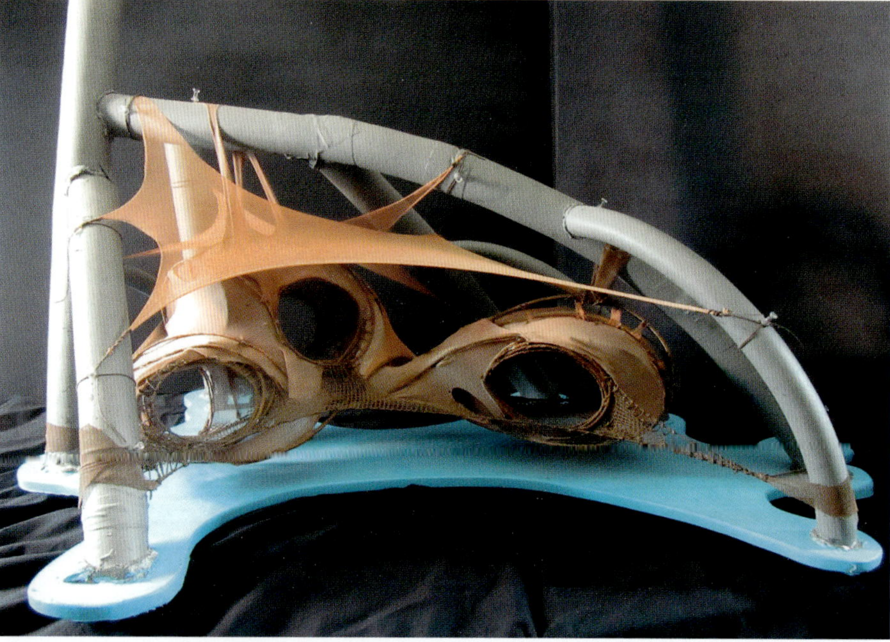

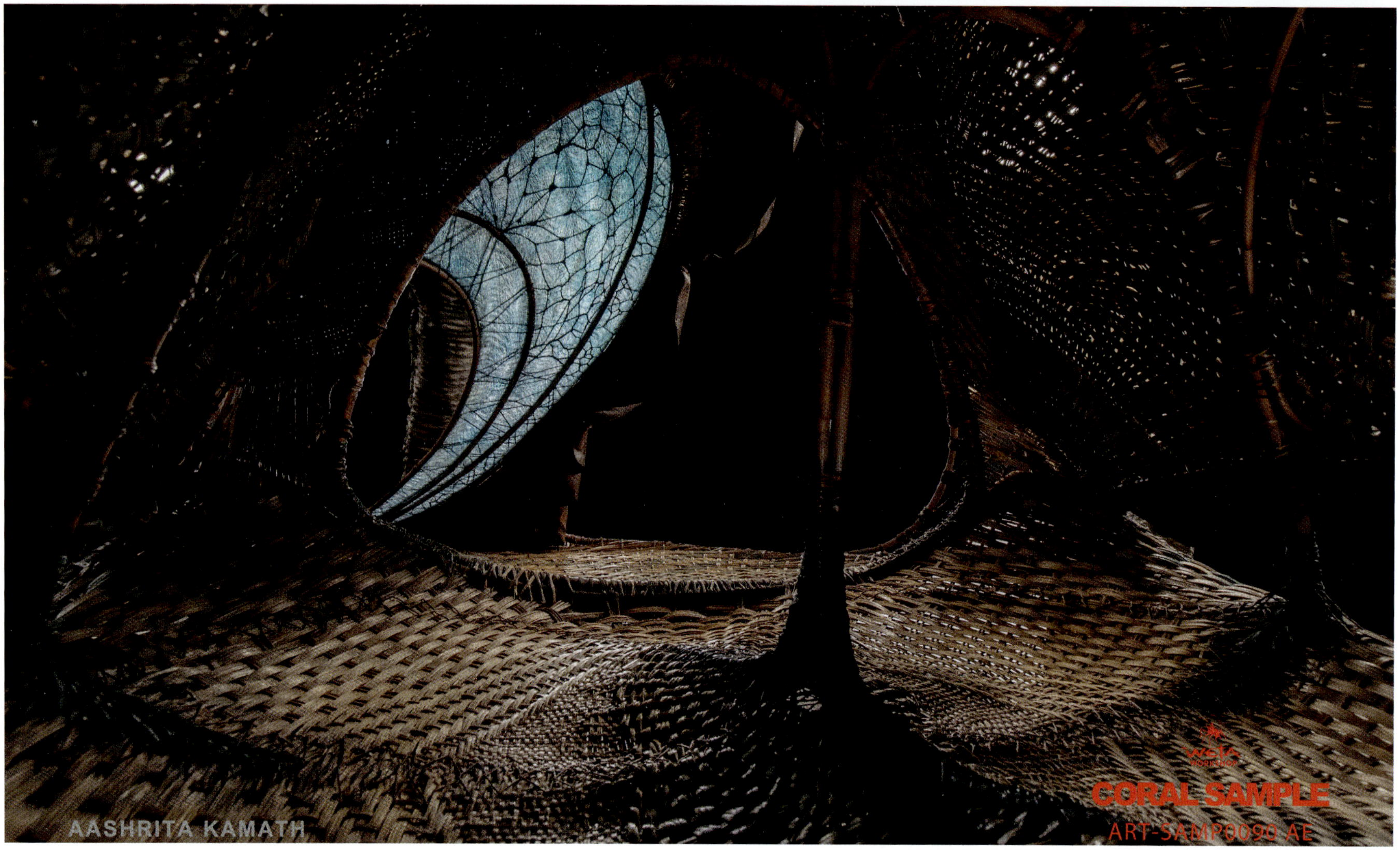

AASHRITA KAMATH
CORAL SAMPLE
ART-SAMP0090 AE

The emphasis on real physics extended to the sets as well. The Metkayina village was one of the production's most elaborate sets, a network of woven walkways, suspended over the shallow lagoon and connecting their homes (*marui*, in Na'vi). The whole thing needed to flex beneath the actors' feet, like walking on a trampoline. The walkways were built using black nylon cargo-net straps, that were tensioned by cables strung between steel columns, using tons of force to keep it all from sagging. The actors could walk through the entire village along this meandering walkway, bouncing naturally as it flexed under their weight. 8 year-old Trinity Bliss loved this scene, bouncing along like a kangaroo as Tuk explores the Metkayina village.

Across the two sequels, a large number of scenes took place inside the Sully's marui, the home gifted to them by the Metkayina clan. This was a large yurt-like woven house stretched between the massive roots of a Cyclopean mangrove tree. The Sully *marui* was part of the Metkayina village, connected to the other family *marui* by woven walkways. Note: the plural of *marui* is *marui*. Just as the plural of *ikran* is *ikran*. One *ikran*. Five *ikran*.

Because it is the home set for the Sully family, appearing in multiple scenes across the two sequels, it had to be complex and intriguing. The production commissioned Weta Workshop in New Zealand to create a detailed model of the Sully *marui*. Working from concept art by Dylan Cole's team, Richard Taylor and his model makers strove to evoke a sense of indigenous craftsmanship in the construction of the Sully's reef home. "Jim wanted a sense of tactile reality," noted Taylor. "We've got a war-cry here at Weta Workshop: 'Ecological plausibility.' We think of it as a line drawn on a whiteboard: at one end is documentary reality, and [the fantasy film] *Krull* (1983) is at the furthest. Pandora sits almost on the documentary line. That's how plausible it is. We wanted to create the notion that there are many Na'vi clans spread around the planet and that all the materials they use derive from the land, or the animals they hunt."

Weta artisans built the Sully *marui* in miniature, at 1/6-scale, spanning 17 ft. "First we welded together an aluminum tubular frame," Taylor explained. "We then worked with stripped flax, rattan, and wicker. We brought in every possible material, some from the people of Aotearoa [the Māori name for New Zealand] and some from other cultures. Weaving styles are dependent on the types of plants that each community grows or has access to. If you look at Ancient Egyptian boats that were used for navigating the Nile, they were originally

Opposite page, top left and below: The marine environment of the Metkayina clan took shape in sketches by Jonathan Bach and John Park that defined the construction, layout, and textures of an elegant structure known as a *marui*.

Opposite page, top right: *Marui* model built by Jeff Frost and Adam Mull at Art Dept.

Right: The Sully family arrives at the Metkayina *marui*, a network of habitats painstakingly constructed from wicker and oceanside materials suspended between mangrove-like roots. Performance-capture sets were rigged and dressed for realistic interactions that Weta emulated in digital environments.

Above: The Metkayina greet a school of highly-intelligent cetaceans—*tulkun*. The *tulkun* return to the reef every year as part of their migratory pattern. Concept art by Dylan Cole.

Left: *Marui* village concept art by Jonathan Bach.

Opposite page: Weta's *marui* model spanned 17 ft in diameter, built from wicker and rattan over a steel frame. The miniature provided filmmakers and visual effects artists at Weta with tactile visual reference for surface tension, reflectivity, and material properties of the structure.

made from a certain type of hollow reed. Chinese culture used bamboo for irrigation, scaffolding, or making paper. We wanted the same principle to apply to the Na'vi and their *marui*." The model-making team drew on its familiarity with New Zealand crafts. "We found people that did complex weaving, wicker, and rattan work. Our model makers trained with them. It was a massive piece of model making. You could run your fingers across the walkways [of our miniature] and they would spring and bounce like the side of a wicker basket. Our theory was that the Na'vi were so focused on these crafts that they would add ornamentation to indicate and celebrate their position in society. They wouldn't make [their work] simply utilitarian. They would invest the beauty of their own culture in their complex weaving patterns to create extraordinary, beautiful work."

The *marui* miniature featured among more than 3,000 Na'vi artifacts that 300 Weta Workshop artisans created for the production. The team worked hand-in-hand with the costume and art departments, employing leather tooling skills, multi-shaft loom weaving, shell and wood carving. Specialty items included 50 Na'vi prop knives and axes derived from materials that resembled rock-crystal and coral structures.

It's important to remember that none of this painstaking work actually appears in the film directly. It was all done as reference, so the VFX team at Weta could scan it, photograph it, study it, and create the CG model of the Sully *marui* with the level of detail and authenticity that the film demanded. The physical model's detail also informed the CC models of the other homes and structures in the village. Even though all were unique in shape, they all employed the same Na'vi fabrication techniques.

The design of the reef village was a major undertaking for the art department. It started with a gestural sketch Cameron drew on a whiteboard, of pod-like structures suspended under the arches of a vast mangrove tree's roots. Cameron didn't want anything resembling human architecture. No cut lumber forming rectangular shapes, which the Na'vi would have found horrifying, not just aesthetically but because it meant mutilating trees. The director envisioned "tensile structures"—essentially woven tents and tarps stretched between the rigid tree roots. The Na'vi would also use "tension hoops," bent rattan members that formed curved ribs, between which woven floors and walls could be stretched in tension. The whole thing would have an organic feeling, almost like a living creature. The director imagined the village flexing gently as the inhabitants moved through it.

Cole and his team ran with those provocations, coming up with a myriad of intriguing designs for the pod homes and the walkways, from which Cameron selected a handful. There were many iterations of the layout, to get the exact meandering feeling for the walkways stretched between the marui and the pillars of the mangrove roots. A miniature of part of the village was made out of coat hangers and panty hose, so that the art team could explore the tension and flexion forces acting on the homes, walkways and ramps. From this more detailed designs were created with *maruis* designed in connected clusters. Detailed final 2D art was created, taking care to contrast the warm earth tones of the woven architecture with the turquoise of the tropical water. Those connected clusters were then modeled in 3D and this formed the building blocks for the village layout.Finally it seemed like a real place, one that expressed the Na'vi aesthetic of artisanal construction, with curved organic shapes and tribal patterns. Most importantly it was a place that the audience might fantasize wanting to live in.

Costume designer Deborah Scott also conducted extensive research into cultural references for Na'vi clans. "We researched indigenous peoples from all over the world," Scott remarked. "We found a tremendous wealth of information. It is remarkable how trends, including modern fashion, resonate worldwide. For instance, tattooing is a global practice, and body art goes back centuries."

Cameron's Metkayina mandate included long, flowing black hair to honor the Polynesian cultural influences in the film. Weta Workshop and Legacy Effects created Metkayina designs and maquettes, which Deborah Scott and the Costume Department artisans used as reference. "The Omatikaya people wore braids, whereas the Metkayina wore curls," said Scott. "We used real human hair to make wigs and found ways to braid and twist hair. We shot footage to show how long, curly locks would look dry and wet. When the Metkayina swam around, their hair tended to straighten out. When they came out of the water, we saw how the curls re-established themselves in wet hair. We logged all this information for the animators and the visual-effects artists. Working with Jim, you've got to follow designs all the way through so that you have a full

Above: The production experimented with the physicality and movement of Na'vi hair by crafting physical items. This Metkayina wig by Weta Workshop was used for early hair exploration and water tests.

Above: The wardrobe department conducted underwater tests of physical materials to determine textures, weight, and motion of Metkayina costumes.

understanding. And we did that with pretty much every garment. How did each one behave underwater? How much water would a certain material absorb? We had to be very mindful of the qualities of handwoven fabrics—if we wanted them to sink, swim, or float. It was a science lesson in the natural world."

Metkayina costumes featured ocean-sourced materials of seaweed, shells, fish skins, and coral, which Deborah Scott's team created using driftwood and shells from the Wellington seashore, as well as modern manufacturing processes of molding, casting, and 3D-printed objects. "It was interesting to compare a 3D-printed item with a real object, like a shell," said Scott. "The real shell won every time. We ended up using a mix of real and fake shells, and we also did a tremendous amount of carving, weaving, knotting, and beading. The Metkayina people are more ornamented than the Omatikaya, we surmised, because they have more leisure time at the beach to sit around and weave. They have a fancy, more complicated way of expressing themselves. We tested all those pieces on the performance-capture stage. The costumes informed the action and the movement of the characters. For instance, Jon Landau often referred to Kiri's shawl, which she liked to hug around her shoulders—Sigourney could have mimed that, but we made a real shawl for her to wear on set because miming that behavior would have never had the same effect."

As Richie Baneham always says "Pantomime is the enemy of truth." Cameron also called for greater realism in battle scenes, and enlisted armorers John Welch and Robert Golatti to bring a new level of realism to the gun action. "In many cases, actors were pulling triggers on real machine guns firing half-load blanks," property master Brad Elliott revealed. "That meant that mag changes had to be honest. They had to push a button, pull out a mag, flip it away, load a new mag correctly, and charge the bolt. They weren't pantomiming that action. They had to do it for real. And, more important than the technical accuracy, it was visceral and loud."

To create the sensation of live fire in combat, the production fitted real guns into mockup props based on Lightstorm designs. Working weaponry included Airsoft electric air guns. For more furious firepower, the production selected the Magpul ACR—"adaptive combat rifle"—a U.S. military weapon. The receiver and trigger areas of that particular firearm most closely fitted into the art department's RDA designs.

Firearm scenes followed strict safety protocols, training actors to understand and respect the weapons, and equipping cast and crew with shields and earplugs. "Jim has a keen awareness of how important gun safety is on set," asserted Elliott. "We were never pressured into doing anything unsafe, we were never rushed, and we were always accommodated when we needed to move witness cameras out of the 20-foot danger range for blanks." The effects of real blank-fire in performance capture were palpable. "When Sam was taking cover behind a gray tube representing a fallen tree, it was so much more for him when on the other side of that tree there were three people with machine guns making a lot of noise." It was also important for Sam to handle the weapon like an experienced war-fighter when he returned fire.

Worthington had no military or weapons training before being cast in *Avatar*. So the director had him train with former US Marine John David "JD" Cameron, the director's brother, who had seen intense combat action in Operation Desert Storm. In a three-day crash course at an abandoned ranch in the Malibu hills, Sam was put through a grueling boot-camp by JD and two fellow Marines. From belly-crawling through the mud, to weapons handling, to small squad tactics, JD drove Sam mercilessly like the drill sergeants who had trained him 15 years earlier at Camp Pendleton. When the director checked in on a training session, he found Sam gasping for breath. "They're fit f—kers, I'll give 'em that," Sam wheezed, in his thick Aussie accent. But over the course of the production Worthington mastered the weapons handling, becoming a lethal machine. He could snap through a reload in under two seconds, and advance with precision footwork and perfect form as he pivoted from target to target.

Interactivity of a much more peaceful nature was required for an early montage in *The Way of Water* where the Na'vi celebrate the birth of Jake and Neytiri's first son, Neteyam. Sam Worthington performed Jake's triumphant ceremonial gesture—raising the infant aloft to honor *Eywa*—with a placeholder doll. Weta animation supervisor Stephen Clee then drew on his personal experience when animating the blue squirming baby. "Stephen and his wife had just had a

Top: Sam Worthington as Jake takes aim with an RDA firearm.

Left: For RDA weaponry, Weta designed an arsenal of futuristic guns in collaboration with the property department. These included blank-firing automatic weapons, and a 30-caliber door gun manned by RDA Sec-Ops corporal Wainfleet (Matt Gerald) on the Samson Tilt-rotor aircraft.

Left: Weta reference—and the joyful performances of Zoe Saldaña, Sam Worthington, and baby Oliver Moore—inspired a touching family scene where Jake, Neytiri and members of the Omatikaya clan celebrate the birth of the Sully family's first-born son, Neteyam.

"The *marui* set was fully dressed. We added a basket of toys and a lot of other props..."

Brad Elliott, property master

baby," Richie Baneham recalled. "Stephen videoed his baby waking up. That gave us his way of stretching and other behaviors." Closeups of Baby Neteyam featured three-month-old Oliver Moore, the son of actor Joel David Moore (Norm). "Baby Neteyam was Joel's little fella, Ollie. Joel brought him to the set. We didn't put markers on Ollie, but we shot video reference. And then, Stephen Clee animated from that reference."

One of the sequels' most affecting performances emerged from an acting challenge that Cameron posed to then 69-year-old Sigourney Weaver: to play a teenage girl. As Kiri, the orphaned daughter of Grace Augustine's avatar, she would have to become an awkward, introverted fifteen-year-old. This was an example of the amazing new possibilities of performance capture. Actors could transcend their bodies to play any character they can imagine.

Sigourney took this challenge very seriously. She started her research by spending weeks in the company of adolescent girls, observing their speech and gestures. Through that preparation, she was able to access her own internal teenager, whom she had suppressed her whole adult life. Sigourney was known for playing hard-edged, intelligent, steely-eyed women of power. At six feet tall, she commanded a room. She had played queens, CEO's and alien-killers. She needed to dig deep to find the vulnerability and insecurity of a teen girl, and that sense of powerlessness that could flash in an instant into defiant certainty and outrage. She saw Kiri as living very much in her imagination, happy to be alone communing with plants and bugs—comfortable in her own skin, except when she was around others.

Stunt double Alicia Vela-Bailey worked with Weaver to develop body language that expressed Kiri's sometimes petulant charms. "It was amazing watching Sigourney ply her craft," Baneham remarked. "Honest to God, when Jim called 'action,' she turned into a 15-year-old girl. She had a lightness to her movement and a joy to her character. There were some things we did augment—no matter how fit an older person is, our knees and hips are not what they were when we were 15."

Cameron, who is close to Sigourney's age, sympathized. He found a solution to the differential between the springiness of a fifteen-year-old and the reality of even a very fit 70-year-old. "I made a deal with Sig. I said, 'You figure out what you want to do, how you want Kiri to be expressed. You act every scene, feel the moment, lay down a bass track, if you will. But if there's something you can't quite do physically the way you know in your heart Kiri would do it, like say spontaneously jumping up onto a log to perch like a cat, then ask Alicia to do it. You direct Alicia. I won't do it. I won't go around you. You tell her what you want, and you watch her until you feel it expresses Kiri your way. I take myself out of it.' I knew that since *Avatar*, Sigourney and Alicia had grown close creatively, and that Sig trusted her."

Sigourney acted every single scene as Kiri, throughout 18 months of capture for both A2 and A3, including all of her underwater scenes. Only the occasional augmentation from Alicia was needed, such as springing up out of a deep

Above: On her arrival at the Metkayina reef, Kiri (Sigourney Weaver) hugs her shawl around her. Weaver's portrayal of the teenage offspring of Grace Augustine's avatar resulted in one of the film's most affecting performances. Weta screenshot.

Na'vi squat, or leaping across big gaps between tree limbs. When Alicia was called in to enhance, she channeled Sigourney's emotional performance flawlessly in her body language, from Signourney's typical teenage eye-rolls and disgusted huffs, to hurt slumps of the shoulders.

"Kiri is trying to figure out who she is," Sigourney Weaver observed in an interview with Collider. "She's trying to figure out who her father is, how she belongs in this world, why she feels so different from other people. I wanted her physical being to reflect the see-saw of emotions that she feels, from great joy to great feelings of injustice, and all those things you feel when you are 15."

Vela-Bailey also doubled Sigourney for stunt action, as she had for Zoe. "There's nothing new about using stunt performers on action movies," noted James Cameron. "Stunt people double actors all the time, if their character is going through a window, getting set on fire. Some actors are more physical and are better at doing their own stunts than others." Sigourney was game for anything, and always made sure she first figured out the emotion and movement of Kiri in every scene. But when it came time to leaping 10 feet from tree limb to tree limb, fast-mounting an *ilu*, or getting dropped 15 feet to face-plant on the deck of a ship, she left that to Alicia, whose bones seemed to be made of rubber.

Alicia had an uncanny way of code-switching her movement between the two characters of Kiri and Neytiri. From one scene to the next, she would channel Zoe's lethal jungle-cat intensity, then switch to Sigourney's teenage gawkiness. In addition, Alicia was tapped to double Oona Chaplin for stunt action. As Varang, Alicia would code-switch yet again, channeling Oona's confident hip sway, and her low crab-walking feral postures. Alicia also had to play her own character, Ikeyni, leader of the Ikran People of the Eastern Sea, which she did with yet a fourth distinct movement style—the haughty carriage of a warrior queen. Across all four characters, Alicia achieved a remarkable feat of physical interpretation.

Another troupe artist who played multiple characters across the three Avatar films was Kevin Dorman. On *Avatar* Kevin distinguished himself as a versatile actor who could play any character, and with broad emotional range. He became a mainstay of the troupe. Kevin rose to prominence on the sequels as Sam's double during flying and action scenes, and especially during live-action shooting, while acting on Sam's behalf in scenes with Jack Champion. Jack came to rely on Kevin to recreate Sam's performance of Jake for him. In Jack's mind Jake was a composite of both Sam and Kevin, and both actors conveyed Jake's strength, courage and fatherly demeanor. Between the first film and the sequels, both Sam and Kevin had become father's themselves, and could convey those parental emotions authentically, drawing from real life. Kevin became the male equivalent of Alicia, the star troupe performer who was a

Swiss Army knife actor. Kevin code-switched fluidly between doubling Jake and Quaritch, whenever additional motion was required for the two leads. He was the first choice for playing all of the male secondary characters. Across the three films Kevin played uncountable other characters—human, Omatikaya, Metkayina, Tlalim and Mangkwan, whatever the day's capture required. When Cameron wanted an actor to take the place of Payakan's eye, to interact emotionally with Britain Dalton playing Lo'ak, he chose Kevin. The troupe actor gamely made up his own version of *tulkun* vocalizations, and took his place in the Payakan mock-up, during scenes captured in the tank.

Other troupe players distinguished themselves across the sequels, during Capture, and as blue-suited doubles and puppeteers during live action. Courtney Rosemont, Kevin Henderson, dubbed "K2" to distinguish from the other Kevin, Johnny Alexander, Jake McLean, Devereau Chumrau, Shawn Driscoll, Brandon Melendy, stuntman Steve Brown, and New Zealand-based Tarikura Kapea all contributed their unique skills and heartfelt talents to bringing the Na'vi to life. Kacie Borrowman remained a rock-steady core member of the troupe in both Capture and live-action phases.

***

The most challenging aspect of *The Way of Water* was the story's immersion in the oceans of Pandora. Cameron's commitment to capturing authentic performances informed by real-world physics required a massive investment in R&D. It also put new demands on the actors' physical abilities.

The Metkayina were ocean-adapted mammals that could hold their breath for many minutes at a time, like seals and otters. And the Sullys would learn the techniques for long free-dives from the Reef People, as the story progressed. So all the actors had to learn to hold their breaths. For a really long time. This included 70-year-old Sigourney Weaver, seven-year-old Trinity Bliss, and everyone in between.

It was always known, from Cameron's first proposal of capturing underwater, that the actors would need to master freediving, the art of breath-hold diving. It was intrinsic to their characters. What the production needed was a world-class expert on freediving, to train the cast.

Years earlier, dive specialist Kirk Krack—pronounced "kr-ahk"—recognized Cameron when they were randomly on the same plane together, and introduced himself. The director said "I know you! You're the guy that did that underwater parkour film, 'Defending the Vandenberg.'" Krack had put together a troupe of underwater performers and shot a short film of them performing radical breath-hold action around the massive wreck of the Vandenberg, a Navy radar ship that had been sunk as an artificial reef. Cameron was impressed by the dynamism of the underwater stunts and asked Krack for his card. Later, when crewing up for the Avatar sequels, Cameron invited him to join the team. Krack's fascination with diving dated back to his boyhood in Saskatchewan, Canada, where he was instinctively drawn to snorkeling and sailing.

> "We're born of the oceans. From conception to birth, we mimic human evolution."
>
> **Kirk Krack, dive specialist**

"I remember a swimming lesson when I was eight years old," he related. "We were in four feet of water, which was over my head. We had to go underwater, kick off the wall, and glide. I felt like I was Superman." After working as a dive shop owner and as a SCUBA instructor in Cuba, Belize, and Mexico, Krack began freediving using controlled breathing exercises, called a "breathe-up," followed by breath-holds of several minutes. "I noticed that my breath-holds for the first hour were hard, but in the second hour, it became easier as my body adapted. That's called the mammalian diving reflex."

That reflex in humans is the legacy of terrestrial life having evolved from prehistoric water-dwelling creatures. "We're born of the oceans," noted Krack. "From conception to birth, we mimic human evolution. In the mother's womb, at some point, we have gills, a salamander-like tail, and other water-organism features. And we can adapt to extreme environments, including the bradycardic

Right: Resting on the center island in the big tank on Stage 18 at Manhattan Beach, dive specialist Kirk Krack (left) prepares principal performers, checking his wrist chronometers for their "breath-hold" dives.

response, the slowing of the heart, which is an oxygen-conserving mechanism." While training world-champion free-diver Tanya Streeter, Krack discovered that after performing deep-breathing exercises using 80% nitrox, a breathing gas mixture consisting of 80% oxygen and 20% nitrogen, he could perform breath-holds while submerged for seven or eight minutes, or even longer.
In 2006, Krack worked with the magician David Blaine on a water submersion stunt—dramatically headlined as "Drowned Alive"—using nitrox breathe-ups that led to extraordinary endurance records, including Blaine's 24-minute breath-hold during a rehearsal. Krack applied this experience to dive-competition safety divers, which allowed extended breath-holds followed by surface recovery breathing using high oxygen mixtures. "That's when I developed technical freediving," said Krack. "It allows us to comfortably stay down longer, recover quicker, and reduce decompression-stress fatigue."

Cameron was aware of the history of oxygen-enriched freediving. It became clear that this form of technical freediving was an exciting solution that would allow actors who were new to diving to work comfortably for minutes at a time underwater.

"Jim explained how he wanted to do performance capture with the Metkayina and other Na'vi," related Krack. "I wanted to know if the Metkayina had evolved or adapted. Jim explained they were adapted, with a little bit of evolution, which gave them their salamander-like tail. He explained the problems [the crew] were having trying performance capture with bubbles in the water, and he wanted to reduce that. My suggestion was to get rid of the bubbles completely and train everyone on technical freediving—camera operators, grip team, safety divers, and cast. Jim asked me how I would do that. We spent two hours talking about all the procedures and the protocol. By the time I got back to my hotel, I got the call, 'Okay, you're our guy.'"

Cameron and Landau enlisted Krack to begin orienting production personnel to freediving training months in advance of underwater performance capture. As casting proceeded, the principal actors joined the training sessions. Krack taught cast and crew Zen-like deep-breathing exercises, lessons in body chemistry, and dive safety. Inductees included the established cast and a new entourage of young actors, all of whom had to commit to extensive training. The actors would be joined in the tank by support divers, underwater camera operators, and rigging crew. On most underwater shoots, this crew would be on scuba. But underwater performance capture required crystal-clear water, without bubbles. Scuba regulators emit bubbles, which would be seen by the mocap system as false markers, adding noise that would overwhelm the capture system. So standard scuba was ruled out for the underwater crew. Cameron considered having the dive team use "rebreathers"—closed-loop breathing systems that recirculated the air, without emitting bubbles. Rebreathers however were complex to operate and required advanced training, so the production chose a simpler solution. Hold your breath. The crew would all need to be accomplished breath-hold divers, as well.

With so many people in the water, holding their breath for several minutes at a time, safety was of paramount importance. The cast and crew needed a "guardian angel."

Marine-unit coordinator John Garvin oversaw all water operations, both in the ocean and the tank. He had worked with Cameron twice previously, once as dive supervisor on the cave diving thriller *Sanctum*, produced by Cameron and shot in Garvin's native Australia, on the Gold Coast. For that, he had to train and keep a motherly eye on actors who had never dived before, who were required to wear full-face rebreather masks for dive scenes deep inside sets of submerged caves. Later, on Cameron's Deepsea Challenge project, Garvin was put in charge of developing the life support system for Cameron's deep diving sub, being built in Sydney, Australia. Garvin used his extensive experience as a technical cave diver and rebreather instructor to design a life support system for the sub based on rebreather technology. That sub would take Cameron to the deepest spot on the planet, on March 26th, 2012, to a depth of 35,786 feet. Cameron's life was literally in Garvin's hands. Cameron had utter faith in Garvin's ethos of safety. On the build of the Deepsea Challenger sub, Garvin wound up running the entire "Sphere Internal Team", those responsible for everything that went inside the 42" diameter steel sphere that Cameron would cram himself inside to set a world record. That including not only the life support system, but all the electronics, control systems, navigation, sonar, communications, and camera systems. There was no room for a cup-holder.

Garvin built a simulator sphere, complete with life support and every electronic system, in which Cameron could make mock dives, sometimes up to twelve hours, going through every procedure like an astronaut in training. The simulator was installed in a large freezer, so that even the numbing cold that would be encountered at extreme depth, only two degrees above freezing, would be faithfully simulated. Garvin conducted drills during which Cameron dealt with every conceivable emergency, including an electronics fire that might fill the tiny capsule with smoke, requiring him to switch to a full-face breathing mask in order to stay alive. On the Avatar sequels it was Garvin's job to coordinate all underwater operations, and to work closely with Kirk Krack to instill a disciplined culture of dive safety in cast and crew.

"You go for the performance first."

Margery Simkin, casting director

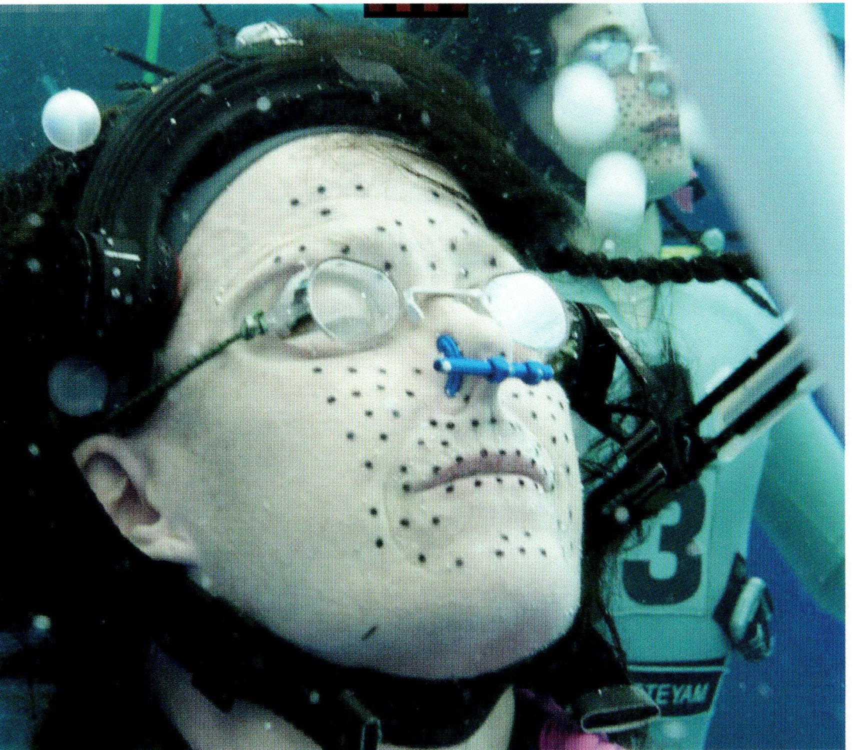

Above: Sigourney Weaver adapted to underwater performance capture process with skill, courage, charm and wit—all of which informed her portrayal of Kiri, infusing Dr. Augustine's enigmatic teenage Na'vi offspring with sublime grace.

To assess underwater capabilities, Garvin and Krack tested groups of the young actors being considered for the roles, six at a time, in one-hour pool sessions. "I was looking for 10 criteria," recalled Krack. "First off, do they like water? Can they listen? Can they act on instructions? Can they put their face underwater? Do they have a little bit of a breath-hold? Could they learn how to 'equalize' their ears? I then graded them in a point system of one to ten to rate their water skills and ability to learn."

"You go for the performance first," casting director Margery Simkin told Backstage magazine, regarding this unique casting challenge. "We did physical and water tests to know a person's baseline for what training had to be done, or who could do what. [Casting] decisions were made not based on that; decisions were made based on who was the better actor. When you do those kinds of tests, you find out things about their pluck, energy, and how they operate as a group."

The production weighed aquatic abilities against dramatic talent. Krack remembers that "One of our most accomplished young performers, Bailey Bass, I ranked second from last. Yet her character, Tsireya, was supposed to have been born in the water. That was a challenge. Cast members had a wide range of water comfort, from [those with] phobias to snorkelers and SCUBA-certified people who loved the water. Some had to go from 'never having been in the water' to 'born and spent their life in the water."

Once the roles were cast, and the actors were in training, they spent long days in the tank. "Most movies would want to spend the minimum amount of effort to make it happen on the day," commented Krack. "That wasn't the case with Jim and Jon. Avatar was our reality, and real physics had to apply. They gave me a tremendous amount of resources, time, and trust to make that happen."

"Jim's brief to me was very, very simple," John Garvin explains, "He says, 'I want the actors to be able to do the stunts themselves, and more importantly, I want them to look comfortable underwater like they belong down there.'"

As freediving training advanced, performers became increasingly proficient. "It was like getting a bunch of actors to do a Western, and nobody's ever ridden a horse before," James Cameron observed. "You start at the dude ranch teaching people how to ride. We had to teach everyone how to hold their breath. And some, like Kate Winslet's character [Ronal] and Bailey Bass' character [Tsireya], were supposed to have been in the water their whole lives. It was not only about getting them to be able to hold their breath; they had to act naturally with it. Before every take, I had to remind actors to hold their breath at the glottis—in the back of the throat—to leave their mouth open, because their lips had to be free to emote."

Above: During the action climax of *The Way of Water*, Kiri comes to the aid of Neytiri and Tuk, who are trapped in the sinking SeaDragon, by wrapping her body in a gill mantle and summoning a school of bioluminescent squid. Sigourney Weaver wore a weighted, sheer cape to stand in for the gill mantle during underwater performance capture. Kiri render and screenshot by Weta.

Above: Stereo head-rig cameras captured three-dimensional records of Weaver's facial performance, which captured nuances of Kiri's facial animation. Weta then generated a 3D model 'creature bake' using colored areas to delineate revisions. Final screenshot by Weta.

Sigourney Weaver, playing teenage Kiri, recalls, "I remember when Jim said, 'Oh, yeah, yeah, yeah, you're going to have to hold your breath for about three or four minutes.' And I said, 'Jim, I can't hold my breath for 30 seconds.' And yet, at the first lesson that Kirk gave us, I held my breath for a minute and a half." Academy Award® winner Kate Winslet had been cast to play Ronal, the matriarch and shaman of the Reef People, who would have been born and raised in the water. Kate, throughout all her films, does intense research in order to inhabit her characters. She embraced the freedive training as her way into Ronal.

"It was a very intense training process," she says, "It started with just simply being comfortable with holding one's breath for long periods of time, which is something that you really have to be trained to do. Learning how to do that, learning how to breathe that way, learning how to oxygenate your entire system so that you are able to hold your breath for longer is very, very technical." Sigourney was becoming adept at long breath-holds. "You have these involuntary sort of shudders when you've been holding your breath for two or three minutes," she explains. "It's quite strong, and Kirk calls them the dirty villain. You kind of say to them, Yes, yes, body, I see that you want to breathe, but in fact, you still have lots of oxygen in you, so it's just the desire to get rid of carbon dioxide, and each time you do it, you remind your body that it can last longer."

"You have to learn how to empty your mind... it certainly isn't something that comes easily to me," explains Kate Winslet, " In life now, when I'm feeling stressed, I'll go and get in a pool and actually do a couple of breath holds." Sigourney ultimately set a cast endurance record. In a static apnea test, lying face down in the water and not moving, Sigourney held her breath for six and half minutes, under Kirk's watchful eye.

Kate Winslet took this as a personal challenge. Due to other commitments, Kate had joined the party late. Kirk had to fly to England to train Kate in her home swimming pool, in a one-week crash course. Nevertheless, when Kate reached LA and joined the others in the tank, within a week she set a cast record of seven minutes and fifteen seconds, in a static apnea breath-hold. This actually beat Tom Cruise's much-vaunted best time, set when he was training for *Mission Impossible*: *Rogue Nation*, which Kate made sure everyone knew, including random people walking down the street.

Top: Stunt water performer Chris Denison.

Left: Cameron reunited with another long-time creative collaborator in casting Kate Winslet as Ronal, matriarch of the Metkayina clan. In a scene cut from the theatrical release of *The Way of Water*, Winslet performed an extended breath-hold, walking on the bottom of the Manhattan Beach Stage 18 water tank, for a First Breath ceremony, a sacred birthing ritual in which Ronal strode across the bed of a lagoon.

Above: (Clockwise) Kate Winslet, Cliff Curtis (Tonowari, Ronal's mate and *olo'eyktan* of the clan), Sam Worthington (Jake), and Zoe Saldaña (Neytiri) emerge from a surface-layer of reflection-damping spheres between takes in the tank on Stage 18.

"There is a huge amount to think about in underwater performance capture," Winslet recalled in a press junket interview. "Fortunately, I am comfortable in the water, so I felt at ease training with Kirk, and I was never afraid. I got to a point where I was determined to be very, very good at it." Kate did become very very good. Her zen-like calm in the water, and her natural emotional affect while holding her breath, infuse her character with authenticity as a native ocean-dweller. Where she appeared terrified in the freezing Atlantic in *Titanic*, she looked utterly at home in the tropical waters of Pandora.

Krack's training soon gained the younger performers' confidence. For the youngest freediving cast member, 7-year-old Trinity Bliss, Krack enlisted his daughter Kaila, who was the same age, as a stand-in. While training Bailey Bass, using freediving computers to keep track of timings, Krack experienced a breakthrough when the young performer overcame her initial reticence. "We were rehearsing in buddy teams," Krack recalled. "One person went down, the other stayed on the surface, and they'd 'safety' for each other as I was overseeing. I gave them a game to help them forget their breath-hold so that they could bring their characters to life. Bailey dived and, at a minute and a half, I could see she was still comfortable, with no urge to breathe, and she was having fun in the water. Then I saw her stop. She looked at her computer—she was at a minute and a half, already a long time. And then I realized, Oh my gosh, she's going to go to two minutes! After two minutes, she came to the surface and it was perfect. After her recovery breathing, I said, 'Okay, that's it for today.' And Bailey replied, 'Aww, do we have to stop?' I was so happy."

"I hated the water when I started filming," recalls Bailey Bass, "I barely knew how to swim. I hated putting on the wetsuit, and I just wasn't good at it, but I really worked hard, and Kirk was so proud of me when we wrapped because he said, 'You were arguably one of the worst swimmers, and you became like one of the longest breath holds of the cast, one of the strongest swimmers, because you really put your mind into it'"

The actors were flown to Hawaii, for more freedive training in open water, on a real coral reef. This carried on a tradition started on the first *Avatar*, when the cast spent three days in the rainforest on Kauai, memorizing how they would move and interact with the natural world. How they would climb barefoot on steep muddy trails and interact with plants, vines and tree roots. How they would track each other by sound in the forest, how they would push through large ferns, allowing them to brush past their bodies, even how they would wrap a fish in leaves and cook it in an earthen oven. Zoe was very proud of the fish dinner she served to the rest of the cast, after cooking it native-style.

It was all an elaborate exercise in "sense memory." They were not just learning to be indigenous people in a rainforest, but paying close attention to movement and sensation, so that they could bring that sense memory back into the sterile gray soundstage. They had to keep that forest alive in their minds, ever present with them, in the subsequent months as they moved through the jungle of Pandora which only the virtual camera could see.

In Hawaii, on the reef, Garvin and Krack continued the cast training, which was now joined by recently cast Jack Champion. All of the actors were also taught to scuba dive, becoming fully certified, so that they could explore and commune with the real underwater world for longer periods, then bring that sense memory back into the sterile volume for their work. Cameron often said, regarding his 1986 film *Aliens* "The Alien Queen was a rubber puppet—a damn good one created by the best creature team in the world—but we believed that puppet was real because Sigourney made us believe it. We saw it in her eyes. That thing was alive and breathing, right there in front of her, and it was terrifying. It's the acting that makes the fantastic elements real, no matter how good our effects may be." So the cast were in Hawaii to learn "the way of water," then keep it in their hearts as they came back to the Volume. As a final culmination, the cast did a night dive at a manta ray feeding station. The majestic animals would glide in out of the darkness into their lights, and swoop gracefully through the bubbles from the actors' regulators, only inches away from their faces. Cliff Curtis, training to play Tonowari, chief of the reef clan, describes it as a spiritual experience.

"That's one of the best things I've done in my life and my career," said Cliff, "was we went to Hawaii and I got to swim with the manta ray, and it just blew my mind, I was on a huge high." Cliff, a Maori, born and raised in New Zealand, has many tattoos including a large ray across his abs—his spirit animal. His close encounter with the mantas felt like a blessing from the sea, empowering him to play this role.

Finally, it was time for the actors to take what they'd learned and start capturing actual scenes in the tank. As the director walked in all the actors were in the water, wearing their futuristic silver wetsuits and head-rigs, up to their chins in white plastic balls, giggling with anticipation. Recalls Cameron, "It was kind of amazing the first day I walked in and the tank was ready to go and we were ready to start capturing. And I thought, this is a pinch-me moment, you know, we actually built this thing and it's really working."

John Garvin's duty station was a control desk above the tank equipped with monitors and in-water 'comms.' Cameron used a comms headset connected to a submerged diver-address speaker to talk to his submerged cast and crew. They could only respond to his direction by sign language. After each take he would view video playback of 16 HD witness cameras. The reference cameras were either operated shooting through the windows of the tank, or by camera operators actually submerged in the tank and holding their breath. Underwater cinematographer Peter Zuccarini operated a RED camera in a waterproof housing to gather close-up reference.

Each water-capture session began with a warm-up, averaging 30 minutes, to acclimate the actors' heart rates and to settle into the desired state of mammalian diving reflex. While J.D. Schwalm's special effects team readied the wave-makers, and final adjustments were made to underwater set-pieces, the

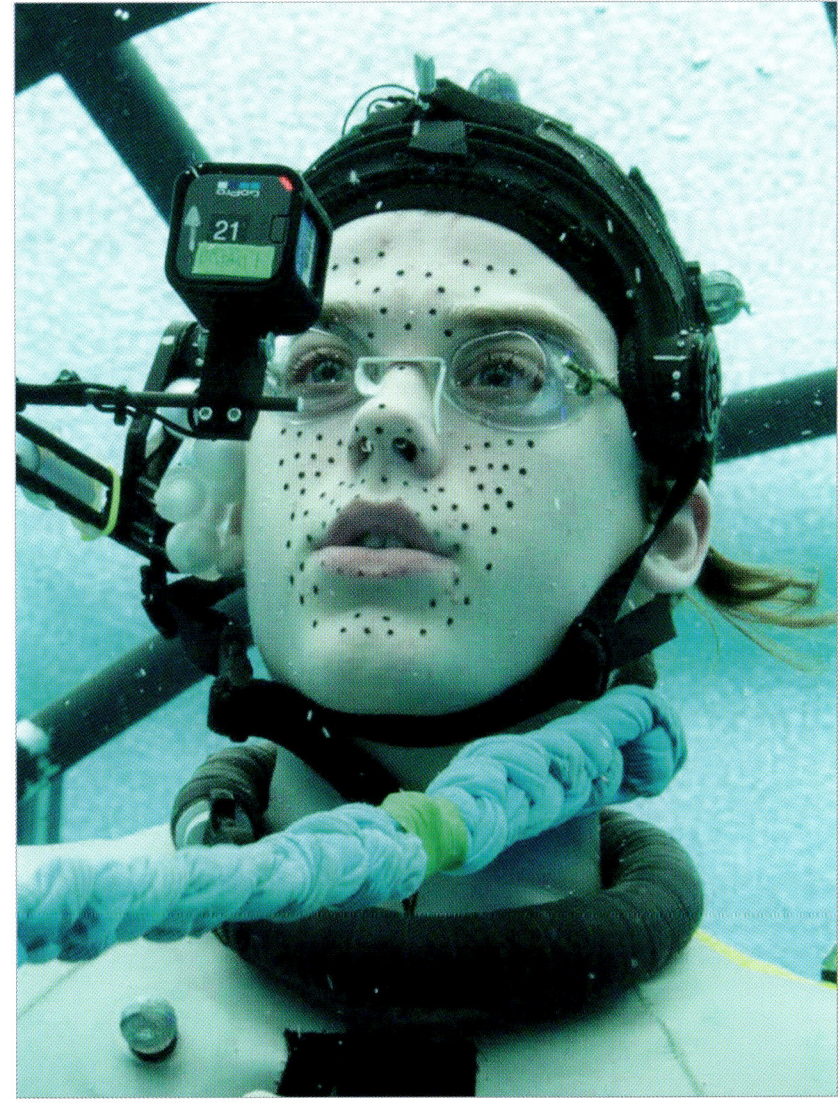

Above right: Britain Dalton performs as Lo'ak in the Manhattan Beach water tank, floating beneath a layer of white plastic balls that suffused the tank with even lighting and eliminated surface reflections for performance-capture sensors.

Right: Kirk Krack assists Britain Dalton's positioning in the tank, while (left) water-safety stunt performer Katherine Klosterman assists, and (right) Peter Zuccarini operates an in-water reference camera; other camera operators aim additional reference cameras through windows in the tank walls.

dive team took performers through breath-holds and practice dives. Maria Campbell and Cameron briefed the cast on the dramatic requirements of the scene, and Krack applied weights to help the actors maintain the right buoyancy.

The final breathe-up for each dive began when the big countdown clock on the wall started, usually three to four minutes before the dive. The cast would start calmly inhaling nitrox from tanks floating on small rafts at the surface, doing long, slow exhales—visualizing their breath just flickering a candle flame—as Kirk had taught them.

The time was called out by First AD Maria Battle Campbell at every thirty seconds. "As that clock was counting down," Krack recalls, "we were breathing on regulators with our 50- or 80-percent nitrox mix. As Kate was breathing up, I'd gently remind her of key points in the scene. That was part of my job, listening to Jim's directions and interpreting them from a practical dive point of view. If Kate had any questions, I was her advocate."

As the countdown progressed the tank stage became silent except for the slow, deep breathing of the cast and crew. "The actors are breathing up, the camera operators are breathing up, " recalls Cameron, "They're slowing down their heartbeat. They're blowing off their CO_2. They're saturating their capillaries with oxygen, getting ready for the dive. And they go into this kind of zen state. Any kind of tension will cause the heart rate to speed up. You may have a record for holding your breath for six or seven minutes. But when you start swimming around and using up oxygen, that number comes way down really fast."

The safety divers were most concerned with the danger of "shallow water blackout"—sudden unconsciousness caused by hypoxia in the brain. The actors were fully trained, and understood the danger and how to avoid it by surfacing before their diaphragm started strongly contracting. Cameron had repeatedly cautioned them to continue acting only as long as they were comfortable, and to feel fully empowered to surface when they needed to, whether the action of the scene was done or not. In addition, every cast member was watched like a hawk by the safety divers during a take. It was a highly disciplined approach, proven on movies like *The Abyss* and *Sanctum*, and representing Cameron, Krack and Garvin's decades of underwater shooting, all with perfect safety records. "The last thing we wanted was for an actor to black out," says Krack. As Garvin states it, "We wanted to make sure that we could get through the production with all the thousands of hours and free dives that we had to do safely, and that any cast member or any stunt member could do 40, 50 dives a day consistently and safely."

On most shots, Cameron would take over the count-down for the last few seconds on the PA system. "10-9-8-7-6, okay last breaths! 3-2-1. Regs out." The cast would spit out their nitrox regulators and calmly submerge. Once they were

"That was part of my job, listening to Jim's directions and interpreting them from a practical dive point of view."
Kirk Krack, dive specialist

under, they could hear the director on the diver-address speaker. "Okay, drop down nice and easy and get in position. Looking good, everybody." Cameron kept his voice calm and unhurried, not wanting to break the relaxed mental state the actors needed for long dives.

At this point Cameron would be watching on his handheld virtual camera, standing on a bridge that spanned the tank. He had found that the v-cam provided better overall situational awareness than trying to figure out what was going on from 16 different reference images, all shot from different angles. Underwater images can be very disorienting. As Cameron saw the characters get into their starting positions, he'd say, "Okay, here we go. Three, two, one, action." Nothing was rushed, nothing was stressed.

Underwater, Krack moved with the performers wearing an un-markered suit that made him invisible to the motion-capture system. Occasionally, Krack used "magic hands" to adjust performer positions in the tank, manually guiding their depth and positioning, so they didn't have to think about buoyancy control while acting.

The first capture scene done for *The Way of Water* was the scene in which the Sully kids jump in to join the reef kids, and see the myriad creatures teeming in the crystal clear shallows. Kiri becomes mesmerized, reaching out touch the life around her. Support divers gave her eye-line targets using little jerry-rigged "creatures" on poles. These were made from bathtub toys and whatever was lying around. There was a red plastic lobster with a tail made from a scrap of tulle nicked from the wardrobe department, which Cameron dubbed the Lobster Princess. It would later become a bulbous-eyed CG octopus that jets away when Kiri reaches for it. Though Kiri has been withdrawn since Spider was captured and she had to leave her home in the forest, her beautiful smile returns as she interacts with the wonders around her.

"It was one of the first scenes we did for Kiri," Sigourney says, "The time on land had been frustrating for her. And then as soon as she dove in and she was with all these remarkable beings underwater, she felt such a connection to them. I felt so at home for Kiri. I had so much energy built up in me as an actor.

Right: *The Way of Water*'s immersion into ocean realms featured water tank performances captured in California and New Zealand. For the latter, stunt troupe performers joined Jack Champion, as Spider, for live-action water surface scenes. Standing outside the tank (left to right): second-unit director Garrett Warren, first assistant director/coproducer Maria Battle Campbell, Cameron, and supervising master diver John Garvin.

Below: In the Manhattan Beach water tank, Jamie Flatters (Neteyam) becomes accustomed to Metkayina ways.

Above: In the water tank at Manhattan Beach, dressed as a Metkayina beach, Neteyam (Jamie Flatters), Kiri (Sigourney Weaver, and Lo'ak (Britain Dalton) face off with Ao'Nung (Filip Geljo), eldest son of the Metkayina chief, and his pals. Silver wetsuits were easier to see underwater and at the surface than black ones. The body markers for all water scenes were a more highly reflective and waterproof material than those used for dry capture suits.

So much need to feel at home somewhere, that when I got down there and I felt so at home, I just was like, this is going to be okay. I can do this film. But also, oh, Kiri is going to be okay because she's found herself in this new place on Pandora."

Weaver took the lead in Kiri's climactic scene in *The Way of Water*, in which she summons a school of bioluminescent squid to guide her through the sunken wreckage of SeaDragon to rescue Neytiri and Tuk. The scene of her searching the wreck for her mother and little sister required Sigourney's longest breath-holds as an actor.

Weaver requested an eye line as she interacted with the squid. Kirk Krack assigned Chris Denison, a freediving stuntman, to do the eyeline and keep a close eye on her as she gazed about at the circling squid, which were small bits of ribbon on the ends of rods waved by the support divers.

"I was down there and summoning them," recalls Sigourney. "It's sort of my favorite thing I ever got to do in the water. And I just stayed down there a long time. And gosh, it was such a treat to do all that. I was making it last as long as I could."

As Kirk Krack tells it, "At the one-minute mark, it was looking good. I could see that Sigourney had no contractions (of her diaphragm). At a minute and a half, I could see Chris getting urges to breathe. Sigourney still had nothing. Chris gave me a look, 'How much longer is she gonna go?' At two minutes, Chris had stronger contractions. Sigourney was still rocking it. At three minutes-plus, Jim called 'Cut!' When we got to the surface, Sigourney calmly went into recovery breathing. Chris was with another safety diver about 20 feet away, and he was gasping. Sigourney just absolutely killed it. It was a testament to the focus she brought to the training. She loved the breath-hold component."

Training to be calm in the water paid off for Zoe Saldaña and Trinity Bliss in the same climactic sequence in *The Way of Water*. The SeaDragon ship has capsized and sunk with them inside it. They wind up trapped in an air pocket, in almost pitch darkness. Before Kiri's squid reach them and they are saved,

Above: Screenshot of Lightstorm Lab render of Lo'ak's *ilu* ride, with (inset) reference image from the Manhattan Beach water tank showing performance capture with Britain Dalton powered by a stunt department Jetovator rig piloted by Mike Avery.

they jammed up against the ceiling in the tiny airpocket. Tuk is gasping with fear, and though Neytiri speaks to her calmly, we can see she too is terrified.

To capture the scene, a set with "non-occluding" steel mesh walls was lowered into the water on the tank's platform, with the actors inside it. "It was scary," recalled Saldaña, "It was definitely a stage... you know you're safe and you trust the process and you use it. You use it all. So if you're feeling fear, I'm pretty sure that's what Neytiri is feeling. If you're feeling claustrophobic, if you can't breathe, all of those things."

"I felt very safe with all the crew members and trusting them," Trinity affirms, "But I also felt very safe with Zoe because she's so caring and not only the best mom to her kids but an amazing on-set mom because she's right there with you and there for you. So it was fun to get to be in that scene with her and improvise together."

For underwater scenes where the Metkayina used their powerful tails to swim like a crocodile, the technicians built underwater jet packs for the actors. Marine coordinator John Garvin's team strapped Scubajet Aquaboost scooters—small thrusters roughly the size of a domestic fire extinguisher—to the actors' backs.

A lot of work went into perfecting the Metkayina way of swimming. William Truebridge, a world champion freediver from New Zealand, was brought in to consult on the swimming stroke.

"I'm a freediver," he explains, "I dive as deep as I can for a living. I've been focusing specifically on "no fins" (a class of competition diving)... and this is essentially what the Na'vi people need to do in their day-to-day lives. So I'm basically like looking at how the Na'vi might move underwater efficiently and powerfully, trying to design a movement - a stroke for that." For competition, Truebridge had perfected a stroke called the "keyhole", a frog kick with a modified breast-stroke that ended in a powerful two-handed push aft that hurled the swimmer forward. What normally happened next was a glide phase, where the swimmer coasted forward a few feet before the stroke was repeated. But a human swimmer doesn't have a powerful tail like the Reef People. So the jet pack was used to extend that glide phase to over three body lengths of

Opposite page: In Metkayina culture, a friendly diaphanous invertebrate known as a gill mantle plays an important role in life on the reef, enabling Na'vi to breathe underwater. Concept art by Constantine Sekeris.

Top: The big tank in Manhattan Beach represented deeper ocean realms, including studies of stunt performers enacting *tulkun* motion. Underwater cinematographer Peter Zuccarini, clad in dive-suit camouflage that made him invisible to ultraviolet motion sensors, uses a high-definition 4K RED motion picture camera to shoot animation reference.

Right: Water performances extended to tank shoots at Kumeū Film Studios in Auckland, New Zealand. James Cameron addresses Jack Champion (in full-face breathing mask), supervising master diver John Garvin (far left), dive specialist Kirk Krack (right), and safety diving team prior to shooting a scene of Spider navigating a submerged section of the sinking SeaDragon set.

“The actors were not pretending to swim underwater.”

Eric Saindon, Weta VFX supervisor

powered flight, during which the actor needed to waggle their hips as if a powerful tail were lashing back and forth from the base of their spine. The jetpack was triggered by a microswitch in the actor's hand the moment the glide phase began, then the hips would be undulated, then the switch was clicked again, stopping the thruster, and the swimmer would repeat the keyhole stroke. Rinse, repeat.

"Stunt performer Léa Catania was remarkable," related Dan Barrett. "She could swim with a sinewave down her body through her hips. We learned a huge amount from Léa's performance and applied that to other characters as we animated their tails." Next the actors playing the reef kids—Bailey Bass, Duane Evans Jr, and Filip Geljo—had to learn the keyhole stroke and crocodile shimmy. This took a lot of practice, but the actors perfected it. When the animated tails were added in VFX post, the effect was seamless and looked completely natural. Not only that, but no character in a movie or TV show ever swam that way before, not even The Man from Atlantis. It was a unique look, but seemed utterly correct for the ocean-adapted Na'vi.

"The actors were not pretending to swim underwater," noted Weta's Eric Saindon, "their arms were really pushing against the resistance of the water. And that also gave us reference for the motion of their hair and clothing. Combining all of that together, we were able to make it feel like characters were truly moving through the water." In a later interview he said, "I was skeptical at first (about underwater capture) and to be honest, after seeing the underwater scenes, it was well worth it"

***

The actors would also need to learn how to ride various ocean creatures. Two species had been tamed by the Reef People: the fierce skimwing, and the playful and social *ilu*, which looked like a long-necked plesiosaur crossed with a manta ray. Its aft fins were wide and ray-like, with a thick middle fin, and small flipper-like canard fin just behind the neck, which the Na'vi grip onto with their knee when they ride.

Working from art department designs, Weta creature animation supervisor Eric Reynolds generated *ilu* motion studies from nature reference. "The *ilu* needed to appear quizzical with a lot of character, peering around with its long neck," Reynolds recalled. "We wondered, 'What other water animal can do that?' The answer was a seal. They're inquisitive, and they're sleek. I found a clip of a seal playing, swimming and looking around, and that became our *ilu* reference."

But before the actors could be trained to ride an *ilu* or a skimwing, the production had to figure out two things: how do you create these ocean creatures in the real world? And how do you ride them? It could have all been faked with animation, but Cameron was adamant that "in the Avatar films, whenever you see a character in action, a person did it for real. Somebody actually performed it, whether it was an actor or a double. It's not animated." The mandate was clear: there would be real human beings really riding some version of an underwater creature at high speed.

The stunt and marine departments had to create vehicles that could match the speed and hydrobatic maneuvers of the creatures. No electric-powered thrusters could deliver the sheer horsepower needed to move that fast underwater. So the vehicles would be propelled by powerful jets of water, delivered by a nearby high-performance jet-ski, through a long hose. The water shot out of jet nozzles that could be directed by the pilot of the vehicle to hurl it forward and twist it into hydrobatic loops and rolls. The designs were based on the Jetovator, a sport rig typically seen at ocean resorts, that allowed the rider to fly high above the water and do acrobatic loops.

"I'd seen people go out on the water with these jet-boot-style devices and do all kinds of tricks," recalled Garrett Warren. "Jim asked me to do some homework. So I called Jetovation, we put our heads together, and found a way to make it work."

Previous pages: Concept art of a Na'vi riding an *ilu* under the Pandoran waters by Dylan Cole.

Right: Stunt performer Bryan Marsh extends a small waterproof camera from a marine support raft, helmed by stunt performer Chris Papajohn, capturing video reference of stunt artists Léa Catania and Emilie Siemer on board an *ilu* rig.

Jetovation Inc., in Redding, California, was the company that built the resort vehicles. The owner and chief engineer at Jetovation, Rob Innes, was tasked with building two completely new designs based on their core water-jet technology, one for the *ilu* and one for the skimwing.

"The Jetavator is based on a hydroflight technology," explains Innes, "Basically you get on it just like a bike, and then it uses the thrust of the jet ski to propel you into the sky."

The *ilu* needed to skim along at the surface, then dive and be able to do loops and rolls underwater. The skimwing, which was basically a giant flying fish, was more challenging—it had to swim fast underwater, then leap out of the water and fly 10 feet above the surface, then nose sharply down and dive back in—all with a rider on its back.

Cameron outlined concepts for the *ilu* with whiteboard sketches. "Jim wanted it to move like a little Loch Ness monster," explained Garrett Warren. "It had to move like a sea otter or a seal. It had to be able to turn back on itself and move around. Jim suggested we position two sets of jets, one by the pilot's hands and another by the pilot's feet, so he could turn the jets to make the head go one way while his feet pushed another way. That was our first version."

The pilot, wearing a crash helmet and holding his breath, lay inside the machine, under a molded fiberglass form that matched the shape of the creature's back. While the stunt rider, on top, pretended to control the creature, it was really the pilot who was in control.

"So we had a person that was invisible to the motion capture that was inside the vessel," Innes recalls, "They would be manipulating all of the controls and making it move like the creature."

Stunt performer Mike Avery was the test pilot for the water-jet rigs, starting in San Pedro Bay, just off the Los Angeles coast. For the *ilu* rig, the stunt team provided Avery with two compressed-air regulators, one at shoulder level and a safety backup lower down, with Avery strapped into to the frame. "Mike was my hero," said Garrett Warren. "We went out to San Pedro, with Mike riding on the surface behind a jet-ski. On the jet-ski was a huge pump that created the water flow for the hose below. Mike went forward, did an oval [in the bay], and made the creature fly around. It could go more than 20 knots, but at that speed, the force of the water pulled your goggles off, and you couldn't see. So, we limited it to 20 knots."

Poor visibility in San Pedro harbor complicated the test. "The water was like a toilet bowl," said Warren. "You could [just] see your hand in front of your face. It was horrible."

Legacy Effects created another in-water rig featuring a section of a *tulkun*, designed for Lo'ak riding on Payakan's fin. "Jim wanted to put performers through what the Na'vi would do," noted John Rosengrant, who led the Legacy team with other Winston Studio alumni. "He wanted to capture the way Na'vi hair and clothing moved with the resistance in the water. He asked water-expert stuntmen to move the rig around underwater as Payakan."

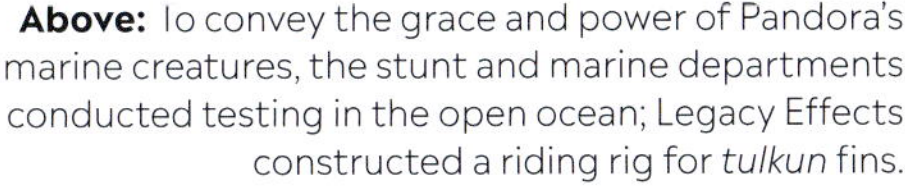

Above: To convey the grace and power of Pandora's marine creatures, the stunt and marine departments conducted testing in the open ocean; Legacy Effects constructed a riding rig for *tulkun* fins.

Right, top to bottom: The Bahamas provided stunning clarity for water-creature rig tests. Stunt performer Rene Herrera pilots a personal watercraft chasing "hydroflight" stunt performers Chris Denison and Mike Avery in a skimwing test; Denison and Avery conduct a Skimwing dive.

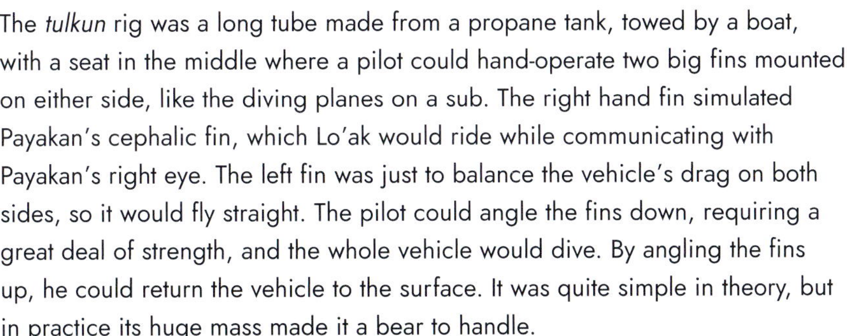

The *tulkun* rig was a long tube made from a propane tank, towed by a boat, with a seat in the middle where a pilot could hand-operate two big fins mounted on either side, like the diving planes on a sub. The right hand fin simulated Payakan's cephalic fin, which Lo'ak would ride while communicating with Payakan's right eye. The left fin was just to balance the vehicle's drag on both sides, so it would fly straight. The pilot could angle the fins down, requiring a great deal of strength, and the whole vehicle would dive. By angling the fins up, he could return the vehicle to the surface. It was quite simple in theory, but in practice its huge mass made it a bear to handle.

"When we were testing the whale fin," Garrett recalls, "Brian Marsh was the stunt person, and he went so deep in the water that he buried it into the ground like an anchor. All of a sudden, we heard the engine go Wwraaaaaaaa and the boat slowed down. But Brian found his spare air, and he was fine. Nobody got injured. Our first and most important consideration was water safety—and that boiled right down to Jim. He always insisted on spare air in two different places [one on the rig, one strapped to the diver], and a quick release for the operator to get out. It was always safety first and design the rest from there."

The production conducted additional open-water tests at Catalina Island, for better water clarity, then they packed the prototype vehicles up and shipped everything to the Bahamas for operational testing in the warm, clear water there. The test runs were filmed from chase boats, and by operators on jetskis using GoPro cameras mounted on poles held under the surface. In addition, underwater cameraman Pete Zuccarini did his best to keep up, swimming flat out with his long-bladed fins.

Here the testing went to the next level. Now that the pilots had learned to fly the vehicles, it was time to study how a rider would actually ride them. It took a while for the *ilu* vehicle's buoyancy to be trimmed so that it could run at the surface with the rider's upper body out of the water and the waves just rolling over their thighs, the way Cameron wanted it. Some scenes called for two riders, one behind the other, such as Kiri with Tuk. The buoyancy needed to be adjusted again, to get the right "freeboard" for two riders. But soon it was all working smoothly.

"Garrett's like, 'Dude, can you stay on that thing?' I'm like, 'Yeah, I'm trying!'"

Chris Denison, stunt performer

Left: Herrera and Avery observe hydroflight sports champion Joseph Natale Jr. perform an *ilu* leap.

The next challenge was to figure out how someone would ride an *ilu* underwater. Just sitting on it like a horse wouldn't work, you'd get blown off immediately by the force of water. But by gripping a hand-hold, supposedly part of the creature's tack, the rider could plane out with their body parallel to the creature, and glide along at high speed.

Underwater performers Léa Catania, Emily Siemer, and Benoit Beaufils, all alumni of Las Vegas water extravaganzas like O and La Reve, were turned loose to figure out how to ride the *ilu*, experimenting with different riding positions. It was found that by hooking one leg, tightly bent, over the creature's forward "canard" fin, with the other leg stretched straight out behind like a rudder, they could strike a posture with a beautiful graceful line, and the appearance of being closely attached to the creature in a stable position. Soon they were doing graceful loops and rolls, then surfacing to breathe, and diving back down for more hydrobatic fun. Their riding style was perfected over a couple days of testing, and would later be taught to the cast by Léa, Emily, and Benoit—skills that would be used in the wind-tunnel of the tank in Manhattan Beach.

Cameron was also interested in the effects of water flowing over the characters. Later, in the tank, the capture system could only record the actor's "skeleton", not the water itself. Nor could it capture the transient fluid effects of water interacting with hair and wardrobe. These flow effects would need to be accurately recreated later by the Weta animators, using CFD (computational fluid dynamics) "sims"—physics-based mathematical simulations. So shooting detailed reference video was essential.

Emily, Léa and Benoit were fitted with wigs matching the thick Polynesian-style hair of the Metkayina, and wore costumes with fringe and trailing streamers, all of which fluttered in the powerful slipstream, and was recorded on video with underwater cameras. The test footage also showed that, at speed, the flow of water violently undulated the performers' skin and muscles in waves, and buffeted their facial features. This was invaluable reference footage for Weta to later recreate those flow dynamics on the characters, such as when Lo'ak rides Payakan's fin.

To test Jake and the other Na'vi riding atop the needle-nosed skimwing as it breached the water, flew above the surface, then dived back in, stunt performers rode a larger 'cockroach' rig. That vehicle had a rigid metal-mesh shell to support the rider on top, while under it was the pilot, crammed into a tubular frame, gripping the jet nozzle handles. The skimwing rig was also piloted by Mike Avery, while Sam Worthington's stunt double Chris Denison rode on top. Chris had to literally learn to ride a skimwing, no easy task in real life, just as it wasn't for Jake in the movie.

The machine would scream along underwater, pop up and fly along on the thrust from its nozzles, like a Harrier jet, 10 or 15 feet above the water. Because it was quite unstable, it even wobbled in a way that nicely simulated the tail-propelled wiggle of the skimwing. Then it would dive back under, hitting the water with tremendous force at over twenty knots—about the speed Titanic was going when it crashed into the iceberg.

Above: Skimwing riders. Concept art by Dylan Cole

On his first flight, Chris could barely hold onto the squirrelly rig while flying above the water, let alone balance well enough to perform in character as Jake. When he dove back in, he took the full force of the ocean square in the face and it knocked him off the rig. When he surfaced, he said "It was like getting hit in the face by a two-by-four." Cameron replied, "Then you better figure out how to do it right."

"We're spy-hopping the skimwing," recalls Chris Denison, "coming out of the water, breaching and then going straight back in. I kept getting ripped off. Garrett's like, 'Dude, can you stay on that thing?' I'm like, 'Yeah, I'm trying!'" After a few tries, Chris mastered diving back in. He would snap his body straight, tucking his head to take the full force of entry on the top of his skull while pressing his face hard into his bicep to shield his eyes from the impact, like a high diver going off the cliffs of Acapulco. He called it "head-butting the ocean." Soon he could rocket along underwater, then breach the surface and do a surfer's "pop" to hop up into a stable riding stance. Once that hurdle was passed, they moved on to figuring out how Jake would manage firing and even reloading his assault rifle while riding the unruly beast. It took days of repeated dives, but Chris managed to become Jake, heroically riding his hell-beast during a battle at sea.

Chris was rigged with an X-sens suit to record his motion. Since they had no capture volume out in the open ocean, this suit worked on a different principle. There were IMU's (inertial motion sensors) attached to each limb, recording to a central pack. It was important to analyze the effects of impact and flow on Chris's body, and the fine motions he need to balance on the creature when airborne.

Later in the capture tank in LA there would be no room to do this kind of flight motion, it could only be done in the open ocean. So Chris's stunt tests became the definitive motion for riding a skimwing, at least for impact and breaching. Chris's bruising journey of discovery closely matches what Jake goes through in the story, when learning to ride the warrior mount. Chris would coach Sam through the exact techniques, but Sam was able to do his flying and diving on a flying rig in the dry Volume.

They also tested a refined version of the Payakan rig. In San Pedro they had learned how to fly the massive beast, but not how to ride it. The Bahamas tests involved Chris, now doubling for Lo'ak, figuring out how to ride the fin. He took to it instantly, holding onto the leading edge of the fin and flapping like a flag as he used his free hand to "sign," to Payakan's eye—which had been drawn in with a magic marker on the side of the rig. Chris didn't know Na'vi

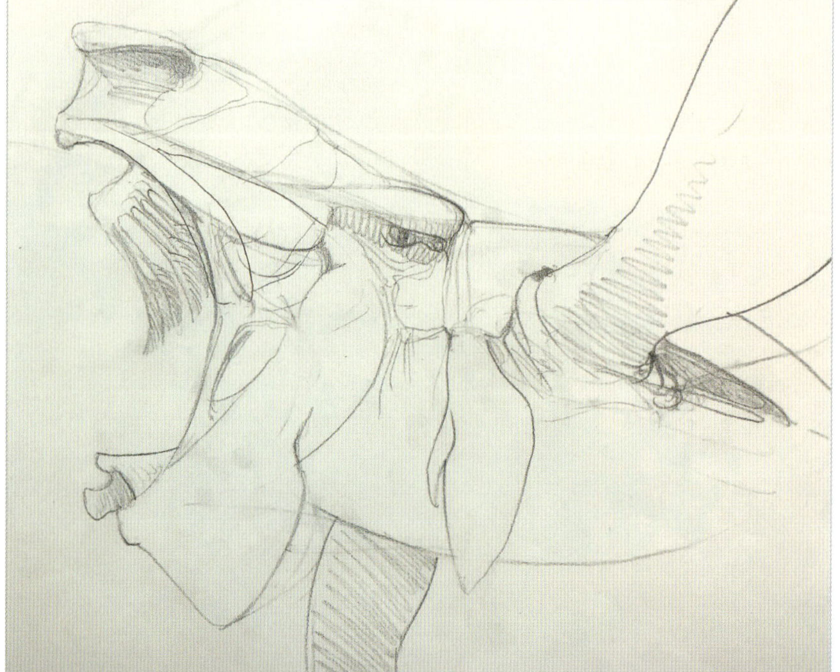

sign language, because it would be another year before it was even created, by deaf actor CJ Jones (*Baby Driver*). So he just made up any old thing in the moment. But it proved the idea, and was amusing in dailies.

In just a few hours, Chris was doing X Games-style tricks—riding the fin like a hood ornament, planed out like Superman, and doing spins and flips. Some of Chris's signature tricks were later incorporated into the scene in which Lo'ak and the reef kids play with their *tulkun* brothers and sisters, near the beginning of *Fire and Ash*.

In The *Way of Water*, one memorable shot shows Lo'ak stretching out with one hand to create a trail across the mirror surface of the water. This was adapted from a bit of improv in the Bahamas where, as the *tulkun* rig dove and glided over the white sandy bottom, Chris spread his arms and reached down to trail his fingers through the sand. A moment of grace and beauty. Later, on the camera stage, Cameron decided to invert the motion and have Lo'ak trailing his hand along the water surface from below, rather than the sandy bottom. But it was Richie Baneham who provided the final inspiration, by inverting the camera itself, so at first the image is of Lo'ak and Payakan gliding in a dreamlike impossibility, above a shimmering surface. Then the camera rolls and you realize it's the ocean surface, seen first upside-down, now righting itself. This magical shot became a core image of the first teaser trailer for *Way of Water*, which wowed fans worldwide. Their first glimpse of the wonders of Pandora in 13 years.

Before they left the Bahamas, other reference footage was shot. Pete Zuccarini did an amazing shot of South African champion swimmer Liz Parkinson doing the "crocodile swim" across the sandy bottom. She used Truebridge's keyhole stroke, which stirred up the sandy bottom in puffs with each stroke, showing the true power of the hand-thrust. Her six-foot frame undulated in a way that didn't require much imagination to see a powerful tail propelling her forward. Liz would later become an integral part of the water team in LA, playing a number of Reef People characters.

As they returned to LA, exhausted, the water team knew they had mastered the art of underwater creature riding. They wouldn't put these skills to use in actual capture for another year, in the tank in Manhattan Beach. But what they learned in the open ocean informed all the water capture that followed, and provided priceless reference for the animators at Weta, as well as the software engineers who would create the CG water itself. The last stage was to master the ways of water in the computer world, not just in the real world.

Left: Mid-process sketches by James Cameron of the creature that would become the graceful *tulkun*.

In 2018, when the big tank on Stage 18 became operational, the stunt team had 900,000 gallons of water, with 100′ runs, to race their creature rigs around in. "We went nuts," remembers Warren. "We had dogfights in the tank, creatures zooming around each other, fighting, shooting guns, and stabbing. It was like X Games underwater."

The water troupe—Léa, Emily, Benoit, Liz, Chris and Mike—also played a variety of secondary characters, just as the other troupe in the dry Volume did. They played other Metkayina, as well as sometimes doubling for the principals when the action required specialized water skills.

And not all of these secondary characters were Na'vi. To capture a sense of the *tulkun* socializing—touching fins, swimming in family groups, protecting their young—Cameron wanted a way to direct them in real time, without having to deal with cycles of animation reviews. Benoit, Léa, Liz and Emily were given mono-fins for their feet, and wing-like "pectoral fins" for their arms. After a bit of practice to "get into character", they were swimming together as *tulkun* while Cameron talked them through their social interactions. It was pure creativity, in real time. Instinctive, truthful. Beautiful. They even worked out the broadstrokes of *tulkun* dance moves, briefly seen in *The Way of Water* during the *tulkun* reunion scene.

Above: *Tulkun* mother and calf, realized in a conceptual rendering by Ian Joyner and a collective of artists who contributed to the design of Pandora's highly intelligent and gargantuan cetacean species, three-times larger than terrestrial blue whales.

Right: Richard Baneham captures *tulkun* swimming paths with a *tulkun* wire-frame puppet.

"For the *tulkun*," recalled Garrett Warren, "we had people being whales. We [also] had stunt people driving Seabob water scooters at them, like hunters trying to separate a mother from her calf. We had a scene where the *tulkun* Payakan was angry and slammed his body into the sea floor. Liz Parkinson was just perfect as the mother *tulkun*. For her calf, we used a smaller lady, Léa Catania, who was a synchronized swimmer from Paris."

Lightstorm also blocked out *tulkun* performances using small wire-frame models performed by hand in the dry Volume. All of these gestural motions, from dry and wet capture, were then given to Weta animation supervisor Eric Reynolds and his team to build upon.

"We were able to take performances that Léa and Benoît had given us," related Richie Baneham. "It felt both fully physically represented and weirdly emotional in the movements that they gave us. Léa and Benoit brought the [*tulkun*] to life in a very meaningful way, with head gestures and fin motions to create the idea that there was a sensory element. The wire-frame puppets allowed us to place the creatures where we wanted them in space. Having to encapsulate that performance into a 100-foot long *tulkun*, and to make those scenes feel intimate was very hard to do. Payakan did not have a lot of articulation in his face, we just had his eye and some mouth gestures, so we had to [convey his emotions] through broad body language."

Conveying a *tulkun*'s personality was challenging, especially in scenes of Payakan befriending the Sullys' younger son, Lo'ak. Payakan's animation focused on his enormous, soulful eye to convey necessary depth of emotion, and the animators found ways to make his face surprisingly emotive. Animator Eric Reynolds observed: "Payakan was treated harshly—exiled by the Tulkun Council for attacking RDA hunters—and Lo'ak feels he was treated harshly, too, and so they connect."

Lo'ak's bond with his *tulkun* "brother" is both touching and transporting. It becomes the heart of the story in *The Way of Water*. As the director puts it, "There are many important relationships in the film, clearly, but one could argue that when Payakan meets Lo'ak, that's the place where the film really tells you what it's trying to be. Because everything that happens from that moment on happens because of that. It's also a joyful experience to see that relationship developing. They can barely communicate with each other, but you get it. You go on that journey and you see it." Britain Dalton, who was 15 when he started playing Lo'ak, puts it like this, "Hearing how people feel about the relationship between them, that just moves me. And I can only speak to what Lo'ak is feeling. Lo'ak is alone. He is feeling outcast, but you know when the right person comes into your life at the right time, that's what Payakan was for Lo'ak. It's like a spirit. He's the most loyal, understanding best friend that I think we all wish we had. You get lost in that scene. You get lost in the moment of watching the beauty of Lo'ak and Payakan."

Capture of Britain riding on Payakan's fin, signing to him, joking and playing, were combined with the *tulkun* motion that had been created by merging Benoit and Léa's motion, with the Weta animator's skills. The resulting *tulkun* scenes are graceful and mesmerizing. While reminiscent of real Earthly whale interaction, it is also distinctly unique to these majestic creatures of the imagination.

***

For *Fire and Ash*, the arrival of the Wind Traders at the reef village required the stunt team to devise new performance capture rigs. The Tlalim are nomadic traders navigating Pandora's atmosphere in gondolas suspended from enormous airborne medusoids.

As in the ocean realms, Cameron demanded authentic behavior and action as the Wind Traders crew their vessel. Working from art department renderings, the filmmakers built a physical set of the Tlalim gondola in the Volume at Manhattan Beach. The set rivaled the grandeur of an Errol Flynn pirate epic. "The Art Department built a big, huge gondola," related Garrett Warren. "We had the entire ship's crew, with people going up and down the rigging. We had people going from different levels, underneath, and climbing back up to the top. It was amazing."

The gondola set vindicated the huge Volume that had been created for the sequels. It filled the stage from end to end, and used every inch of the mocap grid's height. On the first *Avatar*, the height of sets had been severely restricted by limitations of that early Volume. To simulate the gondola's flexible woven decks, the stunt team used an air-filled gymnastic mat known as a Tumbl Trak.

"Payakan was treated harshly... and Lo'ak feels he was treated harshly, too, and so they connect."

Eric Reynolds, animator

Opposite page: The production constructed a pirate-galleon-like set at Manhattan Beach Studios to represent dizzying new realms of *Fire and Ash*, an airborne conveyance of the nomadic Tlalim clan—the Wind Traders—who appear in the skies above the Metkayina reef in a flotilla of giant flying gondolas.

> "The Art Department built a big, huge gondola. We had the entire ship's crew. It was amazing, and we shot all that for real."
>
> **Garrett Warren, 2nd unit director/stunt coordinator**

"Tumbl Trak is inflatable so when you roll it out you can change the tension," Warren explained. "If we wanted it to be super tight, we could add more air. And [the mats] were long and wide so we could fill the stage. When you walked on that surface, it felt like walking on a membrane, or a trampoline-like effect that people could walk and jump and land on." When the Ash warriors land on top of the medusoid and start to cut into it with flensing lances, Jake lands near them and takes them out with his assault rifle before they can bring down the ship. The Tumbl Trak stood in for the medusoid's upper membrane, as the ash riders land and roll. Then Jake's stunt double dropped onto the membrane at high speed, rolled and came up firing.

For scenes of Mangkwan *ikran* riders swooping onto the Wind Trader gondola, the Tumbl Trak proved invaluable. "We first tried hauling a stunt person on a stunt pad and having them jump off and roll and come up," Warren recalled. "Jim instantly said, 'Nah, that's not real.' The amount of speed it needed to fly in on the *ikran* before the jump and impact was not working. He needed the rider to land, bounce, and jump back up to counteract the speed. It had to have forward momentum. Jim challenged us to do better." Warren proposed strapping an *ikran* rig to the top of a golf cart. "Jim thought we were crazy, but he said, 'Do it.' Stunt performer Steve Brown sat on top of the cart. We drove that into the set as fast as we could, 30 miles an hour, with the Tumbl Trak beside it. Steve jumped, hit the inflatable floor, bounced and rolled, came back up, and started fighting."

For scenes of the Mangkwan riders attacking the gondola with firebombs and flaming arrows, stunt players would need to enact the battle on flying rigs. With the lessons learned from *Avatar*, Cameron and Baneham knew it all started with flight-paths. Again the two boys got out their little wire-frame *ikran*, and started flying them around the Volume, attacking a mockup of the ship.

Sequence supervisors Steve Deane, Andrew Moffett, and A.J. Briones added animated motion to the creatures, and orchestrated the entire raider attack, creating a master scene. This was then used by the stage team to guide the stunt

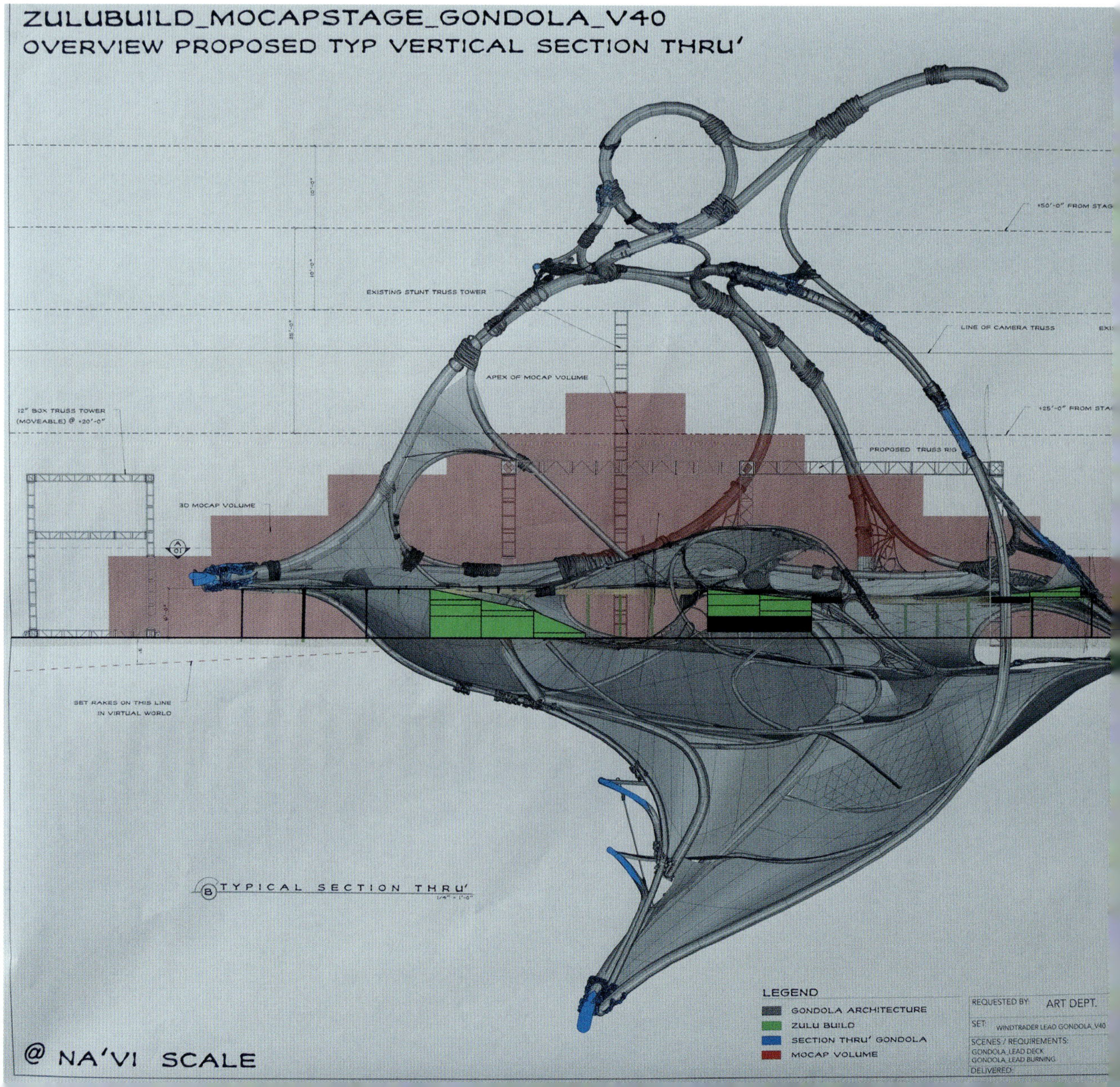

Top and right: The Wind Traders' gondolas are borne aloft and propelled by giant gas-filled creatures. Weta screenshot and gondola practical stage build plan.

Top: Wind Trader set pieces included key props and gondola structures that simulated sections of the giant airborne vessel, including a covered area in the center of the main deck known as the "deck *marui*," where the Wind Traders prepare food.

Above: Gondola defenses included meticulously crafted, giant-crossbow-like ballistae.

stunt capture of individual riders attacking with bows, spears and fire bombs. "If an *ikran* was diving at a certain speed and displacement," related Richie Baneham, "we could show the rider where the gondola would be on our Eyeline system. That allowed stunt performers to take their mark and shoot their arrows. Alicia Vela-Bailey's skills with the bow were fantastic. When you see the complexity of the scene, with 75 to 100 *ikran* riders, you start to understand the complexity that our Lab and our sequence supervisors ran into."

To convey the physical impacts of Mangkwan attacking Wind Traders, Brad Elliott's property department rigged varieties of weapons—some made of foam rubber, others made of PVC pipe—as Mangkwan projectiles that stunt performers could throw. "If we had to hit anyone in the face or head, we use the foam rubber," said Garrett. "For jumping, falling, and shooting, we needed weapons to be lighter so that's when we used PVC props. For our 'hero' look, wherever we needed a performer to shoot an arrow, we made sure [the bows really] worked."

As Jake Sully attempts to repel the Mangkwan raiders, Varang dispatches a flaming suicide diver to kamikaze into the hydrogen-filled medusoid and blow it up. Jake is forced to leap into space, falling hundreds of feet and hitting one of the creature's sail-like vanes, which he slides down. To arrest his slide, Jake stabs into the membrane, ripping open a long slit—a self-conscious homage to a famous Douglas Fairbanks stunt in *The Black Pirate* (1926).

"Whenever we needed a performer to shoot an arrow, we made sure [their weapon really] worked."

Garrett Warren, 2nd unit director/stunt coordinator

"We hung a length of Tumbl Trak up high, suspended vertically," said Warren. "Sam's stunt double jumped and slid across a slit in the material, as hard as he could go. He held a dummy knife that he used to act like he was stabbing. We had a wire on his wrist. As soon as he hit that knife, we gave him some resistance as he slid down."

Mangkwan raiders ultimately cause the fiery death of the medusoid. Its destruction was a bravura sequence for the Weta effects and animation teams.

Right: Varang leads an aerial attack astride her nightwraith, unleashing a hail of firebombs, spears, and arrows on the Wind Trader gondolas. Weta screenshot.

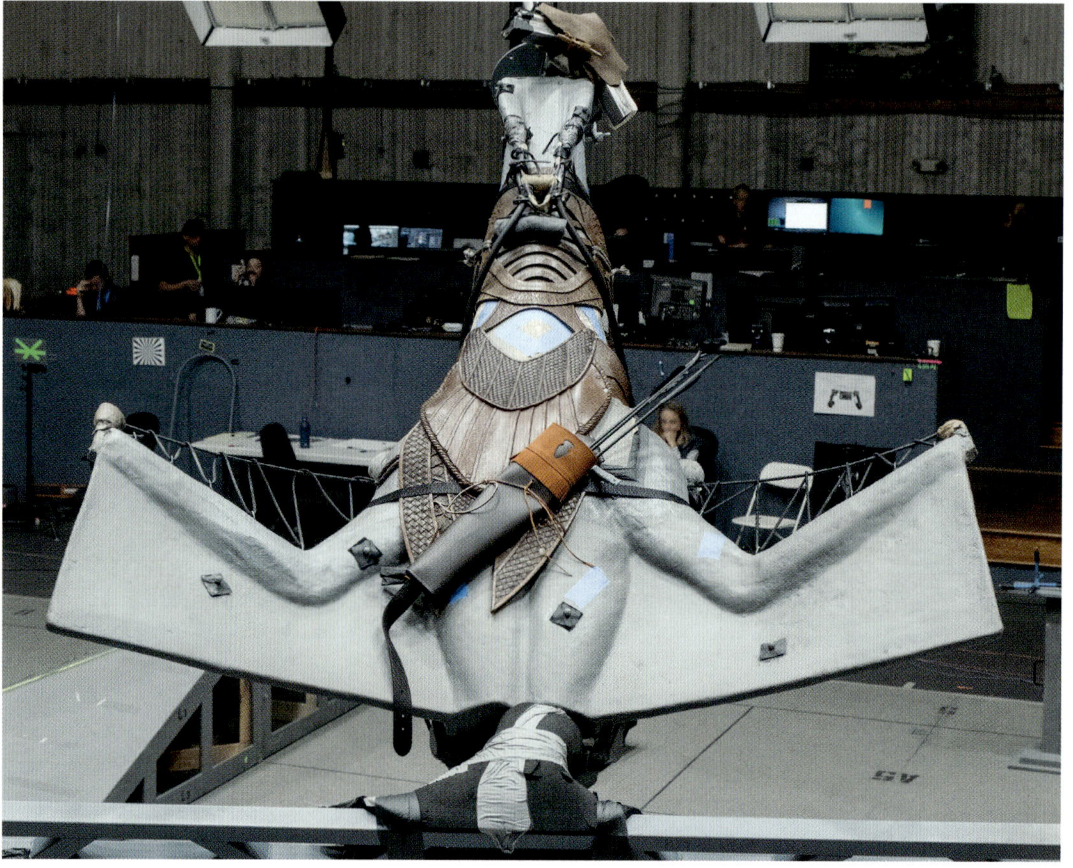

Above: Trinity Bliss (left) and Sigourney Weaver, with a small human placeholder, ride an *ikran* rig for Tuktirey and Kiri's escape with Spider from the Wind Trader gondola.

Right: The *ikran* rig, adorned with the saddle for its Na'vi rider and equipped with a quiver for holding arrows to be used in battle.

Opposite page: (Clockwise from top-left) troupe and stunt performers; Warren engages Alicia Vela-Bailey; Warren attacks Stephen Brown; stunt rigger Randy Haynie uses a cable to displace Chris Denison beneath Brown; Michael Homick grapples Ariel Cronin.

"The medusoid crash followed the look of the Hindenburg explosion," stated Eric Saindon, "We simulated chambers exploding within the creature as it went down. Like the Hindenburg, the chambers ignite and burn through, and so the medusoid stays afloat for awhile after it catches fire. And as the gondola goes down, the windray is still flapping, trying to keep up. The medusoid drags behind the gondola, crashes to its death into the rainforest treetop canopy, and the whole thing is on fire. It is quite a scene."

Fire and Ash also contained ocean scenes featuring a terrifying new creature: the nightmarish, squid-like *tsyong* that menace Lo'ak when he is in search of the outcast Payakan. Cameron tasked the stunt department to devise ways to simulate the creatures' attack on the performance-capture stage.

"We had been talking about the *tsyong* for years," recalled Warren. "Jim reminded us he hadn't seen any video tests, and so we finally got around to show him some ideas. We treated it like the squid from *20,000 Leagues Under the Sea* (1954). We had people getting grabbed and lifted here and there. Jim was not happy. He said, 'This is not that movie!'" Cameron illustrated his point with video of Humboldt squid, 6ft long cephalopod pack-hunters from the eastern Pacific Ocean, which have been known to attack fishermen by leaping out of the water, using water jet propulsion. " Jim challenged us to create something completely different that could believably strike with tentacles to suck you down into the water, grab and twist your head off, or eat your whole body. He wanted this to be dark."

Cameron wanted his squid to be fast, not only underwater but on land as they swarm onto the RDA Factory Ship. They needed to leap from the sea propelled by their water-jet siphons, then move like lighting up the ship's ramps, yanking themselves forward "hand over hand" using whip-cracks of their tentacles. The director showed everyone reference video of a small octopus leaping out of a tide pool and overwhelming a crab in less than two seconds, from several feet away—a devastating attack that left no time for escape. This wasn't going to be the flailing and ponderous leviathan from *20,000 Leagues Under the Sea*.

Rather than attempting to rig mechanical tentacles, the stunt department relied on manpower and the brute force of blunt instruments, leaving the tentacles to the animators. "We had stunt people with 'kill sticks,'" said Warren. "We made big, huge, heavy, padded sticks and used those to strike and smash with heavy

Above: A dangerous swarm of the *tsyong* prowling beneath the surface of Pandora's waters in this illustration by Dylan Cole. Tsyong design by Constantine Sekeris

hits. We used wire harnesses to redirect the body, move people around, jolt, and pull them back and forth. The stunt performers would try to fight these things off."

"The *tsyong* were an animator's dream," remarked Eric Saindon. "Jim wanted them to explode out of the water. They shoot out tentacles to pull themselves along and seem to have no structure. The animators had a blast." Said animator Dan Barrett, "The *tsyong* is a complex creature. Underwater, it's like a Humboldt squid; but it's also capable of moving tentacles-first at scary speeds across the ground. We did a bunch of motion tests for that. That informed design changes that happened after we got the *tsyong* in our hands here at Weta."

Across the two sequels, young Britain Dalton fearlessly battled Pandora's top ocean predators, first escaping an attack from a shark-like akula in *The Way of Water*, and then a swarm of *tsyong* in *Fire and Ash*. "The key for us was to engage the actor in a manner where he could visualize what was happening," noted Richie Baneham. "That gave us a truthful performance. The akula was a really fun one." After the fearsome design was locked in by the creature concept team, the animators had to bring it to life. As always, Cameron started in the Volume. A mock-up of the coral reef was set up, and Baneham and Cameron acted out a "flight path", this time with a wire-frame akula chasing a little wire-frame Lo'ak. With that general blocking captured, the animators applied the creature's movement—powerful tail strokes to drive it forward, trifurcated jaws gaping, black razor-sharp teeth snapping shut like a bear-trap. Its body would flex and twist violently as it tore the coral apart trying to reach Lo'ak. Cameron was very specific, inspired by a tiger shark he had once seen on a scuba dive, tearing apart coral to get at some small prey, its head disappearing in boiling clouds of debris.

The animated akula determined the direction and timing for the stunt players to simulate the attack for Britain Dalton in the underwater capture. "The animation

drove the (actor's) performance," said Baneham, "Garrett and his stunt crew scared the bejesus out of young Britain." Dalton did most of his own underwater stunts for the akula attack, lashing out at a hand-puppeted set of jaws with his speargun, and pulling himself hand over hand through a reef mocked up with foam-padded tubing, all while holding his breath.
Since Lo'ak was supposed to be almost out of air in the scene, Britain was acting as if having violent diaphragm contractions. Unfortunately this is the actual sign that someone is really in trouble underwater. A "cut" signal had to be devised so Kirk Krack didn't intervene every time Britain pretended to be in distress. Britain was told to slash his hand across his throat repeatedly if he really needed help. But he did it all flawlessly, acting like he was almost dying, but with perfect underwater aplomb the entire time.

"The *tsyong* [attack] was similar," says Garrett, "We had different tools for tentacle engagement, and we got a little more 'hands-on.' We did all that for real. When Britain started those scenes, he asked us, 'How are you gonna try to kill me this time?'"

The *tsyong* appear again, in a sequence during the climactic battle at the Cove of the Ancestors, in which Kiri uses her powers to summon *Eywa*'s forces. Kiri's communion with *Eywa* turns the tide of the battle as creatures rally to crush the RDA and Mangkwan aggressors. Leading the attack are the *tsyong*, now working for good, whom she dispatches to "Go to the Sky People. Kill them all." Kiri uses her own biolume dots to flash this message to the lead *tsyong*, dubbed The Alpha, who responds with flashes of his (her?) own biolume patterns.

"The *tsyong* have amazing camouflaging effects that shoot neon lights down their body," observed Weta animator Eric Reynolds. "Jim had us use that as their language. They 'talk' using patterns of light that cycle through their skin." This effect required a long process of "look-dev," look development, at Weta.

***

With the still untitled A2 and A3 being captured together as one massive production, actors would go from Reef scenes to Ash scenes to forest scenes on a daily basis. Scenes with the Ash sorceress Varang conveyed the savagery of the Ash People's rage against Pandora's natural order, which Na'vi call "The Great Balance."

Neytiri confronts Varang again while attempting to rescue Jake, whom the RDA has incarcerated at Bridgehead. This leads to a highly charged confrontation that highlights the different fighting styles of the two Na'vi warriors. "Neytiri and Varang are dripping with bad intention," said Garrett Warren. "Varang's fighting style is vicious. She has two blades on her back, whereas Neytiri has a bow and an arrow; then later Varang uses a flamethrower. Varang's fighting

Right: Oona Chaplin perfectly conveys Varang's aggressive nature.

style is weapon-based. She also attaches her *kuru* to her opponent's and she uses that to zap their brain with a debilitating shock. Then she'll slice off your *kuru*, and eat your heart."

Lightstorm sequence supervisor AJ Briones assembled performance elements for Neytiri's rescue, which kicks into high gear when marine biologist Dr. Ian Garvin (Jemaine Clement) commandeers a 44-foot-high, 200 ton, robotic bulldozer to smash open Jake's cell. "The bulldozer was a character in itself," noted Richie Baneham. "We took animation of the bulldozer and created a whole choreography around how that would work to free Jake. Neytiri becomes the distraction, Garvin breaks him out, and then Neytiri gets him to safety. In the structure of that, the bulldozer was the impetus for the escape, but we also had a huge crowd of onlookers that we had to stage and choreograph before we could shoot a couple of hundred RDA extras scampering away, and soldiers reacting, as this massive bulldozer breaks Jake free. We first established the choreography of Jake and Neytiri, then rolled back and did all the performance capture to fill out all the interactions of RDA guys running away, soldiers arriving, Skel Suits standing guard, turning and engaging, chasing down the bulldozer as Jake escapes and the bulldozer crashes through a building."

For the Bridgehead rescue, Weta collaborated with ILM—working with ILM visual-effects supervisor Nigel Sumner and company—when Neytiri frees Jake from imprisonment. "Nigel and his team joined us here in Wellington," Eric Saindon revealed. "They adapted their animation system and the look of the environments to match scenes that we'd been planning. It was a great sequence set in this industrial city environment, with an RDA bulldozer smashing Jake's cell, and scattering the crowd." Weta created the Ash People encampment at Bridgehead, making use of Ash Village assets combined with ILM models, and Saindon himself in a cameo. "I played an RDA construction worker. They dressed me in cargo shorts and sweatshirt, which is my usual attire. I was

Top: Oona Chaplin, as Varang, performs a Fire Dance in preparation for a Na'vi blood sacrifice. Small foam bricks on the performance-capture stage represented burning chunks from the fire.

Right: Chaplin wields props representing sharp-pointed buugeng sticks used in her ceremonial dance.

Top: After the RDA takes Jake into custody at Bridgehead, RDA scientist Dr. Ian Garvin (Jemaine Clement) commandeers a remote-controlled bulldozer to facilitate Jake's escape. Bulldozer concept art by Jonathan Berube.

Right: Work-in-progress of the practical bulldozer cockpit, built under the supervision of set decorator Vanessa Cole. Design by Jonathan Bach and Jeremy Love.

04/07/25
1030

02/07/25

3275_0005_v0236
Weta FX
v0236
04/07/25
1074

3276A_0010_v0170_HUD_RE
Interocular:2.8 Convergence:237.45 Lens:33.35

3275_0080_v0219
Weta FX
v0219

3305_0070_v0273

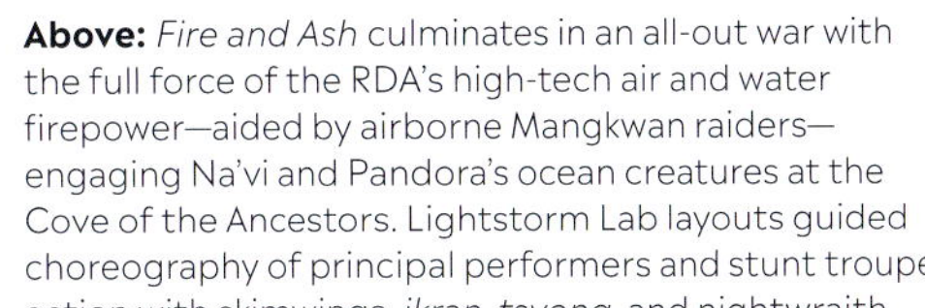

Above: *Fire and Ash* culminates in an all-out war with the full force of the RDA's high-tech air and water firepower—aided by airborne Mangkwan raiders—engaging Na'vi and Pandora's ocean creatures at the Cove of the Ancestors. Lightstorm Lab layouts guided choreography of principal performers and stunt troupe action with skimwings, *ikran*, *tsyong*, and nightwraith.

"We started with conceptual artwork, built [virtual] environments, and then choreographed huge, epic mêlées that were an amalgamation of performances, stunts, and animation, all coming together..."

Richie Baneham, VFX supervisor

Left: Zoe Saldaña performs a scene at the end of *The Way of Water* that mirrors an earlier moment when Neytiri honors the birth of Neteyam by singing a tribute to her first-born. Saldaña voiced Neytiri's sad song in Na'vi dialect on the performance-capture stage.

Opposite page: Cameron staged the mourning with almost identical framing—Neytiri in left profile, softly lit by firelight—the tragic mirroring her celebration of Neteyam's birth. Weta screenshot.

embarrassed and wanted to be way deep in the background, but Jim said, 'Nope, you're not doing that.'"

The integration of captured performances became even more complex in the final battle sequence, the culmination of the third act. This brings to a climax the Sully family drama, the threat of the Mangkwan alliance with RDA, and Jake and Quaritch's conflict over the fate of Spider—which plays out during Pandora's daily eclipse at the sacred site, the Cove of the Ancestors.

Elements included a gathering of *tulkun* elders, fleets of RDA *tulkun*-hunting ships, squadrons of rotor-craft, the swirling magnetic fields of the Flux Devil, airborne Mangkwan raiders, and hordes of ocean-going predators that add to the havoc. The Flux Devil was a new element in the story, a planetary phenomenon unique to Pandora, related to the powerful magnetic fields in Avatar that levitate the floating mountains. It is a towering helix of high-energy plasma that sucks up swirling sheets of atomized water from the ocean surface—since water is a dipole molecule, and can be magnetically levitated. Pay attention: there's going to be a test on this.

The "mother of all sea battles" as it was called in the script, would take literally years of design, capture, choreography and live action photography. The final sequence reached new heights of action filmmaking. "We started with conceptual artwork, built [virtual] environments," related Baneham, "and then choreographed huge, epic mêlées that were an amalgamation of performances, stunts, and animation, all coming together. We then added layers of effects, bullet tracers, explosions—it was an ever-evolving task!" Working with editor Jason Gaudio, Baneham then presented Cameron with Rough Camera Pass (RCP) battle vignettes as raw material for editing. Then Cameron put on his editing hat and shaped the arc of the third act battle. "Jim then restructured the RCPs into a coherent narrative, following the arcs of the characters and the overall arc of the movie."

Weta animators then analyzed this Template cut to determine their narrative requirements. "To accomplish that, Lightstorm Lab did a huge amount of work," stated Weta animation head, Dan Barrett. "and then Jim and his editors put the sequences together. Once we saw the edit we figured out the action within the battle for the duration of the sequence. We then addressed the background—whether it was vehicles, creatures, tracer-fire, or missiles—to make sure everything was playing in a continuous way."

Despite these technical complexities, the performance-capture process remained the beating heart of the production. The actors provided the emotional core of the story, and kept the epic extravaganza grounded in heartfelt stories that you care about. "Every nuance, every blink, those are choices that the actors made," noted producer Jon Landau in a 2024 interview with Deadline. "It was the commitment we made back on the first Avatar. We made a commitment to our cast that they would see themselves up on the screen. When you see Zoe as Neytiri weeping for her child, that is Zoe giving that performance. When you hear Neytiri singing at the beginning and the end of The Way of Water, that is Zoe—she was not doing a voice recording in a booth. She sang that live on a soundstage with a crew around her, and she gave us a heart-rending performance. What you see in that character is her."

Chapter 4

LIVE ACTION

Live Action

Live action (noun)
Action in films involving filming real people or animals, as contrasted with animation or computer-generated effects. Adjective: A live-action film.
Oxford English Dictionary

On *Avatar*, as live-action shooting loomed in 2008, the production had to totally shift gears from Capture to more conventional cinematography. Of course, there is nothing conventional on an *Avatar* film. Even simple scenes, in the labs and control centers of the human base, would require set extensions, holographic displays, and interaction between humans and the giant avatars. Almost every shot in the film, all 2,600 of them, was a VFX shot.

From the dreamlike forests of Pandora, home to the spiritual Na'vi and exotic flora and fauna, it was time to pivot to the human world of high technology, militarism, and corporate greed. Among Weta Workshop's tasks, working with production designer Rick Carter and New Zealand supervising art director Kim Sinclair, was to design and create 22nd-century RDA hardware—from guns, grenades, helmets, and battle armor to breathing packs, medical equipment, and cockpits for futuristic vehicles. High-tech engineering projects included five MRI-like Link Units for the human avatar-drivers in Dr. Grace Augustine's Bio Lab, and two 12-ft steel and acrylic Amnio Tanks, to which Weta later added avatars suspended in digitally generated amniotic fluid.

A heavily featured RDA walking machine, the Amplified Mobility Platform—or AMP Suit—took shape as a 13-ft full-scale prop in California, at Stan Winston Studios. The massive armored exoskeleton—a conceptual cousin to the walking machines in Cameron's *Xenogenesis* and *Aliens*—took shape in TyRuben Ellingson's designs, first in pen and ink, refined in Photoshop, and then translated into SketchUp 3D digital models. "It was a beautiful design," noted John Rosengrant, who oversaw the building of the massive machine at Winston Studios. The full-sized prop consisted of an aluminum-and-steel frame fitted with fiberglass pieces and cockpit controls, used in close-ups and non-ambulatory shots. It would be used for scenes in which Colonel Quaritch climbs aboard and fires it up. The second the suit comes to life though; it was a CG animated figure.

"There were different versions with breakable glass in the canopy," said Rosengrant. "The cockpit interiors weren't easy to make. We went to an aircraft manufacturer, and they made specialty pieces for us." For medium-close-ups in walking scenes, where you wouldn't see the arms or legs moving, Glenn Derry developed a motion-controlled platform capable of supporting the AMP Suit and its driver. This created the simulated motion of the suit walking, turning, and even fighting. The arms were removable to allow Weta to add moving CG limbs.

Concurrently, in the volume in California, Cameron and cinematographer Mauro Fiore scouted virtual models of the sets that would be built in New Zealand, planning their shots and lighting. Production designer Rick Carter then oversaw the building of the physical sets, working with supervising art director Kim Sinclair and the New Zealand construction team. Sets of RDA facilities at Hell's Gate incorporated blue-and-greenscreen backings for areas requiring digital extensions. These included the RDA Ops Center—which had a panoramic vista of the rainforest perimeter—and the Avatar Program Link Room, a circular chamber with a radial array of Link Units, built by Weta Workshop with core design contributions from the LA art department. To save money, this was built as half a set, which would be completed by a digital set-extension in post-production. Contiguous with the link room was the Ambient Room, visible through a bay window. This is where Jake first wakes up in his avatar body.

For scenes of RDA pilots flying tilt-rotor aircraft, the production turned to practical effects supervisor Steve Ingram, whose team engineered various mechanical builds at Stone Street Studios. Working from Lightstorm's designs, Ingram's crew built a full-scale mock-up of the SA-2 Samson "tilt-rotor" aircraft, minus its rotor system. This would be lowered from a massive crane, for landings in jungle and mountain sets. The actors could ride inside, then jump out and walk around the machine. Powerful wind machines would blast the

> "Jim wanted the audience to feel that they could literally be there in this world."
>
> **Richard Taylor, Weta Workshop**

Previous pages: Cameron directs Jack Champion as "Spider" Soccoro during a key scene at the climax of *Fire and Ash*, illuminated by the fiery glow of battle. To root human performances in the Na'vi world, the filmmakers built partial sets illuminated with lighting sympathetic to virtual environments.

Left: Stan Winston, whose studio made a vital contribution to the designs of Pandoran creatures and RDA hardware in *Avatar.*

Above: For live-action scenes featuring RDA's Amplified Mobility Platform—or AMP Suit—Stan Winston Studios created a full-scale, posable version of the robotic exoskeleton. Key model makers John Eric Tucker (top) and Edward Lawton (lower right) test out the AMP Suit prop.

grass and foliage, simulating the downblast from the rotor system. The crane was too big for even the largest soundstage at Stone Street, so the landing scenes at Site 26 had to be shot in the parking lot, with a wall of shipping containers forming a greenscreen wall, as a backing. "Jim wanted the Samson to land," Ingram noted, "so it had to be structurally sound with pickup points and spreader bars so that we could hang it from a 200-ton crane and then sweep it into a forest set. We did that by releasing weight on the back of the rig so it had the angle that Jim liked, like a real helicopter landing."

Despite the spectacular natural scenery of New Zealand, the crew never shot on location there, or in fact anywhere. Every leaf on every tree in *Avatar* was

Above: Stephen Lang (as Quaritch) takes position with costar Kelson Henderson (as RDA gunship pilot) in the cockpit set of the airborne Dragon Assault Ship in New Zealand, 2008.

Opposite page: A Titan crane prepares to hoist a full-scale set-piece of an RDA Samson tilt-rotor aircraft above a backlot forest set at Stone Street Studios in Wellington, New Zealand, January 2008. Wind machines stand ready to simulate tilt-rotor downdraft.

TITAN
TITAN

either shot indoors or computer-generated. There was only one day of outdoor photography in the entire film—landing the Samson tilt-rotor in the parking lot.

Ingram's effects team also used a hydraulic "motion-base" platform to simulate the Samson in flight. "Jim wanted the Samson to go on a motion-base and he wanted to do some movements that were quicker than we could get any motion-base to work," Steve Ingram recalled. "We were still finding our feet with how accurate Jim required things. That was a big wake-up call for us."

Cockpit sets sat atop a cluster of six hydraulic pistons supporting a pivoting platform—which enabled the cockpit to roll, pitch, and yaw. The system used computerized controls developed with robotics engineer Steve Rosenbluth and Lightstorm's Simulcam supervisor Casey Schatz. "That was a massive learning curve for us," Ingram noted, "But there's no other way we could have developed our rigs to do what Jim needed."

In flying scenes the Samson would bank, causing sunlight to sweep across the cabin. To get that effect, it is necessary to move the vehicle or move the sun... On *Avatar*, they would do both. Cinematographer Mauro Fiore mounted a powerful 12K light on a big extensible camera crane, with a remote head that could pivot the light. A witness camera on the light itself allowed the operator of the remote head to keep the light aimed at a moving target. By rapidly extending or retracting the telescoping crane arm, the "sun" could sweep across the Samson mock-up, creating moving shadows from the window mullions onto the actors inside, which usually included pilot Trudy Chacon (Michelle Rodriguez).

To get close-ups of the actors during flight scenes, Cameron would ride the motion-base, often strapped to the side of the Samson set, handholding the 3D camera, whose weight was taken by a bungee cord attached to the Samson. The handheld sway and jitter gave the feeling of being in a real aircraft.

In addition to the bigger practical effects, there were a number of small but important makeup effects, provided by Weta Workshop and Winston Studios. These included Quaritch's signature facial scars, souvenirs of an attack by a viperwolf on his first day in the Pandoran "bush." The three jagged scars on his forehead, arching across his high and tight crewcut, were thin transfer appliances that Stan Winston Studio makeup artist Mike Smithson laid onto Lang's face and scalp.

Jake Sully's live-action scenes also had to depict the effects of the former Marine's combat injury, which had left him paralyzed from the waist down with

Left: The New Zealand special-effects team also rigged the tilt-rotor for outside shooting at Stone Street. James Cameron and co-producer and first assistant director Josh McLaglen discuss a Samson landing scene.

Right: Weta Workshop co-founder Sir Richard Taylor confers with James Cameron flanked by (left to right) senior visual effects supervisor Joe Letteri, production designer Rick Carter, and (far left) costume supervisor Matt Appleton at Weta Workshop, 2007.

atrophied legs. The Winston team engineered a "saw-the-lady-in-half" illusion for Sully's wheelchair, where Sam Worthington kneeled and slotted his real legs through the chair seat, to be digitally painted out later. Stan Winston Studios then attached the pale and withered prosthetic limbs, molded from a real paraplegic, to Sam's hips. These were only needed when Jake was wearing shorts. This gag was seen just once in the final cut of the movie, to really sell the extent of his disability. For scenes in which Jake was wearing pants, a simpler gag was suggested by the director: little vacuum-molded half-shells were set on top of Sam's real legs, under the pants, to suggest the bony shape of his character's atrophied legs.

In many ways the live-action portion of *Avatar* was the most conventional and least problematic part of the overall production, but that was true only relative to the hideously complex and experimental Capture and CG portions of the film. It was nevertheless the most difficult live-action shoot Cameron had ever encountered. It was being shot using experimental prototype cameras—digital 3D cameras designed by Cameron and his engineering partner Vince Pace specifically for this film. Each 3D "rig" was a nine-axis motion control system, with servos controlling the focus, iris, and zoom functions of two 10:1 zoom lenses in perfect synchronization (six axes), plus the convergence of the two cameras (toe-ing in or out to match subject distance). There were two servos to control the interocular distance between the cameras as the subject moved closer or farther away. This would manage the "stereospace" or degree of 3D, so it was always comfortable for the audience. And there was a servo to control the angle of the beam-splitter mirror that unified the two images. All this in a package small enough and light enough that Cameron could operate it hand held. As all of these remotely controlled axes of motion were moving at once, the camera felt alive, flexing in Cameron's hands as he operated.

This miracle of miniaturization and precision worked well enough—for a prototype. Which means it was glitchy and basically a work-in-progress throughout the entire six-month shoot. Cameron had taken the bold step of hanging the fate of one of the most expensive films ever made on a new invention. But what was one new invention, after the string of revolutionary inventions already in play on the movie? Image-based head-rigs, facial algorithms, the v-camera, Simulcam, and so on. Completely re-engineering movie cinematography was just one more insane hurdle on an already demented production.

> "It all seemed like a good idea at the time."
>
> **James Cameron**

But there is a distinction between the battles that you expect and the ones you don't. One unexpected hurdle was the breathing masks that were intrinsic to the story. The Pandoran atmosphere is poisonous to humans. Its CO2 content is hundreds of times higher than in Earth's atmosphere, and a human would succumb to convulsions and death within minutes. So the script called for Sam Worthington, Sigourney Weaver, and the other actors to wear breathing masks for their outdoor scenes. These prop masks weren't really functional. They weren't supplied with pressurized air to an SCBA demand-regulator. They simply had inconspicuous slots that allowed air in and out so the actor could breathe. But the masks all had a curved glass faceplate (it was actually acrylic) so they looked real. But that faceplate reflected every light in the entire studio, which looked completely wrong in what were supposed to be outdoor scenes. The entire overhead lighting grid was reflected. The greenscreen was reflected. The fluorescent tubes creating bioluminescent underlighting were reflected.

When Cameron first encountered the problem, he and DP Mauro Fiore spent hours trying to light a single close-up of Sigourney Weaver, attempting to disguise the reflected lights with leaves and branches—to no avail. It was impossible. After spending half a production day on one close-up, Cameron declared that there would, henceforth, be no glass in the masks. The wardrobe department pulled the glass out of all the masks. No more unwanted reflections.

This solved the problem by kicking the can down the road into post-production. Now hundreds of mask shots would become VFX shots in which the glass was replaced using CG, with reflections of the CG environment around the character being rendered faithfully in the glass. This, like almost everything else on the film, had never been done. But with almost every single live-action shot being already a VFX shot, the production took it in stride.

The later CG augmentation of the live shots would include adding backgrounds outside the windows of buildings and vehicles, extending sets, adding ceilings, adding window glass to AMP Suits and aircraft, adding hologram graphics to the Holotable in the middle of the Ops Center, adding the spinning "scan heads" to the link beds, adding brain graphics to the screens in the Link Room, and generally adding a plethora of video images and graphics—all in stereoscopic 3D—to every single screen and monitor in every set. Cameron wanted Jake's human scenes inside Hell's Gate and the other technical spaces to be as rich and complex to the eye as the rainforest scenes, so the audience wasn't drumming its fingers impatiently waiting for the next scene out in the jungle.

There wasn't a shot in the whole 2-hour-and-42-minute film that wasn't technically complex. Cameron would say with a resigned shrug, "It all seemed like a good idea at the time."

***

Avatar was merely hideously complex. But to raise the bar, *The Way of Water* and *Fire and Ash* would push even further into the unknown. This was especially true with the integration of live-action and virtual elements and characters, which was taken to a whole new level. Production designers Dylan Cole and Ben Procter worked together to identify sets and vehicles that required physical builds. Meanwhile, Cameron brought in cinematographer Russell Carpenter, ASC, to start planning how to shoot the combined live-action production of the two sequels. The director and cinematographer had worked together previously on *True Lies* (1994) and *Titanic* (1997). Carpenter had won an Oscar® for Best Cinematography for the latter film. His first assignment on the Avatar sequels was to shoot screen tests with two young actors being considered for Spider, the character most central to the live-action shooting.

Carpenter had also collaborated with Cameron on *T2 3-D: Battle Across Time* (1996), a 12-minute 3D filmed attraction for Universal Studios. Knowing

Opposite page, top: Jake disembarks at Hell's Gate. Screenshot by Framestore.

Opposite page, below left: Jake's disembarkment, greenscreen element.

Opposite page, below right: To create the illusion of Jake's withered legs, representing the effects of a spinal injury that Sully incurred years earlier in combat, Stan Winston Studios devised an in-camera illusion. They used prosthetic legs that attached to Worthington's hips while the performer's real limbs slotted out of sight through set pieces, including a mobile wheelchair rig.

Costume Focus

Above: Costume designer Deborah L. Scott—Cameron's Oscar®-winning collaborator from *Titanic*—attends to a detail on actor Cliff Curtis in his role as Tonowari, *olo'eyktan* of the Metkayina clan.

"Working with Jim, you've got to follow designs all the way through so that you have a full understanding."

Deborah Scott, costume designer

Below left: Weta Workshop artist Lisa Doherty works on a mantle bearing the tooth of an akula sea predator worn by Tonowari in *The Way of Water.*

Bottom left: During the production of *Avatar*, Weta Workshop artists Claire Prebble, Nadine Jaggi, and Jasmin Van Lithuse work on varieties of fabrics and textile materials, exploring costume textures for Na'vi clans.

Below right: Cameron, Scott, and Curtis review details of Tonowari's ceremonial robes and spear.

Bottom right: Weta Workshop artists Cathy Tree Harris works on an Omatikaya cummerbund for Avatar.

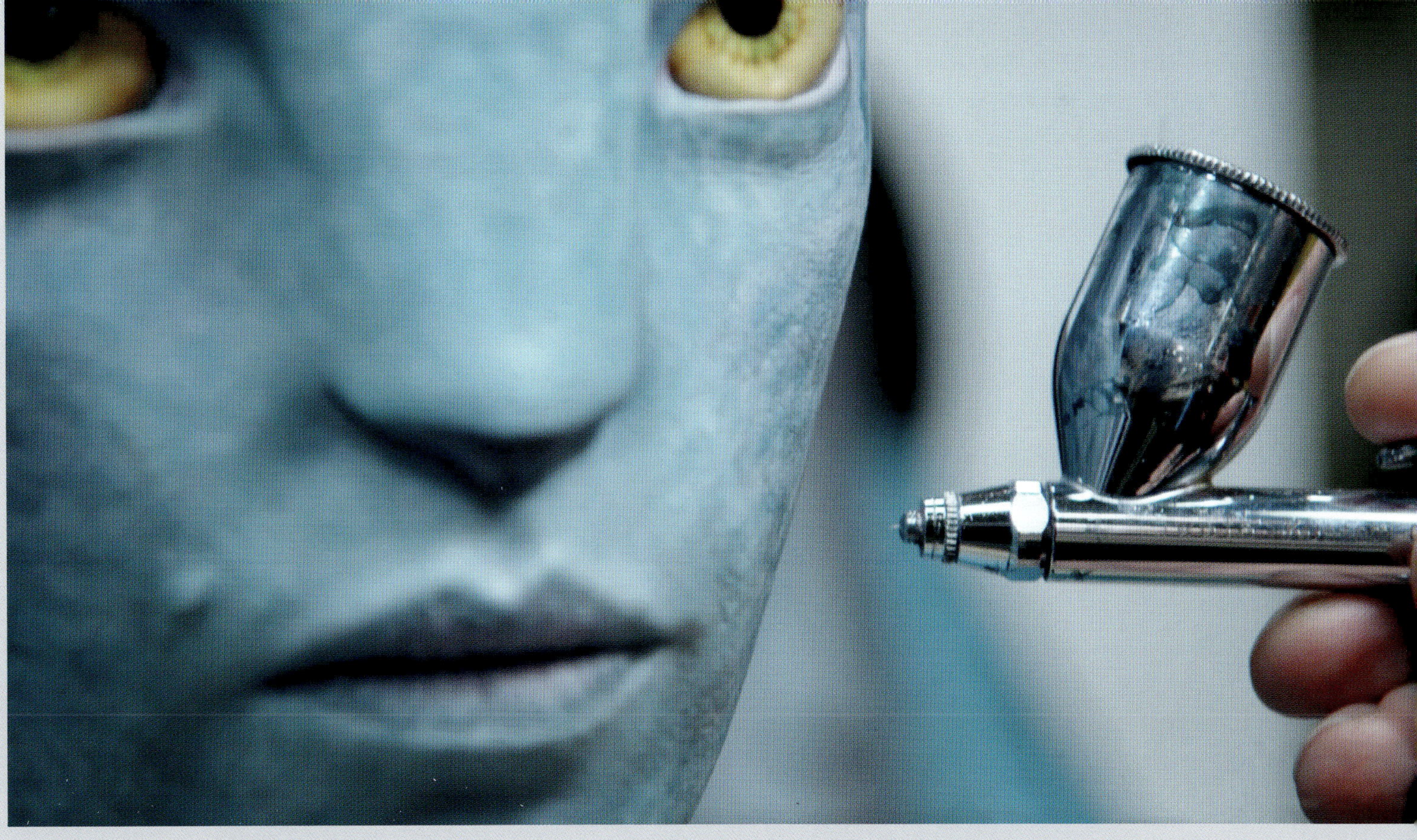

Opposite page: Physical reference of character and hair design informed digital designs, and vice versa. Concepts for Tonowari and his *tsahik* and mate, Ronal, by (top) Joe Pepe, (bottom-left) Legacy Effects, and (bottom-right) costume concept art by Deborah Scott's team at Weta Workshop.

Above and right: Legacy Effects artist Ryan Pintar uses an airbrush to create a physical study of the Metkayina clan's teal-azure complexion on a bust of Ronal.

Cameron's eye for technical detail, and the specific demands of stereoscopic 3D cinematography, Carpenter and his gaffer Len Levine approached the screen test—featuring Spider in a jungle setting—as more than a simple dry run. "I told Len that Jim and Jon wanted to build a small area that was supposed to represent a jungle," Russell Carpenter recalled. "Our set took over about a third of one of the big stages in Manhattan Beach, and Len made a great suggestion. Instead of using conventional movie lights, we built a grid of theatrical lights above the set like they use in music videos. We were able to do what Jim really wanted, which was to replicate the look of an Avatar-type jungle on stage. In fact, he liked our test so much he showed it to his team who were building the virtual jungle. Of course, for the rest of the film, it was the other way around—we followed their template, as laid down since *Avatar*."

Starting a year and a half before the start of principal photography—the art department determined 'Extent of Build' (EOB) for live-action scenes and the Lab mapped out which sets would be partial builds to be completed by CG set extensions. The Lab then delivered layouts to art director Kim Sinclair and the set construction teams in New Zealand, On the first film, the production had discovered that the New Zealand craftsmen did exquisitely detailed work, so going into the sequels they had complete confidence that the sets would look amazing.

In the years since Cameron and cinematographer Mauro Fiore shot *Avatar*—using the Cameron-Pace Fusion 3D system—imaging fidelity had exponentially improved. But the larger sensors in the new cameras required larger lenses, which added weight to each camera. This added significant weight to any 3D "rig" that contained two such cameras, one shooting the left eye image, one for the right. And heavier 3D rigs were the antithesis of what the filmmaker required for his handheld approach to shooting.

"Jim wanted the camera system for *The Way of Water* to be even lighter than the system he used with Mauro on *Avatar*," said Carpenter. "Jim had a partnership with Sony, and he challenged them to bring down the weight of their cameras. Several really smart people worked for a long time on that."

Cameron and Lightstorm Vice President Geoff Burdick, who had a 19-year relationship with Sony, convinced them to create a version of their top-of-the-line Cinealta Venice camera in which the sensor "head" was split apart from the electronics processing "body" of the camera, with an umbilical cable to tether the two together. This would allow the lightweight sensor heads to be in the rig, while the rest of the electronics were offboarded, so Cameron didn't have to lift them. This split system would later be marketed by Sony as the Rialto system, which was used extensively to put small cameras inside jet cockpits on *Top Gun:*

Right: Jack Champion as Spider, kitted out to breathe Pandora's atmosphere.

Maverick. But when the Avatar sequels started, it wasn't even a product. Just an un-named, untested prototype.

3D systems producer John Brooks was tasked with integrating the Sony prototype into a newer, lighter rig. Using new lightweight Fujinon zoom lenses, with their remarkably crisp optical performance, combined with the Sony sensor-blocks, Brooks was able to assemble a rig that weighed just 27 lbs, well within Cameron's target. The director would have to operate with an assistant just behind him, on a 10-foot leash, carrying the processor packs for the two cameras. But at least the filmmaker would have a lightweight 3D rig, with zoom lenses, that he could operate in his agile handheld style.

Cameron was adamant about shooting "native" 3D rather than doing what most studios do, which is convert a 2D film into 3D in post-production. Cameron considers this lazy and believes it results in an inferior product—mediocre stereo depth, with a lot of artifacts that make the image look unnatural. In addition, it removes true creativity in the moment, where the director can author a scene in 3D in real time versus having it applied like a coat of paint in post. He likens conversion to shooting a movie in black and white, then converting it to color later.

Said Carpenter, "The way he designs his shots, how he places actors in the frame, and how he moves the camera, is all targeted toward creating an immersive experience for the viewer. Even in apparently simple scenes, something is constantly unfolding in each frame, revealing new information."

One of the biggest challenges on *The Way of Water* and *Fire and Ash* was the integration of Spider (Jack Champion) into Na'vi scenes, due to the scale differential between his character and the Na'vi. This challenge completely dominated the live-action phase.

The vast majority of live-action scenes in the two sequels would follow the story of Spider, the human kid caught between the Na'vi world and the human world. The complexity of combining young actor Jack Champion with large-scaled characters, including the Sully family and Recom Quaritch, made this a very time-consuming process, especially across the great number of scenes in which Spider appears. Over a year of the production would now be spent on what Cameron called "the Jack Champion Show."

On the first *Avatar*, there were only a handful of shots combining live-action human characters and Na'vi scaled characters—in the Ambient Room when Jake first wakes up in his avatar body and a few other shots dotted throughout the film, including the finale where Neytiri cradles human Jake in her arms. But across the two sequels there would be over 1,000 live-action shots of Jack Champion, interacting with many different Na'vi characters, in both natural landscapes and high-tech sets of labs and ships.

A whole new discipline for shooting scale interactions was needed. On *Avatar*, the virtual camera had been used to scout CG mock-ups of some of the live-action sets weeks in advance, allowing DP Mauro Fiore to anticipate the lighting and camera blocking. But it never became a rigorous form of pre-viz, at least on the first film.

On the sequels, Cameron took that process to a new level. Every single scene that would later be shot as live action was first captured in the volume in Manhattan Beach, with full cast. Jack Champion wound up performing all his scenes twice, once as Capture, and again on the live-action stage, sometimes up to two years later. In Capture, Jack would perform with Sam, Zoe, Sigourney, Stephen Lang, and the others, to lock down everyone else's performances. Jack was there so the other actors could react naturally to his emotional presence as Spider. But none of his work, for a year and half, would yield any of Jack's final performance. Spider was a human character. His final performance would be shot during live action.

During Capture, many tricks were used to integrate Jack at human scale while the other actors were performing at Na'vi scale, 1.6 times larger. This might include Jack acting on his knees, or the others standing on low platforms called "manmakers," to account for the height differential. Sometimes Jack's place was taken in the master scene by Kacie Borrowman, who has diastrophic dysplasia, a rare form of dwarfism, and is only 4-feet tall. In such moments, Kacie would wear a helmet with a video tablet that covered her face, on which Jack's face appeared as he fed in the lines from off-camera. This allowed the other actors to interact with tiny Spider in a fluid and natural way, and on the right eyeline, especially if they were walking around.

Kacie became the go-to solution in many scenes in which human characters interacted with Na'vi or Recom characters. She played many roles, and like all the troupe members, was a gifted and versatile actor who could switch between identities at the drop of a hat. She was ready for any challenge, including some fairly gnarly stunt action. "Once I asked Kacie if it was okay to call her a 'little person'" recalls Cameron, "and she said that was the right term. Then I said, 'well what do you call us?' meaning taller people. 'Average,' she says with a grin." Kacie was anything but average. Despite her size, maybe even because of it, her spirit and heart were enormous. Everyone admired Kacie's indomitable spirit.

"Even in apparently simple scenes, something is constantly unfolding in each frame."

Russell Carpenter, cinematographer

Jack adapted instantly to this bizarre form of production. At 13 years old, he'd never made a movie before, so he just thought "this must be how movies are made. Who knew?" He loved being part of the big, raucous Avatar family, and they all loved him. He was a delight to work with, and was game for anything, no matter how mind-bending.

Once Capture on any given sequel scene was done and editorial selects were made, a performance cut was created by the editorial team. Then, sometimes months later, Cameron would do virtual camera on the resulting loads. Next, with actual shots in hand, the editors could assemble Template scenes. So far, that was basically how it was done on *Avatar*. The difference this time was that the Templates would be used as a highly accurate blueprint for live action shooting.

On *Avatar* a bit of pre-viz had been done in the volume, with troupe performers doubling for the cast. This time around, Cameron would generate cut sequences from principal Capture, not just from scouts. These were the actual performances of Zoe, Sig, Sam, etc., all interacting with young Jack, and complete with Cameron's specific camera angles. These sequences were more than just a roadmap—they were the actual camera moves Cameron wanted when he got to the live-action set. This level of disciplined shot creation was a new layer that had not been done for the first movie.

The Templates proved invaluable to live-action prep. First Cameron would run the scene for the art department, camera department, and Casey Schatz' "tech viz" team. The template provided a very precise guide to the Extent of Build—how much set really needed to be physically constructed? It allowed for detailed tech viz—figuring out all the technical elements of the live-action scene well in advance. For example, Casey could check that the technodolly's crane arm could reach every needed camera position. He could plan the rigging points for the cable of the Eyeline system.

Then, when they got on the live-action set, first AD Maria Campbell could set up the shots in advance, using Cameron's virtual camera moves as a precise guide, and Russ Carpenter could light the set. Simulcam allowed them to see the captured performances of Zoe, Sigourney, Stephen Lang, etc. in real time. Keep in mind that the work of those actors was done. They had already gone on to other movies, or richly deserved vacations. The production was now working with their "canned" performances, fixed in amber. Nevertheless, the director was free to make up new live-action camera moves on the spot, just as he would be during a v-cam session. Simulcam allowed him to see, in his viewfinder, Jake, Neytiri, Quaritch, or Kiri walking around the set.

The Template showed the crew Cameron's exact intention. Often the director would only be called to the live set once the shot was set up and lit, and Maria had run a few rough rehearsals with Jack. That allowed Cameron to work in parallel elsewhere, on the virtual stage, or in the cutting room. A small volume had been set up on the adjacent E-Stage at Stone Street, so Cameron could work alternately in both virtual and live-action worlds on the same day just by walking back and forth between the stages. At the peak of live action shooting, Cameron would be running back and forth between the live set, on huge soundstages, and the little E-stage volume to work ahead on virtual shot creation.

Making a movie is like laying track in front of a moving train. The director had to have Template cuts for upcoming live-action scenes ready to feed into the endless maw of production, so that tech viz and construction could be ready for scenes coming up months later. Sometimes days later.

The painstaking shooting of young Jack came with a ticking clock. "Our big challenge was Spider," noted James Cameron. "I cast Jack Champion when he was 12. Then I needed him for 18 months of Capture for A2, A3, and the first part of A4. We didn't shoot with him in live action until he was 14, and he turned 15 on that shoot, in 2019. Poor Jack had to do all his scenes twice—first he had to perform with Sigourney, Sam, Zoe, and the other kids in the volume in LA. And then, in New Zealand, Jack had to reproduce all of his scenes for the live-action side of his performance, working opposite our troupe players and the Eyeline system. His voice had already changed, in the middle of the Capture shoot. When the COVID-19 pandemic hit, that shut us down for six months, and we hadn't finished Jack's scenes. We had to get back in the saddle as quickly as possible and get Jack's scenes done, before he 'aged out.' Jack had just turned 16 by the time we were finally done, in late 2020. It was almost four years of his life."

Makeup would be another big challenge. Jack was very fair-skinned, but would be playing a kid that had spent his life running around the jungle in a loincloth.

Opposite page: Boom operator Sam Spicer captures dialogue from Jack Champion as Spider beside a stereoscopic camera rig developed for the sequels—updating the 3D camera system on *Avatar*—using a Sony Venice Rialto dual-camera setup.

FLIGHT HEAD APEX
AVATAR

He would, logically, have been deeply tanned. Cameron joked that Jack was the whitest human he had ever seen. When the director cast him, he figured Jack would just go to the beach for a couple of months and get brown. But Jack's mom was a biologist, and legitimately concerned about skin health. She wouldn't allow that. So Jack would require extensive body makeup for every scene, every single shooting day. And it's not like he was wearing much to cover that up.

"Spider had really only one costume change in *Way of Water*," commented Deborah Scott, referring to Jack's loincloth. Joe Pepe came up with the idea that Spider, desperate to be accepted by the Sullys and the Na'vi, would use berry juice to paint himself in blue camouflage stripes.

"Spider's makeup was a journey," concurred hair and makeup lead Sarah Rubano, who joined the team in 2018, a year ahead of live-action shooting in New Zealand. "It had to look like he was trying to emulate the Na'vi, by painting himself with blue stripes. Weta Workshop built full-body and face stencils that we used to apply makeup to Jack each day. It was then about finding the right color blue. We had to figure out the correct shade and level of opacity. We started with a heavy, opaque look; but we came to realize it needed to be quite translucent." Spider also copied Jake's dreadlocks by styling his hair similarly, which Rubano's team created using 12 wigs made from human hair.

> "Spider's makeup was a journey. It had to look like he was trying to emulate the Na'vi..."
>
> **Sarah Rubano, hair and makeup lead**

For the Na'vi characters, who would be realized entirely in CG, the makeup team focused on wound continuity. This required detailed studies of the main characters' cuts, scrapes, and bruises as they progressed through their trials and tribulations. Makeup for the CG characters was just as complicated as it was for any live action shoot, and required the same rigorous attention to continuity from scene to scene. Rubano had to prepare for test shoots, using prosthetic appliances on stand-ins, to create precise reference for the digital artists. "Jim really loves to test everything practically," remarked Rubano, "And so I developed injury progressions for the characters. That involved airbrushing and painting makeups directly onto human skin. The visual effects department then photographed those practical tests and used them as layers in their animation." Na'vi makeups were also needed for cinematic pickup shots, to be used directly in the movie. "We had insert shots, for instance, of Neytiri cutting vegetables, and Jake tying leather straps around his wrists. I painted their arms blue, and then we shot those inserts. Jim loves to sneak in as many practical elements as he can."

Above: Spider (Jack Champion) in full makeup on the rainforest set.

Property master Brad Elliott provided detailed props for other photographic inserts—objects hitherto seen only as virtual elements. This included Neytiri's bow—which she breaks in a rage-fueled attack on the human ship after her son's death. In *Fire and Ash*, Lo'ak reconstructs the bow to restore the Sully family honor. The War Bow—*tsko a'eoio*—becomes an almost sacred object in the sequel story. In *Avatar*, it was given to Neytiri by her father Eytukan, as he lay dying after the RDA attack on Hometree. She has guarded it as a symbol of the strength of the ancestors, whom she invokes when she carries it into battle against the human invaders. When it is shattered by her fury, she loses a part of herself that she can't seem to reclaim. The broken bow is a symbol of her broken spirit.

The war bow is a beautiful example of Na'vi craftsmanship and ingenuity: a nearly-10-foot-long weapon made of shaped and laminated wood, strung with animal gut, intricately wrapped in woven decoration, and equipped with a pair of flight-vanes to aid aiming during aerial combat. The prop team created pieces for the sequence of scenes in which Lo'ak and Tsireya (Bailey Bass) remake the ancestral bow. "We imagined Lo'ak harvesting wood, carving the new 'blank,' sanding, staining, making the glue and varnish," said Elliott.

Initially, Cameron staged the war bow reconstruction with Britain Dalton and Bailey Bass on the Capture stage. The final step was shooting live-action inserts of the shaping and assembly of the war bow. For this, Sarah Rubano had to do blue makeup on the actors' hands. The bow was really shaped and assembled on camera, with every step completely real.

When Lo'ak finally presents the finished bow to his mother, she is overwhelmed. He has channeled the strength of the ancestors. It is a deeply emotional moment for both of them, and a milestone in Lo'ak's life's story. From that moment, he sets out on his own to find his destiny, through a perilous sea voyage. And Neytiri, according to Na'vi tradition, must let him go to follow his own path, no matter how heart-wrenching it is for her. As the Reef People say, "the boy dives deep in the ocean, the man returns."

This level of detail was also applied to the live-action weapons of the RDA. New Zealand property master Melissa Spicer and head armorer Gunner Ashford provided an arsenal of "full flash" weapons that produced fireballs from gun muzzles. For a scene early in *The Way of Water* where Jake, brandishing an assault rifle, leads a Na'vi attack on an RDA supply train, the filmmakers had to consider where Sully could have obtained his Na'vi-scale machine gun. The RDA would need to supply its new army of Na'vi-scaled Skel Troopers with weapons, so that would be where Jake got the guns. However, Jim reasoned the Skel Suits wouldn't need a shoulder-stock because they were robotic and strong, so they would use guns without a stock. So Jake's gun has a Na'vi-carved wood stock, and filmmakers had to figure out how to integrate that into his weapon.

Costumes for human military personnel also received a makeover to convey that years had passed since the Battle of the Hallelujah Mountains. In *Avatar*, RDA combat gear had featured a "Universal Camouflage Pattern" based on a real U.S. military design. In *The Way of Water*, RDA combat fatigues featured a more organic pattern. "The idea was," said Deborah Scott, "if you were flying above Pandora, looking down, one of the main things you'd see is forest.

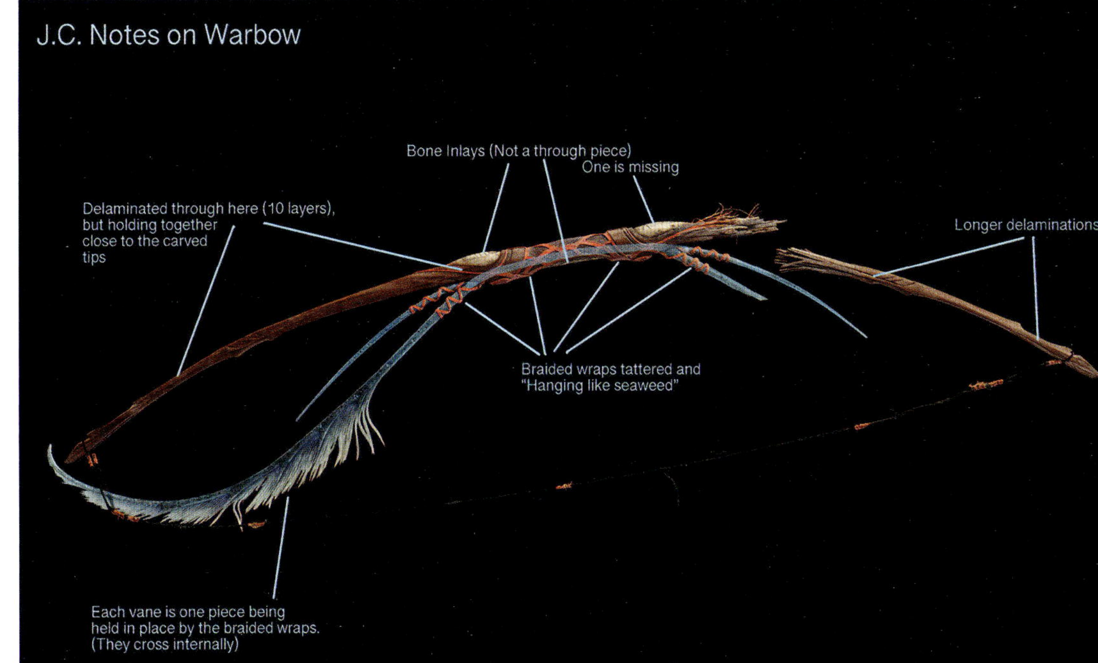

Top right: Cameron's notes on the shattered war bow design: "The weapon takes on mythological significance in *Fire and Ash*. Hewn from timbers of the Omatikayan Hometree, the broken bow symbolizes the death of Eytukan in battle against the RDA and, years later, Neytiri's struggle against the RDA in a sea-raid, where she damaged the weapon and its fragments fell into the sea. Lo'ak salvages the bow to amend his family's honor."

Center right: Prop master Brad Elliott embarked on detailed forensic reconstruction of a human-scale war bow.

Below right: The tactile nature of the prop resulted in a memorable performance- capture session with Na'vi performers Britain Dalton and Bailey Bass.

Overleaf: Diving to the wreck of the SeaDragon, Lo'ak and Tsireya discover remnants of Neytiri's broken war bow. Weta screenshot.

Opposite page, top row: RDA Skel M69 assault rifle modified with wooden stock, which Jake Sully adapts for Na'vi rebel raids, Weta Workshop design with a stock by Dylan Cole and Johnathan Bach; and (right) a Magpul Industries adaptive combat rifle, a modern-day weapon adapted for gunplay during performance-capture.

Opposite page, second row: Recom Hydra .50 caliber machine gun; and (right) Skel AR minus the Omatikaya stock. Weta Workshop designs as oversized weaponry for deceased RDA Sec-Ops troopers regenerated into 10-foot Na'vi Recom warriors.

Opposite page, lower left: OZ-33 United Ballistics pistol, standard .40 caliber human-scale sidearm issued to RDA Sec-Ops and Cet-Ops troopers. Weta Workshop design.

Opposite page, lower right: RDA technicians prepare Na'vi-scale Recom weapons for combat. The production manufactured full-scale weapon props for live-action interactions of human characters handing weaponry to Recom characters.

Right: Blank-round gunfire gives the recoil, muzzle flash and ejection of bullet casings, creating a realistic depiction of an actual gunfight.

So, we used a forest-like pattern. That took quite a while to design and print. The hardest part was working out the scale that would look good on a human and also work on a much larger Recom."

Cameron also wanted the RDA troopers to have a completely new generation of breathing masks, to indicate that this new wave of the human invasion had upgraded technology. This proved to be a deceptively difficult design problem that plagued the production for months. The complicating factor: the new mask had to actually work underwater, not just functionally but aesthetically.

In several important scenes in *The Way of Water*, Spider wears an RDA mask as he dives into the sunken SeaDragon to search for Jake and Neytiri. This leads to him finding his father, Colonel Quaritch, unconscious. He decides, against his better judgment, to rescue him—a critical plot point necessary for subsequent sequels. The mask design from *Avatar* would not work for this due to the shape of its acrylic faceplate, which was quite curved. That shape would miniaturize the actor's face underwater, due to the refractive distortion of a dome in water. Underwater masks require what's called a "flat port." And since Spider would be doing major dive scenes in what was supposed to be the standard issue RDA mask, that mask couldn't be mass-produced for all the other actors and extras until a working dive mask was designed. It was a crisis moment. John Garvin was tapped to solve it. Not only was he an experienced cave diver, familiar with all the commercial dive masks, he had been the designer of the life support system on Cameron's Deepsea Challenger sub. Cameron knew he could solve complex technical problems on short notice. Garvin had even faced a similar problem on a previous Cameron-produced movie, the cave diving thriller *Sanctum*. For that film John created a mask that really worked underwater but was visually kind to the actors' faces.

Garvin brought in a firm he'd worked with on Deepsea Challenger, Sydney-

> "The hardest part was working out the scale that would look good on a human and also work on a much larger Recom."
>
> **Deborah Scott, costume designer**

based Design and Industry. Together they brainstormed with Cameron, who was no stranger to designing underwater headgear that would work for photographing actors faces—the custom-made diving helmets for *The Abyss*. From his experience on that film, Cameron knew he could photograph faces through an acrylic port that was "faceted"—flat on the front and sides. But a completely flat port would have been a serious departure from how the masks had looked in *Avatar*. A compromise was suggested—a faceted mask that had front and sides that were slightly curved overall, to at least reduce the refractive distortion in water.

But the mask had to actually work underwater. A daunting engineering and design problem. The mask had to work safely enough that a 15-year-old actor could use it, and it couldn't miniaturize Jack's face. To supply air, the new mask would require a tiny second stage SCUBA regulator built in. The fake regulators on the masks in *Avatar* were extremely small, assuming technology a century-and-a-half in the future. But now the regulator had to really work. John Garvin found a tiny second-stage regulator, and worked with Design and Industry to incorporate it into a fully functional breathing mask. The new mask had a slightly curved front and sides, and looked reasonably consistent with the first *Avatar*. John put on the prototype and videoed himself in a pool, turning this way and that, then sent the video to Cameron, who loved the design. John reported that the mask had great visibility and was easy to breathe in, an important factor for Jack Champion. Also breathing easier was costume designer Deb Scott, who after collaborating with Garvin and Weta Workshop artist Lans Hansen on the initial R&D for the masks, had had to wait for the completed prototype, before she could mass manufacture.

The mask proved to be safe, camera-friendly and easy to use. It even won a major Australian design innovation award. But there were still a few things to be worked out.

Opposite page, far left: Mansk, a Sec-Ops trooper killed in action during the RDA's attack on the Tree of Souls, was rejuvenated from his Soul Drive consciousness hard-drive storage, uploaded into a Recombinant Na'vi body, and reactivated for service as Recom Mansk (Kevin Dorman). Concept by Weta Workshop.

Opposite page, lower: Bridgehead Ops Center RDA costume concepts by Weta Workshop.

Above left: RDA Colonel Quaritch, killed in action, returns to lead a squad of Recom special forces troopers. Recom lineup concept art by Jeremy Hanna.

Above: Cameron and Deborah Scott discuss details of RDA costume design.

Top: Breather mask prop used by Hell's Gate personnel and Spider. Several variants developed for the sequels.

Above: Spider's exopack, adorned with a Na'vi woven strap

The first problem was Jack's air supply. The "exopack," the typical breathing pack that was well established on the hip of every human character in the Avatar films, was too small to practically contain much of an air supply. It was supposed to be futuristic tech that we don't have yet. So Jack was fed air through a "hookah" hose, a long umbilical that supplied air from a SCUBA tank at the surface. The umbilical would be digitally painted out later.

The second problem was getting light onto Jack's face in dark scenes. Underwater movies always make the same mistake—putting lights inside a mask or helmet to light the actor's face. To anyone who actually dives, this is nonsensical. A light inside the mask would blind the wearer with internal reflections. As a seasoned diver, Cameron refused to accept that solution. So how to light Jack's face at night, inside a dark shipwreck? It was decided to give the mask a HUD, a Heads-Up Display, supposedly built into the acrylic faceplate. The glow of the HUD would softly light his face, especially his eyes. It would be easy enough to add the graphics of the HUD display later as CG, but how would they create that interactive glow on Jack's face? The solution: a fiber optic was threaded into the mask and aimed at his face. It piped in light from a laser light source at the surface, down the "hooka" umbilical, and into the mask. Later the fiber aimed at Jack would be digitally painted out when the HUD graphics were added. Problem solved.

Getting Jack in the water, with all these systems working, had become like a space mission. Jack was a trooper though, and went through the mask training without complaint.

Jack recalls, "I could just be fully in character underwater and have a real full face mask that worked perfectly. If it ever got a little bit of water in it, I could just press down on here (the purge button), and I don't know the science, but it would get rid of the water and make my face dry and everything else. This was a microphone, so whenever Jim was talking to us underwater, I could say whatever and he could hear it." The director could talk to Jack underwater, through the diver-address speaker, and Jack could talk back. This really helped the two of them work through the difficult action of Spider searching the ship and rescuing Quaritch. The resulting scenes look completely authentic, because they were done for real.

Another big design challenge was the Skel Suit, a motorized exoskeleton that gave a human trooper the size and agility of a Na'vi. It had to look completely functional and have the range of motion of a human for running, jumping, and handling any form of weapon. Weta Workshop initiated the Skel design process with broad exploration. A mantis-like, long-armed sketch from Jeremy Hanna caught Cameron's eye, and was painstakingly interpreted into a functional 3D design by Fausto De Martini, who worked out all its ergonomics and mechanics. Legacy and Workshop both assisted with real-world ergonomics tests.

Cameron loved the Skel, and decided Edie Falco's character, General Ardmore, would wear one. It added a dimension to her character, suggesting that she was not a desk-bound officer, but one who had come up through the ranks, with years of combat experience. Falco loved this idea. She'd never done a VFX-heavy show before, and was a bit wide-eyed at all the bluescreen and Eyeline rigs. But she took it all in stride. Her attitude was: acting is acting. Put me in a foam shadow caster or whatever, I'll do my job. "I'll be General Ardmore, to the bone, no matter what "crap" you put on me".

Edie liked the concept that as Ardmore, the On-World Commander of all RDA forces, she wouldn't want some man towering over her. Especially a guy that, in his human incarnation, had been the previous commander of Sec-Ops. She would need to establish her absolute authority immediately, and for that she needed to be eye level. The Skel Suit gave her that stature.

> "I'll do my job. I'll be General Ardmore, to the bone, no matter what..."
>
> **Edie Falco, actor**

For the live-action scenes where Ardmore interacts with Quaritch wearing her Skel, an active-marker system was used (as opposed to the passive reflective markers used in the volume in LA). Under Edie Falco's costume was a network of infrared LED markers, that shone their light right through her camouflaged fatigues. Though the light was invisible to the 3D camera shooting the scene, mocap cameras could see it. So she was actually being photographed cinematically, and captured at the same time. This allowed the Simulcam system to display her, in real time, in her 10-foot-tall Skel Suit. Cameron could operate the camera, following her naturally, and her Skel Suit perfectly matched her action. It was a remarkable technical achievement.

To stage live-action scenes of characters in, around, and under water, the New Zealand special-effects team constructed water tanks in Auckland and in Wellington. "We built an interior tank at [Auckland's] Kumeū Film Studios," noted Steve Ingram, "and then we shot there for about four weeks. In Wellington, we had great success with a system of tanks that we could put up

Top: Skel Suit final 3D design by Fausto De Martini basd on an early concept by Jeremy Hanna.

Above: Skels in rainforest and naval color schemes, by Fausto De Martini

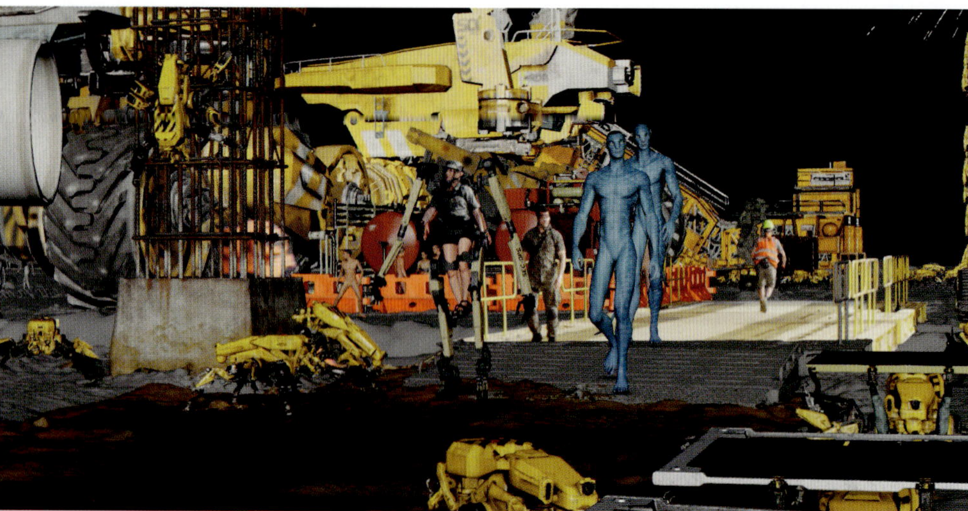
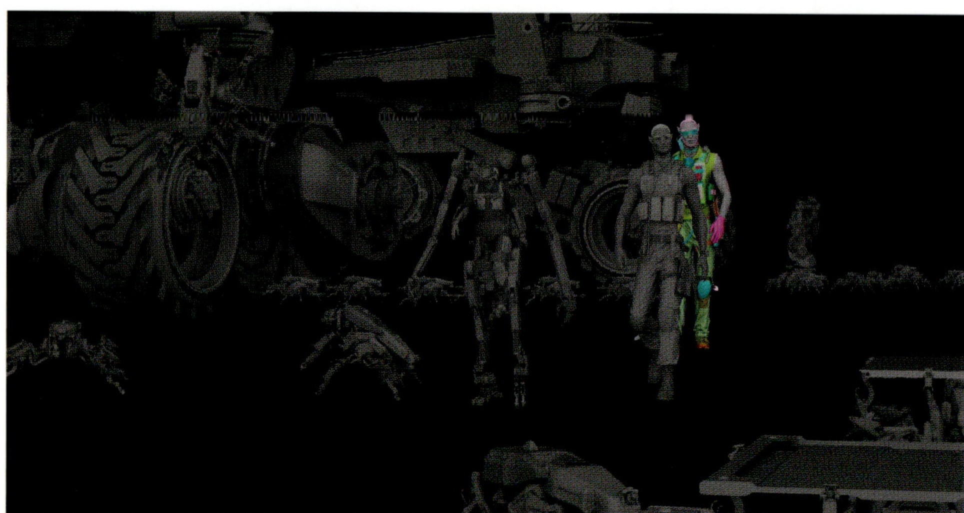

and take down as needed. They were six meters deep and 18 meters in diameter. We used them, too, in Auckland when we needed additional tanks. We could put them in a container and set them up with all the water treatments and filtration in about two weeks. The underwater photography team told us that it was the cleanest and best working water they'd ever been in." These tanks were used, in *The Way of Water*, for scenes of Spider searching through the sunken SeaDragon ship, and ultimately pulling his Recom father's unconscious body out of the wreck. For *Fire and Ash*, scenes of Spider rescuing an unconscious Kiri during the final battle, and later witnessing the *tulkun* hunters closing in for the kill, were shot in a 20-foot-deep circular "pop-up tank" installed on F-Stage at Stone Street. Other scenes in *Fire and Ash*, of Spider riding Payakan's fin, and later an *ilu*, were shot in the "underwater wind tunnel" in the big tank in Manhattan Beach. In all, seven tanks in three cities, in two countries, were used in the filming of the Avatar sequels.

To build practical chase boats for the *tulkun*-hunting scenes, supervising art director Kim Sinclair and art director Alister Baxter drew on the innovative work of New Zealand marine specialists. Watergoing craft included the cockpits of the one-man SMP-2 Crab Suit and two-man Mako attack sub, and a fully working, seagoing Picador jet-boat, plus a full scale mock-up of the Matador harpoon boat, mounted on a six-axis motion-base. "Alister has a great background in modern marine construction," noted Ingram. "The Picador was the smaller of the two craft. The marine crew took it out and did quite a few tests on the ocean. It was an awesome piece of technology. To enhance the speeds and jumps Jim needed, we worked with Alister to put the Picador on a motion-base." Matador and Picador were built in New Zealand. The Crab Suit and Mako sub were built in LA by Wild Factory under the supervision of supervising art director Luke Freeborn. These cockpits were later modified by Baxter to flood.

Shooting the 60-foot Matador harpoon boat, which was done completely on stage on a motion-base—with CG water added later—was a daunting challenge. "That was a massive job," Ingram recalls. His team modified a custom-built computer-controlled motion-base by adding top rotation to Cameron's specifications. "That way, instead of constantly having to move the camera and lights around, we could move the boat through 360 degrees."

Opposite page: RDA General Ardmore (Edie Falco) uses a mechanical Skel Suit exoskeleton to elevate her to Recom eye level. Live-action shoot; simulation of animated elements; layout presentation; animation presentation; final composite. Weta breakdown.

"Instead of constantly having to move the camera and lights around, we could move the boat through 360 degrees."

Steve Ingram, practical-effects supervisor

As a guide to the motion programming of the base, it was necessary to capture motion of a real boat in ocean swells. James Cameron's 33 ft RHIB (Rigid Hulled Inflatable Boat,) nicknamed "Prime Rib," was drafted into service. It was a veteran of his deep ocean expeditions, a powerful machine sporting two 250 horsepower outboards, able to go 55 knots flat out. It was fitted with inertial motion sensors. Then the director's brother, JD, an experienced waterman from his Marine Corps days, took a stunt team out to sea, off the coast of Santa Barbara, California, to put the boat through its paces. The younger Cameron launched the boat hard into waves and surf, getting it airborne and crashing down in teeth-jarring impacts. All this gnarly action was recorded by the motion sensors, and later used by Lightstorm and Weta to drive boat animation. It was imagined that the *tulkun*-hunters would be fearless cowboys who loved their job, addicted to the adrenaline rush of charging their boats around, getting air in the big ocean swells as they hunted the leviathans of the deep.

With true motion, recorded at sea on a real boat, it was then possible to run accurate fluid-dynamics sims to generate the bow waves, impact splashes, and boat wakes. "We captured GPS data from a real boat in the ocean," related Weta visual effects supervisor Eric Saindon. "We then applied that data to a motion-base, which recreated the boat's motion on a stage. We later applied the same ocean-movement data to CG water. That way, our water simulations interacted realistically with the boat. As the boat pushed through the water, its bow wake splashed correctly with the motion of the water. Then we added smaller splashes, spray, and mist."

In the smaller E-stage volume at Stone Street, the production captured action of the crews on the boats. This included Quaritch alongside *tulkun*-hunter Captain Mick Scoresby (Brendan Cowell) on the Matador kill-boat. Cameron then shot v-cam coverage of the RDA boats for the *tulkun* hunt sequence, which were

Left: For oceangoing scenes, the production created full-scale Cet-Ops craft, including the 50-foot Matador harpoon boat and the 32-foot Picador patrol boat. The art department team adapted the vessels to fit in a soundstage set representing the "Well Deck" of the SeaDragon *tulkun*-hunting ship on K-Stage at Stone Street Studios in Wellington, New Zealand. An Eyeline monitor lowered into the set guided the presence of Recom characters in the scene.

Below: Recom Colonel Quaritch pauses to admire the weaponry of the Matador harpoon boat. Weta screenshot.

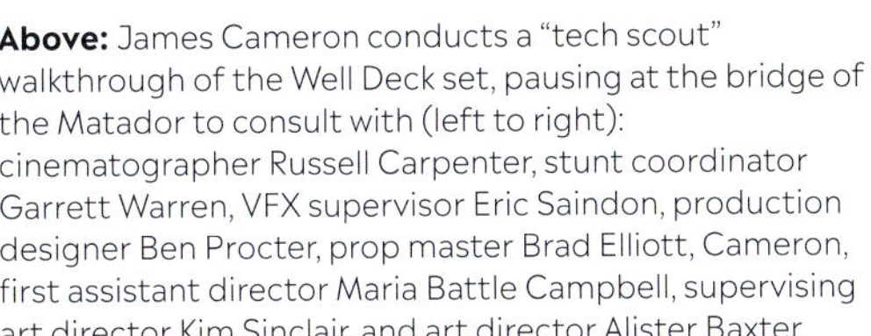

Above: James Cameron conducts a "tech scout" walkthrough of the Well Deck set, pausing at the bridge of the Matador to consult with (left to right): cinematographer Russell Carpenter, stunt coordinator Garrett Warren, VFX supervisor Eric Saindon, production designer Ben Procter, prop master Brad Elliott, Cameron, first assistant director Maria Battle Campbell, supervising art director Kim Sinclair, and art director Alister Baxter.

edited into a rough assembly as a guide for live-action filming. From this, the programming for the Matador's motion-base was derived. Stuntmen playing *tulkun*-hunters, along with actor Brendon Cowell, were then shot on the full-scale Matador as it gyrated on the motion-base. Water mortars provided the downpour, supposedly from tail splashes as the massive *tulkun* mother writhed in agony on the end of the harpoon line.

"We had fire hoses and big fans to blow the water back," said Ingram. "And then we triggered water mortars with the motions of the boat. As the boat's bow went down, we timed the splash to occur at the right time." The ocean would be added later with CG water. Huge advances in water sims were required to create the close interaction of the boat with swells, bow-waves, impact splashes, and wakes. Lightstorm spent millions of dollars on years of Weta R&D to be ready for the task.

Cameron said, "The amazing thing is when you watch the movie, it looks like we were out at sea. There is not one shot of an actual boat at sea in the entire movie. People aren't CG. The boat's not CG, but the water in the ocean is CG."

Top: To simulate oceangoing scenes of Picador action, the New Zealand special-effects team mounted a full-scale vessel on a computerized mechanical motion-base. Motions of the craft pitching through the waves allowed Cameron to capture visceral interactions with the *tulkun* hunters.

Above: The gun of the Picador has a controllable LED lighting rig that can be used to simulate muzzle flare and interactive lighting.

"The amazing thing is when you watch the movie, it looks like we were out at sea..."

James Cameron

In *The Way of Water*, the SeaDragon—a massive *tulkun*-hunting mothership—would become the stage for a ferocious final conflict between Jake and Neytiri versus Quaritch and his Recoms. This sequence was dubbed "Parents from Hell" because of the relentless fury with which Jake and Neytiri storm the ship to rescue their daughters. It is a cinematic tour de force, choreographed by Cameron and Warren on the Capture stage in LA, and finely edited into a Template to guide live action. It was then shot in New Zealand on the SeaDragon set, where live-action "plates" of the many arrow and assault rifle "kills" were filmed in 3D.

Ben Procter and Lightstorm concept artists Fausto DeMartini and David Levy designed the SeaDragon to look almost like a monstrous sea creature, with a broad, mouth-like portal at the front, and manta-ray wings that allowed the giant machine to lift above the water, propelled by four aft-mounted propellers."

The underlying concept for the SeaDragon was a technology Cameron had been fascinated by for years called WIGE—Wing in Ground Effect. In the 80's the Russians had built monstrous seagoing vehicles that were part ship, part aircraft. They had short wings that could only lift the vehicle out of the water a short distance, staying within "ground effect," but this technique made these craft faster by several factors than conventional ships. Cameron took the idea farther—what if it was a ship that lifted itself part way out of the water on hydrofoils? Then, as it accelerated, it would come all the way out and fly on its short wings and ram-air hull shape. The top speed of the SeaDragon would be 180 knots, 10 times the speed of a conventional ship its size.

Ben loved the idea, and came up with multiple designs, including giving it a gaping mouth shape, suggesting a living monster. The problem was reconciling the need for an aerodynamic shape with the broad deck space that would be needed for the battle action, such as when Payakan crashes down on the deck, smashing everything in sight. Ben proposed a "clamshell" design, with a broad foredeck that would open up and spread out flat once the ship slowed down. In the script, page-count for the SeaDragon was very high, so a lot of time was spent designing the ship, stem to stern. This included the moon pool and sub bay, where the Mako chase-subs would launch, and the aft ramp where the slaughtered *tulkun* were dragged aboard to be harvested. Everything had to be accounted for, to service all the action, including the *tulkun* hunt, the Metkayina skimwing attack, the final battle on board, the ship's sinking, and the subsequent scenes inside the wreck. The writers referred to this as the "hot wreck" sequence. In most submerged shipwreck scenes, the wreck is a rusted hulk that's been lying on the bottom for years. In *The Way of Water* it has freshly landed on the bottom, with some of its emergency lights still on, surrounded by the silt of impact, and with columns of air bubbles streaming out of it. A dynamic, and visually exciting setting, promising lots of jeopardy for the characters.

Lighting design helped place the human and Recom characters on the high tech SeaDragon. DP Carpenter lit the massive set with slashes of bright sun and shadow, to appear as very naturalistic day exteriors. "Ben Proctor was so collaborative," remarked Russell Carpenter. "He'd show me his concepts and invite my input. For instance, Ben and I discussed the quality of the light in the scene when Recom Quaritch is walking along the deck and everybody is disembarking. I pointed out how I could put three shafts of light on our set to align exactly with the virtual set extension." Carpenter and his lighting team introduced shimmering lighting effects in the moon pool, where three Mako subs were parked, ready for launch. Weta later filled the bluescreen opening with computer-generated water.

For live-action RDA environments at the city of Bridgehead, Carpenter took cues from concept art to create a hard-edged lighting palette. "This was a world imbued with a sense of power and dominance," Carpenter observed. "It was in stark contrast to the forest scenes, which had a subtle play of light that had to feel alive. For the RDA's Bridgehead base, I remembered growing up in

Opposite page: Mako subs in the belly of the SeaDragon. Concept art by Fausto de Martini.

Above: The SeaDragon, from which the RDA launch myriad *tulkun*-hunting missions.

Right: A proxy model of Recom Quaritch (far right) provides scale reference beside Jack Champion as Spider, while Cameron directs on a partial set representing a portion of the exterior of the SeaDragon bridge.

Above: Recom Quaritch crushes the skeletal remains of Colonel Miles Quaritch. The New Zealand property department created approximately 40 small, crushable prop skulls for the scene, and troupe performer Kevin Dorman enacted the Recombinant officer's pulverizing grip.

Southern California and the lighting you get at night in a parking lot at Kmart, or one of those big box stores in the San Fernando Valley. We made the light feel sharp; nothing was soft."

Lighting for Pandora's natural world featured moments of jaw-dropping beauty, often infused with luminous natural sunlight that emphasized how the Na'vi lived in harmony with their environment. From Carpenter's perspective, the imagery called to mind the "Hudson River School" of late-19th-century American landscape painters. "If you look at the art of Thomas Cole or Frederick Church," noted Carpenter, "there is a romantic feel to their light that makes it feel like a beautiful world to live in. I took that from the first *Avatar*, and I knew I had to support that in our live-action lighting to make contrasting statements of the two worlds, [human and Na'vi]." In rainforest scenes involving human characters, which required live-action sets, Cameron referred Carpenter to the landscape paintings of Maxfield Parrish and J.M.W. Turner. "Jim loved direct sunlight, with a tinge of warmth against the blue in shadowy areas beneath the rainforest canopy. He then wanted to add a third element. Where the sunlight hit a giant leaf, it had to have a green reflection. Even in strong rays of light, Jim wanted to see that green combine with the blue skin of the Na'vi. That turned out to be really beautiful."

In *The Way of Water*, as they roam the rainforest, Spider and the Sully children are captured by the Recoms and brought to the site of human Quaritch's fallen AMP Suit—the place where it fell as Quaritch died in the first movie. There the resurrected Recom Quaritch confronts the skeletal remains of his prior human self. For the Capture portion of this scene, a miniature version of the derelict AMP Suit was placed on the capture stage, where Stephen Lang was captured picking up a tiny human skull, then crushing it in his now giant hand. A wax skull was used, to create the proper shape and resistance.

To shoot the live-action part of the scene later, with Jack Champion, a full-size AMP Suit foot and leg were built for Jack to lean against as he watches his

"Jim loved direct sunlight, with a tinge of warmth against the blue in shadowy areas beneath the rainforest canopy."

Russell Carpenter, cinematographer

Above: Warm lighting creates the effect of Pandora's lowering sun on a riverbank studio set where Cameron directs Daniel Lough, Jack Champion's stunt double, and blue-suited Kevin Dorman.

father confront his mortality. Simulcam was used to compose Jack in the frame with the captured figure of Quaritch. In addition, Legacy Effects built an accurately detailed 2/3-scale miniature of the AMP Suit cockpit, complete with meticulously crafted and aged skeletal remains, overgrown with moss and vines, to be used for insert shots. "The suit was scaled down so that Stephen Lang, playing Recom Quaritch, could pluck out his older human skull and crush it," revealed John Rosengrant. Troupe actor Kevin Dorman, with his hands made up in Na'vi blue stripes by Sara Rubano, played Quaritch, at least from the elbows down. He wipes away the vines revealing Quaritch's stenciled name and signature dragon "nose art" on the outside of the cockpit. Later, it's Kevin's hands picking up a practical 2/3rds scale skull, and crushing it into fragments. The final scene is a seamless blend of full-scale live action with Jack, live-action miniature with Kevin, and performance capture with Stephen Lang.

The first step for all these live-action scenes, on A2 and A3, was to capture Jack Champion interacting with Na'vi characters on the performance-capture stage. This established the emotional truth of the scenes and laid the groundwork for shooting live action in New Zealand. Then, two years later, Jack had to be shot in live action, scaled to appear small next to his (previously captured) Na'vi co-stars.

"Jack Champion was five foot two inches when he joined the cast as Spider," Richie Baneham explained. "We were hoping he'd get to five foot seven inches by the time we shot live action. But he shot up to five foot eleven inches! That skewed our scales, and by the time we were finished shooting he had passed six feet. Jack is a big boy. If you meet him today in real life, he's grown again, and he's filled out. He's a handsome young man that carries his size very well." One of *The Way of Water*'s most seamless blends of liveaction and virtual elements was the story's most emotional sequence—the death of Neteyam, the Sullys' eldest son. The scene featured Spider struggling, along with members of the Sully family, to haul the injured Neteyam out of the ocean and onto a rock island. Neteyam dies in his father's arms, lit by fading light of an eclipse. The sequence began with Jack Champion and the other actors in performance-capture. The scene was actually captured twice, first in the tank, with the actors struggling in the breaking surf provided by the wave-maker. Richie Baneham recalls, "They were standing in water getting hit by waves trying to heave a body up onto the rocks. Obviously they're fake rocks and it's a fake wave. There wasn't anything fake about it for the actors."

For this session, Spider was doubled by Kacie Borrowman, straining with Britain Dalton, Sam Worthington and Bailey Bass, to help lift Jamie Flatters' limp body from the surf. A second pass of the scene was done dry, in the volume. Here the actors picked up the scene after Neteyam has been hauled onto the rock. In the dry capture session, the actors were able to focus on refining their intensely emotional performances.

It was a day they all dreaded in advance, but on the day, they gave their all. After the scene was done, they were uncharacteristically quiet. Sam and Zoe especially, as parents now themselves in real life, were hit hard by imagining the death of a child. Without much said, they went their separate ways, back to their families, to process what they had just been through.

To complete the scene in live action, almost two years later, Jack would need to be photographed coming out of the water and witnessing Neteyam's death. This was filmed in a water tank set in Auckland with Champion interacting with blue-suited troupe members taking the places of Sam, Zoe, Britain, and Bailey (Tsireya). There was also a large blue puppet, weighted to simulate the mass of Neteyam's body, for Jack to struggle with in the surf. The crashing shore-break was created by three tractors with back-hoes pushing plow-like plates that raised a substantial wave in the shallow tank.

The emotional component of the scene was far more challenging than the technical aspects. It is a tribute to Jack Champion that he was able to recreate the emotion of that memorable Capture day, two years before, without any of the original cast present. It is also a tribute to the troupe players—Kevin Dorman as Jake, Alicia Vela-Baily standing in for Zoe, and Courteney Rosemont as Tsireya—that they were able to support Jack with emotional performances of their own. During live action, Jack had adapted to thinking of Kevin as Jake and Alicia as Neytiri. Sam and Zoe had left such a powerful impression on him that, to Jack, Neytiri and Jake were real people. Kevin and Alicia were continuations of those characters that to Jack felt natural. He had come to love and trust them, just as he had Sam and Zoe.

"One of our more difficult things was in the middle of Neteyam's death scene," commented Russell Carpenter. "The sun had to go behind the planet Polyphemus and I needed to know how long that eclipse was supposed to last. Jim replied, 'Well, there's how long it's supposed to last, and how long it lasts in the movie.' And he explained the whole cosmology, and about the layers of gases around Polyphemus." Cameron had calculated the orbital mechanics and proposed that it would take about 90 seconds for the eclipse to reach totality. But in movie time, the scene lasts longer.

Chief lighting technician Len Levine simulated the eclipse by using programmable lighting above the water tank set, creating gently shifting patterns of light through

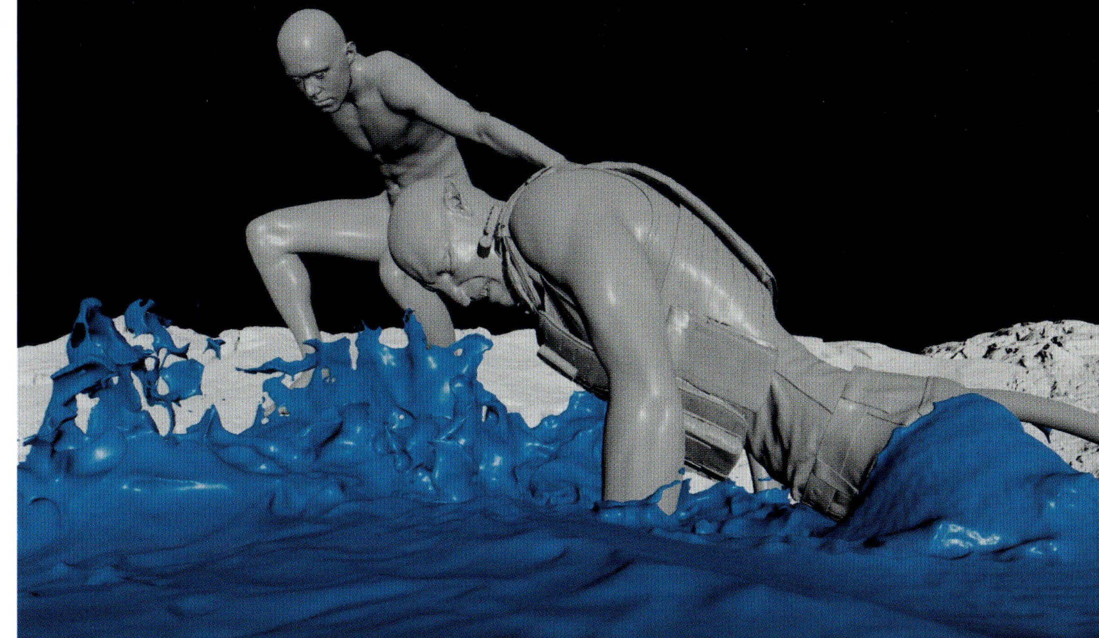

Opposite page, top and center: Tragedy strikes the Sully family when their eldest son, Neteyam, dies battling the RDA. The sequence was one of the most challenging and rewarding for Cameron's animation and effects teams. Weta screenshots.

Right: *The Way of Water* redefined what was possible in the integration of live-action and virtual performances in water environments. The human boy Spider (Jack Champion) shows mercy to Quaritch (Stephen Lang) by hauling the 9-foot (2.7 m) Recombinant from the sea. Weta breakdown of animation, water simulation, and composite.

the scene. "It was one of our proudest moments," Carpenter added. "We built a low sun light off in one corner of the huge stage. At one end of the tank there were large, moving metal plates to make waves on the rocks." LED light panels simulated the flames of a capsized burning Picador nearby. "We shot with Spider in his costume, with other characters in their blue suits. They came up out of the water and onto the land." The film crew monitored the scene via Simulcam, which miraculously placed Jack Champion into the emotional tableau of the grieving Na'vi family. "When I saw the first composite of the arrival on the rock," said Carpenter, "I was knocked out by how realistic it was."

It also proved to be one of Weta's most challenging shots, as they had to integrate characters of different scales, and CG water mixing with a live-action plate shot in real crashing waves.

"It was incredibly well directed," asserted Richie Baneham, "and the performances were great. But Jim did a very good job right out the gate by laying it all out so that we could understand the choreography and staging. That's why we shot that scene virtually first. We worked out interactions with a fully CG Spider, down to how much blood there would be, how much of Neteyam's wound we would show, how we would make it feel like the kids were panicked. We shot all that virtually so we could understand the scene's visual language, including the displacement of the water and the interaction of the camera. We then mimicked that when we shot the live-action version with Spider. That's why it integrates so well. It was so well planned. And we employed the same performers who had featured in the virtual version of the scene in the live-action shoot. They helped to keep Jack in the moment."

"When we were shooting in Auckland, Jim saw that integration for the first time," Eric Saindon recalls, referring to the moment he showed Cameron the finished shots, " It was impressive. He was so blown away, he stopped to address the crew."

"All of the performers gave such great performances," Saindon continues, "Zoe's emotion played against Sam's almost lack of emotion, and his stoic reaction through that scene. It was the performances that made it."

***

For *Fire and Ash*, live-action segments of the Wind Trader scenes required dexterous lighting that Russell Carpenter and Len Levine designed to work on

Below: The sinking of the RDA SeaDragon serves as an apocalyptic backdrop to the drama. Weta screenshot.

Opposite page: The Wind Trader flotilla—a picture of serenity before the Mangkwan attack. Weta screenshot.

stage in New Zealand, taking cues from Lightstorm conceptual designs. "It all starts with a painting," noted Richie Baneham. "We'd look at what Dylan Cole and his team had done and then take it to fruition. We worked out the lighting digitally first, so that I was able to give exact information to the lighting team. Russell and Len could then set up their scenes to match."

Art director Ben Milsom and the New Zealand art department and construction teams built live-action sections of the Wind Trader gondola needed for Spider interactions. These were based on an Extent of Build derived from Template cuts of the captured scenes. As Dylan Cole explained, "Jim did a rough edit, so we could surgically figure out areas where Spider interacted with the set." Interactive shadows cast by gondola rigging and the shadows of attacking Mangkwan raiders required choreographed light-rigs above the set. "There was not only a sun element," commented Russell Carpenter. "The light on the Wind Trader ships was supposed to be dreamy, like Maxfield Parrish illustrations. In some shots, we had Spider run out from under deep shadow from a piece of the gondola and then run into the light. And then, he'd see something burning nearby. So, we wanted to feel that burning element there. Also, the ship was often rotating, which meant our 'sunlight'—usually a light on a crane—moved counter to that rotation."

The lighting team constructed shadow-casting objects using 4 x 8-ft frames that they placed in front of lights to create 'cucoloris' effects—a theatrical lighting term, derived from the Greek kukaloris, meaning 'breaking of light.' "When our light shone through those shapes, and Spider ran by, he passed through those shadows."

"It is such a beautiful environment," commented Eric Saindon, referring to the sequence where the caravan sails through rocky spires just before the Ash People attack, "As they sail through canyons, there's a blue fill light against the

Above: Wind Trader crew spring into action as they leave the Reef Village. Weta screenshot.

warmth of the sun. That gave us the Maxfield Parrish art reference that Jim was seeking, with warm and cool colors in interesting contrasts. In stereo, that sequence is stunning, especially as the medusoid above the gondola catches the blue light through its translucent layers, and the red sunlight creates a gorgeous warm glow shining through. The scale of that scene is immense, traveling through a gorge bigger than the Grand Canyon. And that's where they encounter the Ash People."

The lighting team also used cucoloris effects to emulate dappled sunlight for scenes of Spider and the Sully kids when they are stranded in the rainforest after the Mangkwan attack. The New Zealand team built rainforest sets at Stone Street Studios using elements of terrain and selected foliage, backed by bluescreen. The sets were minimal, always extended to infinity using Simulcam. "Anything Spider touched was right there in the set," Carpenter explained. "If he ran by a fern, we wanted to see him brush by that object. We tried to be inventive, using just enough to create a sense of the jungle."

Spider and his friends, separated from Jake and Neytiri, journey deep into unfamiliar territory to avoid their Mangkwan pursuers. They enter a fast-flowing stream to shake off the Ash trackers. J.D. Schwalm's special-effects team used their huge current-generator propellers to create the moving river in the tank in LA. "It was one of the few live-action pieces that we built practically in our big tank on Stage 18, complete with sculpted rocks and elaborate green dressing" Dylan Cole recalled. "We used the tank in what we called 'Race Track' mode, which made the water flow round and round. We captured those scenes with our Na'vi performers and Jack Champion playing Spider. It then became a blend of live-action and CG; but the close-ups with Jack were practical." Hundreds of pounds of a brown dye was added to the water, to simulate the brown tanin-rich color of tropical rivers.

As the story continues, the river becomes a raging rapids. For this sequence large polymer blocks were installed in the racetrack, to simulate the cascading rapids, and the propellers were turned up full blast. Waterfalls and chutes of up to three feet were created. The safety challenges increased proportionately. Though Jack was game to "shoot the rapids," the other kids were now doubled. Alicia and Chris Denison played Kiri and Lo'ak, respectively, while stuntwoman Juliana Potter doubled Tuk. Pete Zuccarini ran the rapids with them, operating

Right: The production reconfigured the tank on Stage 18 into a narrow channel representing a fast-flowing forest river for a live-action shoot with Jack Champion as Spider and blue-suited stunt performer Emilie Seimer assisting Na'vi character interactions.

the tiny "Nano" 3D camera in its waterproof housing. The shots of Jack shooting the rapids, gasping in his breathing mask, look completely real. And he looks appropriately scared. Acting? Maybe not.

Sigourney, Britain, and Juliana's facial performances were captured using FPR—Facial Performance Replacement. In the universally used process of ADR (Automated Dialogue Replacement), an actor watches playback in a sound recording studio and matches sync with a new voice performance. In FPR the actor, wearing a head-rig, watches playback of their captured character, performed by a stunt double, and provides the appropriate facial performance, including dialogue. The resulting fusion of body and facial capture creates a single compelling performance. It is far better than live-action stunts, in which the stunt double needs to keep their head down or turned away so the audience can't recognize that it's not actually the actor. When all the CG and live elements were combined by Weta, the illusion of the kids buffeted by powerful rapids was seamless.

"The trickiest part was... [the cocoon] had to work almost like a suit."

Christopher Swift, Legacy key artist

A highlight of the forest trek occurs when Spider's air supply runs out and Kiri saves his life by summoning forest mycelium to transform him into "the Airbreather." The tiny mycelium strands rise up and enclose him in glowing tendrils. The scene recalls the cocoon sequences in *Avatar*, in which the Na'vi attempt to save Grace Augustine at the Tree of Souls by trying to transfer her consciousness into her inert avatar. In that scene, the CG bodies of Grace and her avatar are overgrown by bioluminescent cilia. But it was a completely CG effect. However Spider's transformation demanded a practical solution, using makeup and prosthetic effects. "Jim drew many images," remarked Sarah Rubano, "and a lot of excitement and anticipation went into the planning of this scene. Jim has a very long-standing relationship with Legacy Effects, so he wanted them involved."

Legacy Effects co-founder Shane Mahan brainstormed an approach with key artist Christopher Swift to create the glowing mycelium using ultraviolet paint combined with prosthetics and in-camera lighting effects. "The trickiest part," said Swift, "was we had to allow an actor to get into the cocoon, and then, after a certain time, to be able to pull it apart, so they could rest, and then come back later. It had to work almost like a suit."

Champion was scanned, lying on his side. Legacy used the scan to create a physical replica of Jack, then molded the root system to his form on top of a slab of translucent white acrylic, which could be lit from below.

"We were not simply putting lights under there," Chris Swift explained. "We constructed LED strips, and they were sequenced to change color, pulsing inward from the roots, fading out to the forest floor."

The COVID-19 pandemic restricted international travel, so Legacy shipped the mycelium effect to New Zealand, with detailed instructions. Sarah Rubano and Weta Workshop then implemented the effect, applying mycelium strands to Jack Champion just before the cameras rolled.

"We had to do that in a speedy manner and make it look amazing," said Sarah Rubano. "Jim wanted the mycelium to have purpose and feel directional. It was

Costume Focus

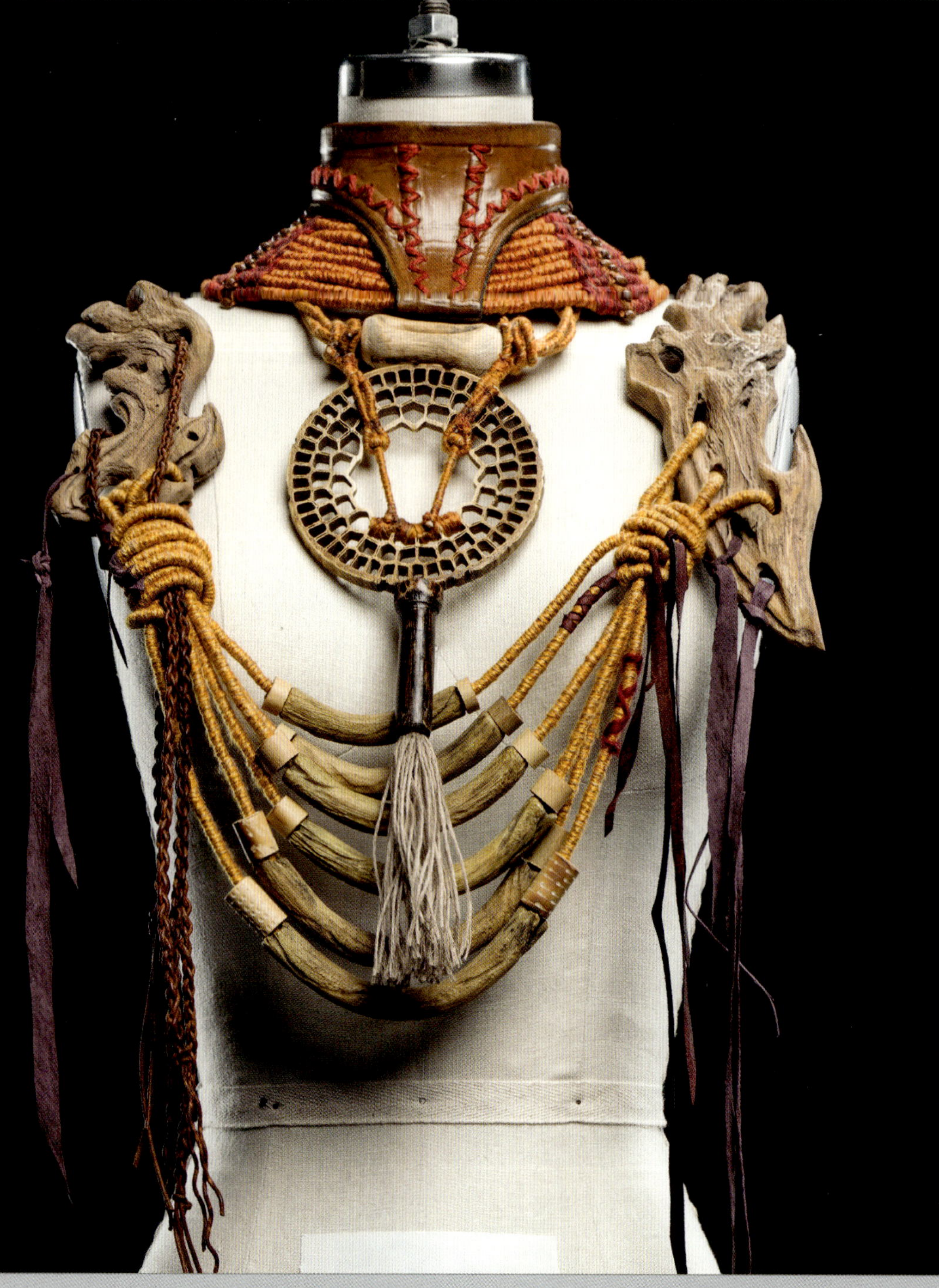

Above and right: costume samples designed by Deborah Scott and manufactured at Weta Workshop to inform the world-building of the Wind Trader design language and act as exquisite reference for visual effects.

Above: A Wind Trader market scene. Weta screenshot.

Left: Studies of the Wind Traders' culture included costume designs that suggested clothing and accoutrements necessary for high-altitude living. Wind Trader cloak features a map of Pandora's trade routes. Concept by Weta Workshop.

Below: A selection of Wind Trader market food items.

Left, top to bottom: Legacy's mycelium prosthetic elevated Jack Champion on a translucent platform rigged with a filigree of self-illuminated ultraviolet tendrils. When Sarah Rubano's team laid the prosthetic onto the performer's skin, the tendrils transmitted light to Champion's body, which Russell Carpenter lit with an ambient glow.

Below: During the rainforest trek, Spider's oxygen supply runs out and Kiri summons *Eywa* to assist, causing a cocoon of mycelium to encase the asphyxiating human boy. Cameron attends mycelium dressing during performance-capture with Jack Champion using Halloween-style spiderweb material as a facsimile for tendril growth. The effect took on further dimensions in a New Zealand shoot, and with visual effects.

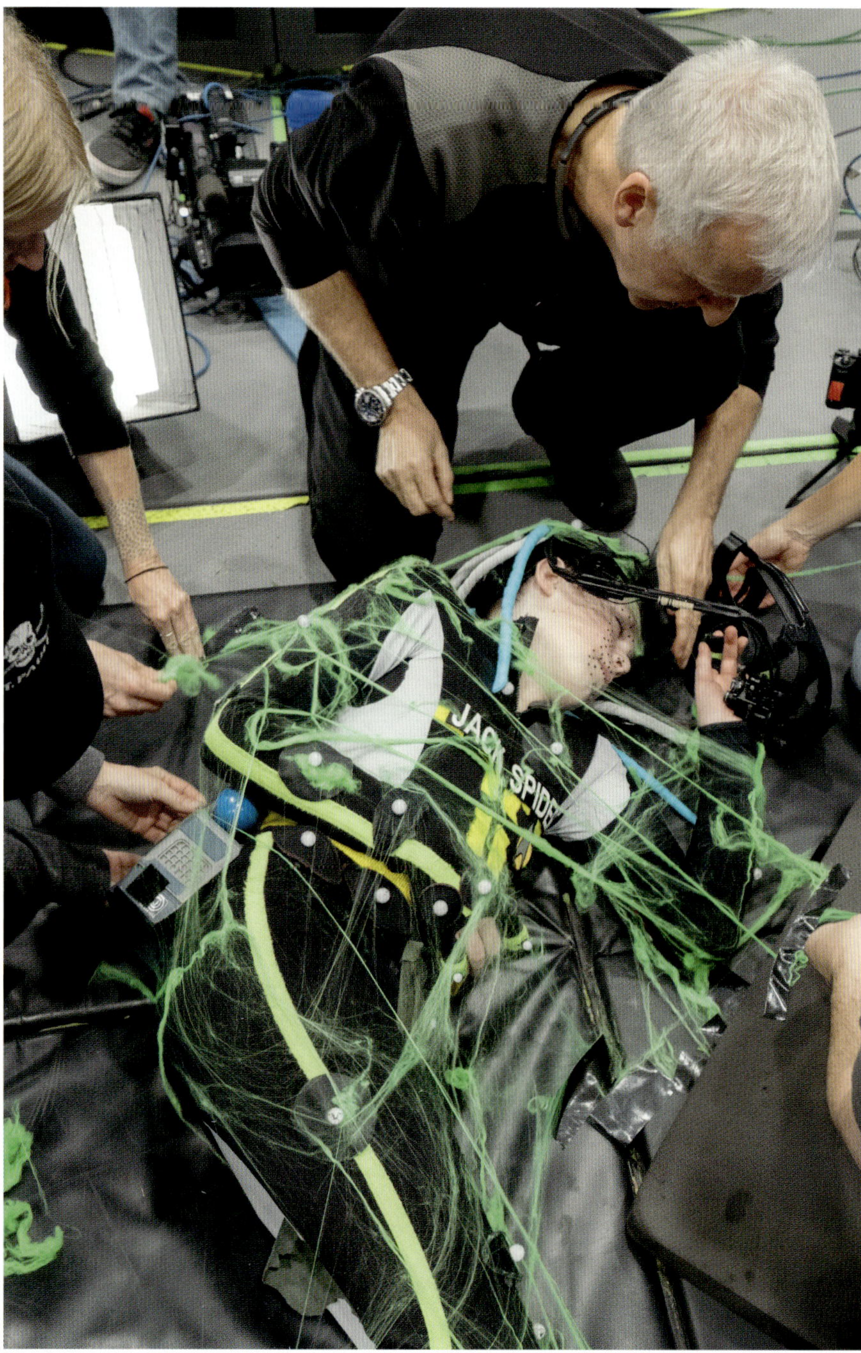

Above: Lo'ak carries Tuk through the swamp. Art department renderings set the mood for eerie swamp-water bioluminescence that united elements of Russell Carpenter's live-action photography with animation derived from performance-capture in Los Angeles. Weta screenshot.

Right: The production staged swamp-crossing live-action elements at Kumeū Film Studios in the shallow tank, which contained root structures and effluvia with underwater lighting. Jack Champion—now without a mask—performed with troupe performer Kevin Dorman standing in for Jake. Dorman wore a blue padded suit to assist Na'vi body interactions and helmet-mounted Na'vi "eyes" to help Champion make eye contact with Jake.

a very delicate process. We worked closely with cinematographer Russell Carpenter so that when the UV lights started pulsating, the UV paint kicked in with a glow that was part of the bioluminescence of the forest."

The entire mycelium sequence was later augmented by Weta artists to give it movement and life. "We animated the mycelium to grow into the makeup effects on Jack," visual effects supervisor Eric Saindon explained. "They had to grow into his nose, mouth, and his internals to cause his body to change."

After his transformation to breathing Pandoran air, Spider sits up and the mycelium fibers are seen tearing away from him, as if he's shedding a silken cocoon. The makeup team used silicone adhesive to attach mycelium to Jack's skin, and for other pieces that were meant to break away they used hairspray to make less resistant tackiness. Jack went along with all this patiently, and gave an incredible performance as Spider wakes up to a whole new existence on

Overleaf: The Sully youngsters and Spider—joined by Jake and Quaritch—try to shake Mangkwan pursuers by trekking through a swamp. The dank rainforest environment required atmospheric lighting, with Jack Champion in partial bluescreen sets that Weta then used to integrate Spider into virtual terrain. Weta screenshot.

Above: *The Way of Water* and *Fire and Ash* presented Bridgehead as a bustling military industrial complex that far exceeds the scope of the RDA's outpost at Hell's Gate. Lightstorm updated the *Valkyrie* landing craft to a new variant, the garuda, with larger engines, small stabilizer winglets, and a darker and more menacing livery resembling a B2-bomber. ILM screenshot.

> "We built those elements based on wherever we had human characters."
>
> **Ben Procter, production designer**

Pandora. When he throws away his breathing mask, that's been the millstone around his neck for his whole life, we feel his exhilaration. He has achieved his greatest wish, of being like the Na'vi, a true native of this alien world that he loves so deeply. This moment of joy is cut short by the arrival of Varang and her Ash warriors, who have been relentlessly tracking the kids. Many complicated shots ensue, requiring Jack's human character to closely interact with Oona's captured Varang performance, and those of the other Na'vi actors. For these scenes, once again Simulcam was the key to getting close, tactile interaction of the characters at two different scales.

Much later in the story, when Jake and Spider have been caught and taken to Bridgehead, Neytiri mounts a daring rescue. The elaborate rescue sequence featured a complex intertwining of live-action and virtual elements. Bridgehead exterior sets included the airfield where Quaritch arrives with the Ash horde and a large plaza where Jake is held captive in a cage built for a

Right: Bridgehead personnel flock around RDA Skel-driver Sec-Ops officers, who hold back a crowd that gathers around a wildlife containment unit cage that holds Jake Sully, former Marine and Omatikaya *Toruk Makto*. ILM screenshot.

Below: Following Spider's mycelium encounter, RDA scientists take Spider into custody and examine him in the Bridgehead Scanner Lab to study the young man's newly acquired genetic mutation and ability to breathe Pandoran air. Live-action sets.

thanator. Interiors included the lab complex, where the scientists study Spider, the Ops Center with its holofloor display, and a holding cell where Spider is held captive.

Other RDA sets included the hunting fleet's largest craft, the nearly 700-ft-long Factory Ship, which dwarfed *The Way of Water*'s SeaDragon. The massive, four-hull vessel contained an elaborate bridge complex, commanded by General Ardmore (Edie Falco), portions of the lower decks where Spider and Kiri infiltrate via a cargo ramp, and the top deck where Quaritch, Spider, and Jake confront each other. "We mapped out what we needed," said Ben Procter, "and built those elements based on wherever we had human characters."

Planning for the live-action coverage of the Cove of the Ancestors battle in *Fire and Ash* began with Templates derived from months of design, capture, and editing. From these an Extent of Build was analyzed to figure out what needed to be built and shot for real. There were scores of boats, including a dozen Matador kill-boats and a fleet of Picadors. The full-scale mock-ups of the Matador and Picador from *The Way of Water* would be used again, this time representing multiple different boats. But a massive new set was also needed. Central to all the battle action was the enormous Factory Ship, 698 feet long. The bridge of the Factory Ship was an ambitious set, with scores of intricately detailed chairs and consoles, and a huge bluescreen "cyc" (cyclorama backing) outside the windows, where the attacking *tulkun* elders would breach upward, blocking out the sky. "For the bridge, we decided against simply having an open-topped set," Procter explained. "We wanted structures above the set to cast shadows on adjacent scenery. We decided to build those ceiling volumes at true scale into the set, which gave Russell Carpenter all the correct shadows."

Above: At the climax of *Fire and Ash*, RDA dispatches its gargantuan Factory Ship to lead a *tulkun* hunt, which results in a full-scale battle with the Na'vi. The production designed the bridge of the immense marine vessel as a partial live-action set. The art department, construction, lighting, and camera teams then collaborated with visual effects to create seamless blends of performers with live-action, digital set extensions, and holographic displays.

The Bridge's panoramic forward-facing windows allowed the lighting department to emulate the cyan and purple glow of the roiling Flux Devil, a major element of the Cove of the Ancestors battle. Carpenter installed banks of lights controlled through a computer lighting board, that could move the cyan and purple interactive lighting around the set, to simulate the effect of the Flux Devil's shifting plasma glow. The correct color and movement of interactive lighting could be judged in real time, using Simulcam. In the Simulcam image, sent to the camera monitors, the animated Flux Devil could be seen writhing beyond the bay windows, towering overhead. Cameron could tilt his handheld camera up to see its full height.

RDA set builds included portions of the SeaDragon and Factory Ship cargo decks and bulkheads, which set decorators aged with streaks of rust and grime. "Alastair Maher was our paint supervisor," said Procter, "We could tell the New Zealand painters, 'I want this to look like a nasty old oil rig,' and they'd nail it. Ally was terrific because he also worked with Weta, helping the visual effects artists interpret surfacing, paint looks, and textures on the digital side, bringing all the knowledge that he gained from working with me on the practical side to the digital environments."

The New Zealand art department were skilled at creating futuristic set dressing. This included recycling used aircraft parts—rare in New Zealand—which were imported from US military surplus junkyards and used as cockpit paraphernalia. The aircraft parts were used as interior dressing heavily on A1, but for the sequels the production mainly used them fo debris dressing—exploded bits of SeaWasp and other aircraft. Some things could be purchased or rented, but all of the elaborate consoles and high-tech chairs on the ships and aircraft were hand-built in New Zealand by the amazing craftspeople there. Because the film was being shot in high-resolution 3D and would be seen in IMAX, the quality of the workmanship on every technical surface had to be flawless.

The New Zealand team also built highly realistic underwater vehicles, including the Mako subs and Crab Suits, introduced in the *tulkun* hunt in *Way of Water*. Action in that film's underwater battle, and at the Cove of the Ancestors battle in

Fire and Ash, required the complete flooding of these vehicles—with sub crews trapped inside, drowning. For safety reasons, it was decided not to try to flood the Mako attack sub underwater in a tank, but to simply fill the interior as the sub sat on a soundstage. The tiny 3D Nano camera, in its waterproof housing, would shoot the interior action as the pilot and weapons officer are overwhelmed by water, trying to escape. From outside, other cameras would see the water filling through the canopy glass. This meant the sub needed to be sealed, and its windows strong enough to hold over two tons of water. Even on a dry soundstage, it was potentially dangerous for the two stuntmen who were actually trapped inside a fully flooded sub. Cameron had a healthy respect for the power of water, from his experience on *The Abyss* and his ocean expedition films. He asked Steve Ingram to devise a large-bore valve that could dump the water out of the sub in a few seconds, in case the stunt actors got into trouble. Noted Ingram, "Jim wanted the subs to very quickly fill with water so the people inside appeared to drown. We built a massive hopper that we could load with the amount of water we needed. Alistair Baxter and his team sealed the subs to be watertight. When we dumped in the water, we had to be able to jettison it very quickly."

Above: As a solar eclipse dims Pandora's sky, the Cove of the Ancestors is lit up by a gyrating Flux Devil—aan ethereal yet dangerous phenomenon generated by the Cove's intense magnetic field, which also drives the shapes and levitation of it's geology. This artwork by Steve Messing depicts a sea vessel—the Factory Ship—exploding inside the Flux Devil.

Right, top to bottom: Concept art for the climactic battle at the Cove of the Ancestors: (top) by Dylan Cole; (center) by Fausto De Martini; (bottom) by Dylan Cole.

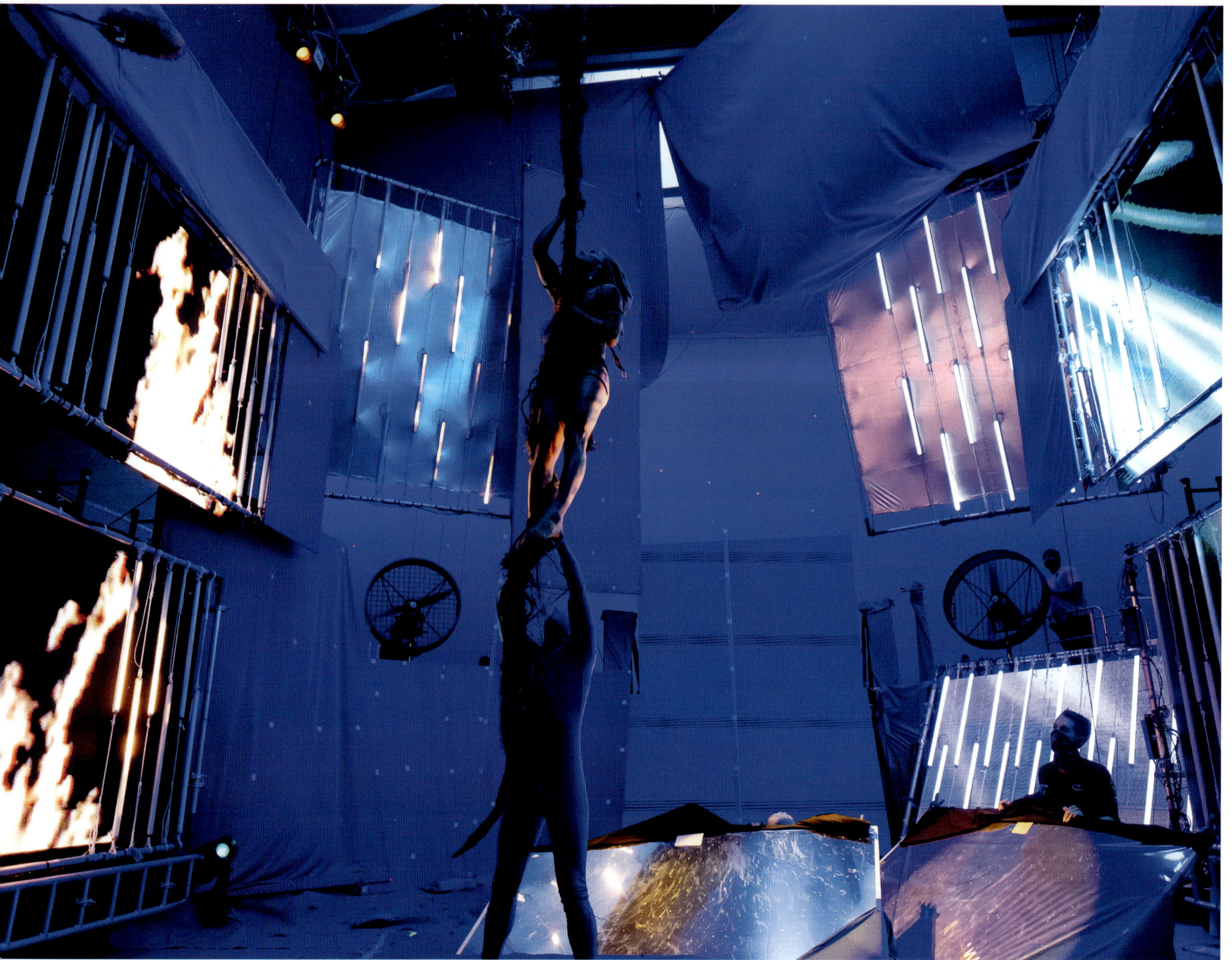

Above: Cinematographer Russell Carpenter and his team rigged interactive lighting to illuminate Jack Champion in climactic scenes where Spider is suspended between the blaze of the oceangoing battle and the pulsing lights of Pandora's Flux Devil.

"This is a human-centric, artist-centric, actor-centric workflow, in every possible way..."

James Cameron

In another scene, Ronal floods a Crab Suit by smashing holes in the top of its canopy with her spear. Kate Winslet was captured in the tank in LA, furiously slamming her spear down onto a mock-up of the Crab's top—a pregnant warrior woman in full beast mode. Her CG figure would later be combined with the practical effect. This was an even more complicated shot, because the Crab Suit was in motion as it reached up with its arms, trying to dislodge her—meaning

that it needed to be shot on a motion-base. This would violently slosh the water around as the Crab filled, an effect Cameron really wanted. Hoses were attached to flood the cockpit from above, and also from below to add water volume quickly, as the hapless pilot struggled to defend himself. Again, a quick release valve was used to dump the water out after the director yelled "Cut!" so the stuntman wouldn't drown trapped inside the cockpit. The stuntmen for these roles were cast only after they were thoroughly vetted by the dive team, to make sure they would stay calm when submerged. They needed to act panicky, but not really be panicked.

"Everybody tried to talk me out of these flooding gags," Cameron recalls, "They were going to be really complicated and expensive. But I thought they would be intense visceral moments, especially in 3D. The classic question from production is always 'Do you really need this?' The correct answer to the question is actually 'No.' You don't really really need it. It's not a critical plot point. Maybe *Ben-Hur* didn't really really need that chariot race either. My approach is that if I you feel in your bones it's something the audience will think is cool, you should try to do it."

At the end of the battle, Jake faces off with Quaritch among the floating islands. The Flux Devil's magnetism draws up the shredded wreckage of the Factory Ship and streamers of its burning fuel, adding to the maelstrom. The two antagonists clash among levitated rocks as purple and cyan streamers of plasma writhe around them, and debris from the disintegrating Factory Ship tumbles upward, threatening to crash into them. Spider dodges flying debris, gouts of burning fuel, and levitating blasts of water, as he scrambles after them with his Metkayina speargun.

"Fire rips through this giant structure," related Saindon. "That added another complexity to our lighting. We had fire, and cyan and magenta plasma all mixing together into different vortexes. Our visual effects simulations had to render all those forces." There, in what looks to become a fight to the death, they wind up ironically having to work together to save Spider as he dangles above the inferno. Sam and Stephen Lang were captured ahead of time, of course; then Spider was added to the scene in the live-action photography.

Jack wore a seat-harness hidden under his loincloth costume, so a cable could take his weight as he appeared to dangle over the inferno below. To create the strong grip of Quaritch holding onto him, a massive stuntman named Michael Homick, AKA "Big Mike," grasped his hand and lifted him up. Jack spent a long day dangling 15 feet in the air on a bluescreen stage, his crotch in agony from the seat harness. But typically, he never complained. To Jack it was all a big adventure, and he enjoyed the company of everyone around him, especially the stunt guys. He and Garrett had a special bond. Whenever they saw each other they would yell "Bruddah!" Then they'd either trade punches, or hug. Sometimes both.

Jemaine Clement (Ian Garvin), Giovanni Ribisi as Administrator Parker Selfridge, and Edie Falco as General Ardmore had come and gone throughout the shoot, and all played important roles. But it was Jack who had been the center of the entire production team's world for over a year of live action. He had bonded with those around him, and come to think of them as a second family. When shooting finally wrapped, he was saddened by the end of his time among his Avatar family. All movie professionals know that when the film ends, the bonds and friendships forged during the shoot often end as well. But Jack had never done a film before, so he was unprepared for the hard emotional adjustment when his long sojourn on Pandora came to an end. He had been in that world for four years. A quarter of his life. Over the following months Cameron, Garrett Warren, and Jon Landau were careful to call and text Jack regularly, to assure him that his Avatar family were still there, whenever he needed them.

***

The live-action elements of the Avatar films were the tissue connecting the narrative elements of a virtual cinema process that, ultimately, relied on performance, artistry, and ingenuity to bring the spectacle to the screen.

"This is a human-centric, artist-centric, actor-centric workflow, in every possible way," declares James Cameron. "I think people think you just wave a magic wand, with some computer. There is no 'generative-AI' in the making of these films. We're not just making up images out of nothing. People work for years on the design, on the fabrication of the clothing, the fabrication of the props." "It drives me nuts," he continues, "when people say, 'Oh, Sigourney voiced

Kiri.' Like on an animated film, you stand at a podium, you do the script, takes you a day, maybe two days to voice a character. Sigourney worked on these two films for 18 months. She did everything. It's about the physicality. It's the entire face, body, voice, breath, performance. It's everything."

"It's very physical, really hard, immersive work," declares Kate Winslet, "And I can imagine how people would think, well, they're cartoons, or it's not really them, or something, but it is really those actors putting life and blood into every single one of those characters, creating that energy, creating that environment, heightened, passionate, fiery people. Everyone's really doing it, like more than you could possibly imagine."

"As much as we use computers and technology, the heart of the film is the heart of the actor, and the heart of the character," Cameron says, "So we have to get to the emotional truth. We hold the actors' choices in the moment sacred. On the Avatar films, we make a religion out of preserving that performance through every step, down to the final render. We don't intercede or embellish, other than adding ears and tails. How Sigourney or Kate or Sam chose to interpret their character, at the moment of capture: that's what the audience will see later. We will preserve that to the best of our human ability. There's nothing sacred about acting in front of a lens. Ultimately, it's all just acting, whether for theater, for a camera, or for performance-capture. Each has its pluses and minuses. I would argue that capture is actually the purest form of acting. Generative AI has the potential to replace actors. But I have zero interest in that, and I don't think it's a choice we should collectively make. I love working with actors, it's what feeds me creatively, as a writer and director. Our process on the Avatar movies is the antithesis of genAI—not replacing acting but celebrating it, in all its glorious detail."

Left: Spider clings to Quaritch while the Recombinant RDA Colonel, daubed with markings of the Ash People, dangles above an inferno. Weta screenshot.

Chapter 5

THE LAST MILE

The Last Mile

Everything about the first *Avatar* was more complicated than a normal movie, even other VFX epics that had gone before. The production spanned two worlds. The design bifurcation between the organic, spiritual Na'vi world and the hard-tech human world was mirrored all the way down the line, with the parallel worlds of virtual production and live-action production. There was a virtual art department and a live-action art department, two completely separate entities, one in LA and one in New Zealand. Often there were two different versions of the same set, one virtual and one live action, in two different scales, built years and continents apart for the exact same scene. There was a virtual camera team and a live-action camera team, also working 7,000 miles apart, and using two completely different forms of technology to make images. One used hundreds of mocap cameras feeding an image to a virtual camera, shooting actors in black leotards covered in Scotchlite markers. The live-action team would use digital 3D cameras and cinematic lighting on fully detailed and dressed sets, shooting actors in makeup and wardrobe. These two completely different teams, making images in completely different ways, needed to coordinate closely with each other so those disparate images could all blend into one movie, one narrative.

There were actors that only worked in the capture volume in LA, like Zoe as Neytiri and CCH Pounder as her mother Mo'at. There were actors that only worked on the live-action sets in New Zealand, like Stephen Lang, Giovanni Ribisi, and Michelle Rogriguez. And there were actors who worked in both phases of production, like Sam Worthington, Sigourney Weaver, and Joel David Moore, who played both their human characters as well as their giant avatars. In fact, the actors playing Na'vi—Zoe, CCH, Laz Alonzo (Tsu'tey) and Wes Studi (Eytukan), would never even travel to New Zealand, or lay eyes on the live-action sets.

Across all this complexity, the editing team (James Cameron, Steve Rivkin, John Refoua) had to bridge both worlds and be adept in cutting both forms of image creation. Editing spanned all paradigms.

Editing is typically a post-production process on a conventional movie. You shoot, then you edit. A linear sequence. On an *Avatar* film, before you can even start live action, you have to shoot the performance capture, then edit it, then shoot the virtual cameras, then edit that. Only after all that can you shoot the live action, and then and only then can you edit those scenes. It is a looping, non-linear process, with many layers. Cameron calls it "four dimensional chess."

> "I don't think there has been a more complicated way to make a movie."
>
> **Stephen E. Rivkin, film editor**

On *Avatar*, the complexities of virtual production redefined the art of editing for Rivkin and Refoua, who shared editorial duties with Cameron. "I don't think there has been a more complicated way to make a movie," Rivkin remarked, joined by Refoua in a 2023 interview with the Advanced Imaging Society. "We came on during the performance-capture phase of the film. We used the reference video as a guide to put together the best performances of each actor in scenes, and sometimes that involved combining actors from different takes. After careful review with Jim, we built a 'performance edit' until the film existed in capture form."

The editors relied on the disciplines of their craft to assemble raw material for best dramatic impact. "That's what you train for," noted Refoua. "You train to remember your first reaction when you read the script. Then, you train to remember your first reaction when you see dailies, or Capture. That is so important. You have to remember which 'take' set you off."

The results of these editorial choices often did not emerge until years later, when Weta delivered rendered images. "There was nothing as gratifying as seeing the final render, sometimes two, three years [later]," said Rivkin. "Suddenly, in all their glory, the actor's performance was back in every little detail in their faces, in their eyes, in their expressions. It was truly phenomenal to see that come full circle."

Previous pages: *Eywa*'s presence spreads across Pandora as bioluminescence causes the moon's surface to glow against the immensity of Polyphemus. Concept art by Dylan Cole.

Opposite page: Neytiri hesitates as a woodsprite from the Omatikaya's sacred Tree of Souls rests on the tip of her arrow. Weta screenshot.

Above: Tuktirey (Trinity Bliss), the youngest of the Sully family, experiences the wonders of the reef while swimming with the Metkayina. Animation render, and final composite. Weta breakdown.

Three years after *Avatar*'s theatrical debut, Rivkin and Refoua regrouped with Cameron and a fourth editor, David Brenner—an Academy Award®-winner for Oliver Stone's 1989 film *Born on the Fourth of July*—for the production of the sequels. The editorial team built on past experience to tackle an even larger canvas: the creation of two movies, each massive on their own, being made at the same time.

"It was a steep learning curve," Rivkin confessed. "David Brenner picked it up very quickly because he was incredibly bright and dedicated and committed to understanding our process. Things got a bit more complicated with the number of characters in the script, the combinations of live action and virtual, and the added layer of dealing with unprecedented underwater performance capture. That was something that had never been done before, and Jim pioneered that."

The dual productions of *The Way of Water* back-to-back with *Fire and Ash* allowed film editor Refoua to build a complete assembly of A3 by the completion of his A2 editorial duties, using performance-capture reference footage and live-action elements. "I had various ways of approaching scenes," he told *IndieWire*. "It was [a work] in progress, but pretty far along. Technically, we were always learning, depending on the parameters of the scenes. The rest of the process was just editing, and I love that part. We're so involved in the collaboration with Jim, that's the part I love about working on these movies."

Despite post-production being dominated by editing, Cameron still had to finish literally thousands of shots on the Camera stage and get them turned over to Weta and ILM. Because Cameron had moved permanently to New Zealand since the first film, this work needed to be done there. The smaller capture Volume on E-stage, at Stone Street, would become the focus of his work for the last year and a half of making *The Way of Water*, and again for the last year-and-a-half of *Fire and Ash*. Cameron would bounce between weeks working in the Volume, with his v-cam, and weeks in the cutting room, creating the final cuts for Weta turnovers.

E-stage was crewed with its own "Brain Bar" team, mostly seasoned veterans of the Los Angeles Volume, such as Stage Operators Buffy Bailey and Dan Fowler, who had been with the films since 2006. Each "stage op" ran a "box," a workstation from which they could control playback of the scene to Cameron. This is where real-time adjustments to layout, lighting, and motion were added. The stage op would constantly adjust the rate of playback, the scale ratio, and a thousand other parameters as the director made new shots. E-Stage was a quiet but intense creative workspace. Cameron would operate in the center of the empty Volume, usually assisted by Jamie Landau, who ran the E-stage team. Jamie, son of Jon Landau, had been on the sequels for seven years, initially working as one of the troupe players. He was a keen observer of how the whole process worked and had demonstrated strong leadership skills over the years. After Jamie's father died, in July of 2024, Cameron started giving him more and more responsibility, moving him up into a role as one of the producers, alongside Brigitte Yorke and Maria Campbell. In addition, Cameron asked Rae Sanchini, who had been the President of Lightstorm two decades earlier, to return to help finish *Fire and Ash*, as executive producer. The director knew that he couldn't replace Jon Landau, one of the most experienced and charismatic producers in Hollywood. All he could hope was that between the five of them, they would able to distribute the load Jon had carried and continue on.

Cameron worked closely with Jamie to grind through the remaining shots for *Fire and Ash*. With years of experience, the E-stage team was a well-oiled machine. The younger Landau would prep the camera by roughing in the camera's "offset", its position in worldspace, for each new shot. The director would lift the camera from its stand and line up his shot by doing a few playback rehearsals. He'd call "Playback," and the stage op would start the scene file running. Cameron would do his dance to create the camera move. After each take, Cameron would view video-playback. He would assess the take and decide if it was good. If not, he would describe to the stage op or the "lighters" what needed to happen to make it better.

Sometimes complex adjustments to creature or vehicle movement were required, and the director would ask them to add "keys," making keyframe changes to the motion. This was animation on-demand. The stage ops were like short-order cooks flipping burgers. "Animation While U Wait." When the changes were made, the operator would sound an "Ah-ooooga!" klaxon, like the alarm for a diving World War II sub, to let Cameron know they were ready for another take. He'd break off from whatever he was doing—usually standing at the Avid editing station—and rush back into the Volume to pick up the camera. The dive klaxon was first done as a joke on *Avatar*, but it stuck, and is now a traditional part of the Camera sessions. This creative process would go on eight hours a day for months on end, as every shot in the film was painstakingly crafted.

The E-stage team found that adding additional stage operators, on additional boxes, allowed Cameron to hop-scotch from one scene load to another. Every time one operator had to tackle a problem that would take time, Cameron would jump to another box, another operator, and keep shooting. This shift allowed them to double or triple their output in a single day. To feed the demand for experienced stage operators, up-and-coming artists were trained in the adjacent room on boxes that were off-line to the main stage. This was called the Back Bar, in the tradition of the Brain Bar. When they were ready, they were put in the hot-seat on the Brain Bar itself. This became a rite of passage, as the director put them through their paces.

> "We're so involved in the collaboration with Jim, that's the part I love about working on these movies."
>
> **John Refoua, film editor**

New shining stars emerged to join the stage-op team, such as Shea Melville (a native Kiwi), Connor Gartland, Donald Dey, and Yoon Young Lee. Each had their own style and their own unique strengths. And each was celebrated by the others as they took over the hotseat and proved their skills.

Cameron was justifiably proud of his E-stage team. They were doing something insanely complicated that nobody else in the world, even at other VFX facilities, could even understand. They represented an internal culture of excellence and loved the challenge of solving hard problems. Though the beating heart of an Avatar film is the actors' performances, it was on this little gray stage in Wellington that the Avatar movies were truly being made. It looked as unglamorous as a shipping dock, with no big camera cranes and bright lights, no assistant directors shouting on megaphones, no hundreds of extras. But some of the wildest action scenes and the most epic images in cinema were being made there on any given Tuesday morning, calmly and quietly, by a handful of artists.

Meanwhile Richie Baneham was working with his own stage ops—Jerry "Ziggy" Zigounakis, Ian Adams, and Nick Taylor—in LA to feed RCPs to Cameron's virtual stage. Hundreds of people in two countries were working feverishly for years to feed an insatiable production pipeline. Even this late in post-production, the Lab was working its way through Capture recorded years earlier that had lain dormant until they could get to it. The Lab would prep the Loads, based on Performance Edits from editorial. Then Richie would wade in, trouble-shooting each Load and making RCP's, the rough cameras that suggested possible angles to the director. The Loads were shipped to New Zealand, where Cameron and his E-stage team would create the actual shots for the movie. The editors would then assemble these into scenes and Cameron would do his fine-cut pass to lock in the final cut of each scene. The locked scenes were then turned over to Weta. This is where Weta's work began. The Weta teams would unpack the Turnover files and begin bringing the scenes to life at photoreal resolution, which could be an additional six to eigtht months of work on a scene.

The term post-production is meaningless on an Avatar film. At any moment, any given scene might be at any stage within this workflow. Post was ongoing, in parallel, throughout every phase, starting with the first day of Capture in 2017. As soon as the first performances hit the pipeline, the post-production process began. The production process was telescoped upon itself so that v-cam, live action, and editing were all happening at once on different scenes. So in a single day Cameron might be shooting a live-action scene with Jack, and also doing virtual camera on E-stage to create templates for upcoming live-action scenes, or final-editing scenes to turn over to Weta. The insatiable maw of Weta turnovers needed to be constantly fed.

If it sounds exhausting, it was. "But it was a joyful exhaustion," says Cameron. "We chose this for ourselves. We loved it. We were doing things nobody had ever done before. Every day we would be doing things even we hadn't done before, solving new problems as they came up, like playing Whack A Mole. Every new scene seemed to have its own new challenges. It was daunting, but exhilarating. And the greatest joy was working with these brilliant young artists and tech people, who thrived on the challenge. They knew they were doing things nobody else in the world was doing."

Another tradition, religiously observed by the seasoned E-stage team, was "Friday Shots." In the early days of *Avatar*, the entire Camera team would celebrate the end of a grueling week with a shot of tequila. Over the years this became quite a ritual. Whenever Cameron declared the last take of the last shot of the day finished, Brendon the video operator would hit play on *Tequila* by The Champs, and the catchy drum tempo and big sax notes would blast over the stage speakers as Jamie and the director set out glasses and poured a shot for every member of the crew. Editorial and Back-Bar artists would congregate at the Brain Bar as the shots were distributed. By tradition, whoever had just joined the team or was about to leave, or anybody who had a birthday that week, was expected to make a toast. No wriggling out of it. Some of these speeches were long and sometimes quite emotional, as people expressed their gratitude for being part of such an extraordinary team and project, and what it all meant for them. Cameron would often cap the toast by telling the team how much he appreciated them, not just for their brilliance and artistry, but for their passion and dedication. Then it was bottoms-up and Cameron would slam his shot glass upside down on the Brain Bar console, signaling the end of another week on Pandora. This group-bonding ritual was observed throughout the years and came to mean a great deal to the whole team. The very last one took place on August 4, 2025, as the team finally wrapped for good, after bagging a few last straggler shots for *Fire and Ash*, including the death of Quaritch as he falls into the fiery maelstrom, and Varang's final shot as she banks away, flying off into Avatar 4. As the gnarly sax riffs rang out, the team crowded around the Brain Bar knew that their 12-year journey of the Avatar sequels was finally over.

> "We loved it. We were doing things nobody had ever done before."
>
> **James Cameron**

As the Camera stages wound down, it was now Weta's task to finish the film visually. They were pedal to the metal, powering along at peak strength to finish their work. On *Avatar*, then *The Way of Water* and finally *Fire and Ash*, this pattern repeated itself. On all three films, it seemed like there was an impossible number of shots to complete in the final months. Over a thousand artists worked tirelessly to bring the scenes to full, vibrant life.

On *Avatar* the challenge was to maintain the highest level of quality across all the characters' faces, despite the hectic pace. All the technology was new and still glitchy, and nobody had done anything on this scale before with this level of emotive photorealism. It took Herculean effort on the part of the artists at Weta to get all the shots in before the deadline, with some coming in just days before the film's delivery. Bleary-eyed artists were stumbling through the halls. It was a tense but exhilarating time for everyone. The amazing magicians at Weta gave it their all, and the results stunned the world. *Avatar* won the hearts of a global audience, to say nothing of the Oscar® for Best Visual Effects.

On *The Way of Water* the biggest challenge was the water itself, and all the new creatures and characters that interacted with it. Great strides had been made since Cameron's experimental CG water-tentacle in *The Abyss* (1989) and the digital oceans for *Titanic* (1997). But the detail required to integrate water with performance-captured and live-action characters was a quantum leap greater challenge in *The Way of Water*. "Water is one of the more difficult environments when you're creating characters," noted Joe Letteri. "When you have a character coming out of the water, you have rivulets on their skin, drips falling from their hair and rolling off their body in really fine detail. But if they're surrounded by a vast ocean, you cannot render the ocean to that same level." To handle scales of detail in simulations, Weta wrote a special software system, called Loki.

"That solver lets us look at whether water was close to camera, or far away," related Letteri. VFX supervisor Eric Saindon worked closely with director Cameron, whose eye was refined by years at sea, to craft and shape the water using the new cutting-edge tools. Fortunately, on this film, Weta had years of pre-production to do R&D well before the final crunch, and the tools were in good shape to created CG water at levels of realism never seen before. The end result was flawless. Despite over a third of the film taking place in and under the water, only a handful of shots (mostly of Spider) actually used photography of real water. The vast majority were simulated, using

Above: Lo'ak, Ao'Nung and others astride a pod of *ilu* in a conceptual rendering by Steven Messing. Computer-generated water—long considered one of the most computationally-daunting mediums to render convincingly on-screen—proved one of the greatest triumphs for visual effects on the Avatar sequels.

computational fluid dynamics. But it looked 100 percent real. The photoreal water combined with the emotively flawless and photoreal characters to suspend all disbelief, and fully immerse global audiences in the wonders of Pandora. It was a virtuoso triumph that the entire VFX community took note of when the film was released. At the VES (Visual Effects Society) Awards in 2023, the film received 14 nominations in 9 categories and won them all in a straight flush.

It was a jubilant night for the Lightstorm and Weta artists, and much tequila was consumed that evening. *Avatar: The Way of Water* also won the Oscar® for Best Visual Effects.

For *Fire and Ash*, the final challenge turned out to be the scale of the Factory Ship and the sheer scale of the battle taking place around it. "The Factory Ship

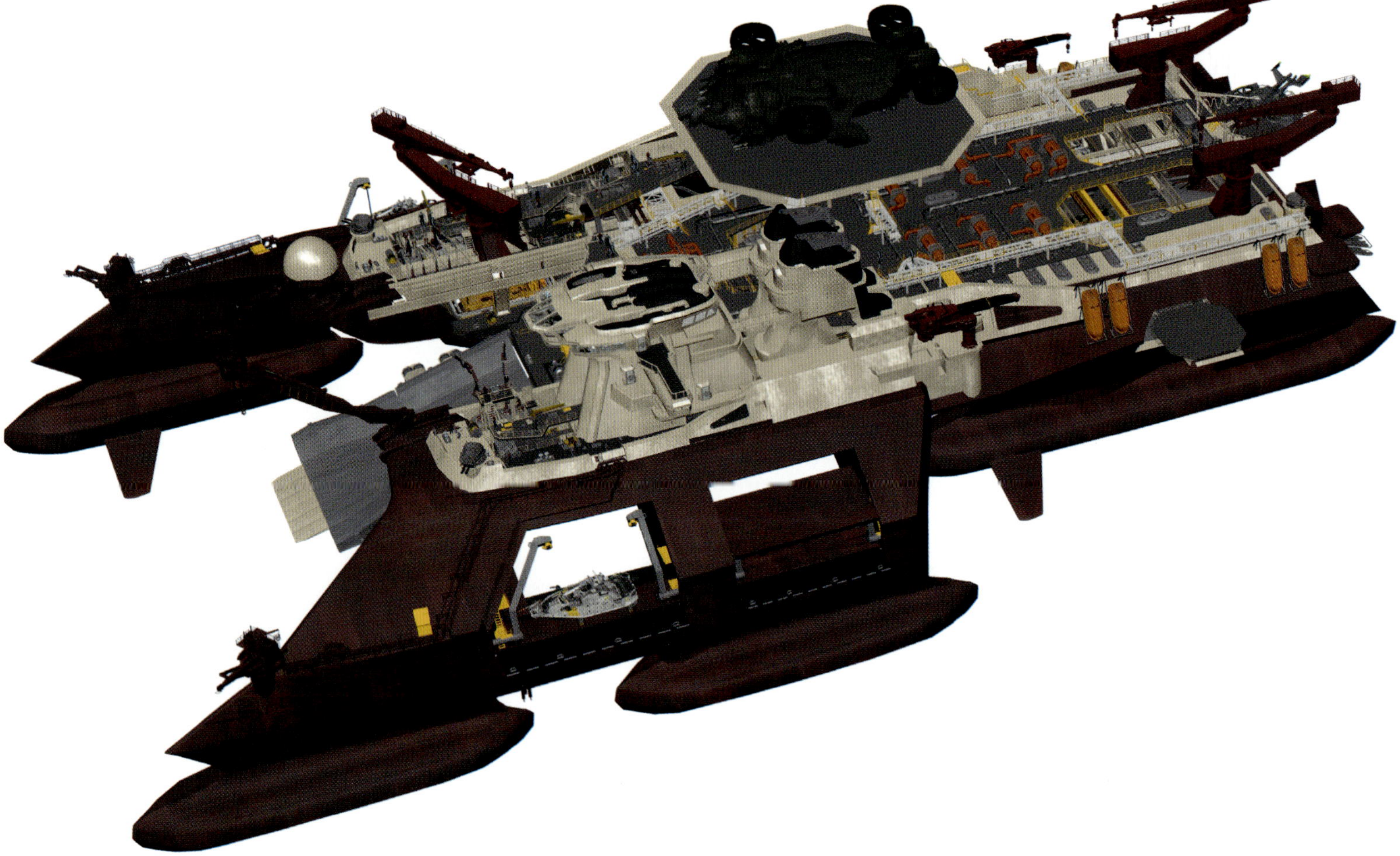

Opposite page, top: Lightstorm Lab and Techvis artists from Proof Inc. plotted the Factory Ship's construction in 3D builds that guided layouts of virtual and practical set construction and the internal workings of the giant vessel.

Opposite page, bottom: The RDA unleashes its full firepower on the Na'vi, including battalions of Crab Suit amphibious vehicles that disembark a massive Factory Ship at the Cove of the Ancestors. Concept art by Fausto De Martini.

Right: Simon Franglen helped to create a rich musical score to accompany the drama on Pandora, combining orchestral textures, exotic instrumentation, and electronic synthesizer tonalities.

was four or five times the size of a SeaDragon," commented Eric Saindon, "and because it gets completely ripped apart in the end battle, we had to build both the outside and all of its internal workings." The geometry of the Factory Ship overwhelmed the capacity of Weta's modeling program. The total data exceeded all previous Weta records, measured in petabytes (a petabyte equals one million gigabytes). "Back on the first *Avatar,*" Weta digital asset supervisor Marco Revelant recalled, "we presented Jim Cameron with a military dog tag printed with the words 'One Petabyte Club' because we reached a petabyte of data. On *Fire and Ash*, we reached a petabyte every second week with the amount of data we processed, and the amount of rendering we were passing through our facilities. One of our production crew in charge of managing our resources told me, 'I've never seen numbers like this.'"

Despite the challenges, the Weta team was prepared this time. They had a mature pipeline, built especially for the Avatar sequels and tested in combat on *The Way of Water*. Despite the fire in the title of the third film, there was no last-minute crunch with everyone running around with their hair on fire.

As the VFX process thundered toward the finish line, sound design and music progressed in tandem. As producer Jon Landau had noted, the score was "the heartbeat of Pandora." In a 2010 interview with Cameron and members of their sound-design crew at Fox Studios, Landau's praise of James Horner's Academy-Award®-nominated musical score for *Avatar* brought audience applause: "The score that Horner wrote was such a part of the essence of the film. And it was a real challenge, because Jim challenged [James Horner] to do something he had really never done [before], which was to combine classic film scoring with indigenous and tribal music, and make it feel a single integrated piece."

Cameron used two of Horner's earlier scores to put "temp music" to his cut of *Avatar*: the ancient Mayan adventure *Apocalypto* (2006) and rainforest survival drama *The River Runs Black* (1986). Horner's score took shape when his colleague, Simon Franglen—a British-born composer/arranger, and collaborator on *Titanic*—joined him initially to consult on new orchestral textures. "They were heading in a tribal, voices-and-wooden-drum approach like *Apocalypto*," Franglen recalled. "James thought he needed to look in a different direction and he asked me to come in and work with them for a week." Based on Horner's brief and a screening of work-in-progress footage, Franglen recommended the glassy, ethereal sounds of the Indonesian gamelan, a xylophone-like instrument, to evoke the wonder of Pandora. "I suggested a glowing gamelan approach, a shimmering Balinese feel, as an essential part of

Left: *Tulkun* attack the RDA fleet in "The Mother of All Sea Battles." Concept art by Ben Procter.

the texture. The first cue I created with James was for a scene where Jake is alone at night in the forest, suddenly the environment glows, and he sees the beauty all around him. James and I felt like there was a natural harmony in terms of the way that we were working that melodically supported what Jim was doing. I ended up working with James for the rest of that year."

Franglen worked as electronic music arranger on *Avatar* and, with scoring mixer Simon Rhodes, Horner produced approximately 300 minutes of music using a 130-person orchestra with choral, percussive, and synthesized elements. "I wanted this to be a non-orchestral score with orchestral elements," Horner stated in an interview with Avid, the company that supplied the scoring team's music notation and editorial software. "I've been trying to move slowly away from writing conventional orchestral music to writing orchestral music, but incorporating other instruments that don't play orchestrally; and I like to weave those worlds together."

Horner's non-traditional instruments included djembe, doumbek, taiko, dunun, tom-tom, shakuhachi flute, kena, ocarinas, and panpipes. Franglen and Rhodes built elements into premixes with synthesizer sounds, including a Horner flourish of a menacing vocalization that served as the primal undercurrent of Pandora's predators. "That was a sound-patch that James used in some of his other scores," Simon Franglen recalled. "He called it 'Groany Men,' and it was derived from a male voice taken down two octaves." Other vocalizations included singers that specialized in soundtrack accompaniments, including Carmen Twillie, lead vocalist from Disney's animated *The Lion King* (1994). "Carmen has an amazingly wide range," remarked Franglen. "Terry Wood and Clydene Jackson were the brighter voices. We sometimes hybridized them with synths, but those three were the choral voices of *Avatar*."

Sound designer Christopher Boyes and his dialogue, music, and effects re-recording mixers then built Pandora's acoustic world. "This was bigger than anything I'd ever come across in my career," Boyes remarked in a 2010 interview at Skywalker Sound. "Every nuance of the world we explored sonically. Pandora was like a rainforest 10 times over. It had bioluminescent plants, and all sorts of life that were so vivid in their colorization it gave license for a wide range of sound elements, such as insects flying by, or background noises of animals unlike anything ever heard before. And then, in Hell's Gate, where the humans lived and breathed synthetic air, we contrasted that with the natural world. It was an incredible landscape for sound."

Boyes created jungle sounds from field recordings and his library of materials. Concurrently, supervising sound editor Addison Teague worked for three years with Cameron's in-house editorial team to build sounds for editorial assemblies. These became audio templates that guided the sound design. "Jim cuts his own temp mixes," explained re-recording mixer Gary Summers, whose work with Cameron extended back to *Terminator 2: Judgment Day* (1991). "He cut in

Opposite page, top: Sound designer Christopher Boyes at the mixing desk at Park Road Post in Wellington, New Zealand, orchestrating the soundscapes of *The Way of Water*.

Opposite page, below: A key moment in the sound design of *Avatar* occurred during Jake's first encounter with a rampaging thanator. Cameron made clear his brief to the sound editors and mixing team, focusing them on the emotional impact of Jake's gasping breaths amid the frenzy of the giant predator's attack. Weta Digital screenshot.

Above: A music recording session for *The Way of Water* at the historic Newman Scoring Stage at the former 20th Century Fox Studios in Los Angeles, California.

music from the score, temp music, and sound effects fed to him by his sound team, making selections from libraries that Chris and Addison were building. We all then referenced that template."

The yipping calls of viperwolves featured coyote howls that Teague recorded in the Malibu hills behind Cameron's home studio, combined with hyena cries. For mountain banshee *ikran* shrieking, growling, and chittering in reaction to Na'vi riders, Boyes used elements of raptors, wild cats, horses, and the squeals of three-day-old baby pigs pitched down. "If you asked me what was the key component to the sound of the banshees," Chris Boyes told *Indiewire*, "I couldn't honestly tell you. Once I pull sounds from different creatures, I almost forget where they have come from on purpose, because I don't want to be thinking about that. I build from many different elements, and I play with how they fold in and out of each other."

Na'vi dialogue stemmed from performance-capture audio, which Cameron's postproduction sound crew assembled at Skywalker Sound. The mixing team built footfalls and body-motion noises as "Foley"—postproduction sounds, named after veteran Hollywood sound engineer Jack Foley—performed by a team of skilled recording artists reenacting on-screen movements. Rainforest Foley was a subtle art. "The very first time we see Neytiri," recalled supervising sound editor Gwen Whittle, "she's walking through the iridescent forest, spying on Jake, who's making a mess of things. Neytiri was supposed to be walking on spongy ground. That was very hard to figure out. Grass sounded too sharp; mud was too gloopy; we tried people walking barefoot through all sorts of stuff. Then, one of the Foley walkers, Jana Vance, was at the beach, and she saw some kelp. She brought that back to the studio and that's what we used. For Neytiri's walk, that's Jana walking on fresh kelp."

Jake's first encounter with a thanator set the style for balancing sound to narrative intent. "Chris had all the roars and noises of the monster crashing through and running," recalled Gary Summers. "I had one track, which was Jake's breathing laid in with the dialogue. Jim viewed the scene with our premix, and it then was like film school. Jim asked us, 'What's this scene about?' We were all like deers in headlights. He said, 'It's about the threat to the main character. If I lose that, this is just a monster movie.'" Gwen Whittle recut Jake's breath tracks, using sounds derived from Sam Worthington's ADR. "If you listen to that scene, we didn't miss one of Jake's breaths. When we remixed the scene, it had a whole different feel. It connected us with that character."

***

For *The Way of Water*, Boyes and other members of the sound-design team returned, to explore new Pandoran realms including the underwater ambience of the Metkayina reef. "Jim is a diver," noted Summers. "He was looking for a sound that he heard or sensed underwater. Chris came up with a low-frequency bass-tone that became the sound bed for underwater scenes. And then there were elements, such as bubbles and other details, depending on the action in each scene. When characters came up from underwater, the surface sounds were a very clear contrast."

The younger characters' voices were a priority for the sound team, who were tasked with modulating age-appropriate timbres. "Jack Champion was 12 when they cast him as Spider," recalled Gwen Whittle. "He is now in his twenties, but in a lot of his live-action scenes he had his 'baby voice.' Anytime his younger voice overlapped his costars', they brought him in and rerecorded his lower voice."

The voice of Kiri was less problematic, despite the age-discrepancy between Sigourney Weaver and her teenage Na'vi persona. "I researched teenage girls' voices on YouTube," Whittle recalled. "I noticed that some are naturally deep. So, we decided that's her. We did nothing to Kiri's voice. That was Sigourney all the way."

Kiri was one of several key characters that received special attention in the musical score to *The Way of Water* composed by Simon Franglen. In the years since *Avatar*, Franglen had reunited with James Horner to create music for the Walt Disney World attraction at Disney's Animal Kingdom Theme Park: Pandora—The World of Avatar and its Flight of Passage and Na'vi River Journey rides. The assignment was bittersweet. "The idea for the theme park music was for James to write the theme and I'd produce the music," said Franglen. "In 2013, I started working on arrangements for Na'vi River Journey. We were into the early process when James died on June 22, 2015."

Horner, a keen aviator, was 61 when his high-performance aerobatic plane crashed in Los Padres National Forest, California. Franglen honored the loss of his friend and colleague by completing their works-in-progress, including the Pandora theme park music. Impressed with Franglen's work, Cameron invited Franglen to read scripts for four new Avatar feature films. "Prior to that," Franglen recalled, "there had been nothing for James to work to, because there were no scripts. Jim explained this was not one film, but a complete arc. So I sat in a locked room at Lightstorm and, over a week, I read all the scripts. I then started writing tribal music that Jim needed for A2 and A3."

Tribal music included a song in Na'vi, sung by Neytiri at the beginning and end of *The Way of Water* honoring the life of her first born, Neteyam. Known as "Songcord," the concept was partly based on Aboriginal Australian Songlines, where tribespeople use music to "sing" maps and cultural pathways. "We applied that analogy to the Na'vi," said Franglen. "They have threads of beads that represent different parts of a person's life. Neytiri sings the life of Neteyam. I also wrote Songcords for Lo'ak, Neytiri, Grace, and Tuk—each had their own melodies and lyrics."

Na'vi linguist Professor Paul Frommer adapted Franglen's English Songcord lyrics to the sometimes-challenging Na'vi language. "I tried to find words using a thesaurus and Professor Frommer's official Na'vi dictionary," Franglen commented. "I moved words around until we ended up with something melodically and lyrically singable. Zoe sang her Songcord on the performance-capture set. That became our family theme."

To maintain continuity with James Horner's score, Franglen reunited with vocalists Terry Wood and Clydene Jackson. For Metkayina vocals, Franglen adapted Polynesian and Melanesian voices from the Cook Islands and Vanuatu in a choir that he assembled at Park Road Post in Wellington, New Zealand. Metkayina orchestrations featured indigenous instruments made of bamboo and clay, representing material that reef-dwelling Na'vi would find in the sea.

A key undercurrent of the score reprised Jake and Neytiri's love theme that Horner had established with recording artist Leona Lewis for *Avatar*'s end title song *I See You*—evoking the Na'vi greeting. "I used the *I See You* theme in action sequences as our 'Hero Jake' theme," said Franglen. "One of the things that Jim and I talked about was that James had written ten great themes, but he often used those sparingly, or only once. This time, Jim asked me to take a more 'leitmotif' approach to scoring, where themes became associated with certain characters."

Opposite page, above: Ronal (Kate Winslet) and Tonowari (Cliff Curtis) gather with their clan to celebrate the life of the Sully family's deceased son, Neteyam. Franglen composed a haunting melody for the ceremony that Zoe Saldaña voiced as Neytiri's "Songcord" in Na'vi rituals that bookended *The Way of Water*. Weta screenshot.

Opposite page, below: Neytiri releases Neteyam's body to the ocean. Weta screenshot.

> "Jim asked me to take a more 'leitmotif' approach to scoring, where themes became associated with certain characters."
>
> **Simon Franglen, composer**

New motifs included Neytiri's Songcord, which expressed connections between members of the Sully family. The Metkayina theme heard during the arrival of the *tulkun* at the reef underlined those characters' connection with the sea. The *tulkun* loner Payakan received his own theme. "Payakan's theme is based on resonant frequencies," Franglen explained. "Initially, there was an idea that we would hear the *tulkun* sing. Chris and I built *tulkun* vocalizations. I incorporated that into the way I created the melodies."

For the RDA, Franglen created an aggressive, propulsive synthesizer motif, and another for Quaritch. As a flip side to the aggressors, Kiri received a questing, four-note melody that tied to a deeper theme. "Kiri is connected with *Eywa*," Franglen observed. "Her theme occurs in a scene at the Metkayina village where Kiri is dipping her toes in the water, talking to Jake about her connection with *Eywa*—he asks, 'What does *Eywa*'s heartbeat sound like?' She says, 'Mighty.' I used that melody for *Eywa* or Kiri, to show how Kiri can connect with plants and wildlife because she is channeling *Eywa*. Jim liked that so much, he made it the Lightstorm studio logo theme."

Final mixes sampled premixes of music stems and effects. "On a typical action movie," observed Chris Boyes in an interview with *Mix Magazine*, "when a big music sequence comes along, we might gingerly add sound effects here and there. With Jim, it's not that way. Music might be carrying a sequence, but we were articulating hundreds of sound effects, handing one off to the other. We'd go into music elements and dial out elements of percussion so that the sounds of guns had more impact. In underwater scenes, Jim would want to hear tail swishes, and people swimming in such a way that it didn't take away [from] the majesty of the music. Sound supported the visuals, so all the pieces worked in orchestration, telling a story, one shot at a time."

After the release of *The Way of Water*, a double tragedy struck the production when film editors David Brenner died of a heart attack, then John Refoua succumbed to cancer, only months apart. Rivkin paid tribute to his colleagues in press coverage of their work and offered a tribute to Refoua in a *CinemaEditor* obituary: "John's passing is heartbreaking. He left us way too soon. His warmth, humor, and kindness were an inspiration to the entire Avatar crew and all who ever had the pleasure of working with him. He will always be our beloved friend, colleague, and gifted editor." Working from Refoua's rough assembly, Rivkin and Cameron were later joined by film editor Nicolas De Toth for *Avatar: Fire and Ash* in New Zealand, where the director relocated in 2020.

***

Fire and Ash presented diverse musical challenges, beginning with the Wind Traders, whom Simon Franglen likened to Phoenician traders of ancient Mediterranean culture. "The Wind Traders were more sophisticated than other Na'vi," commented Franglen. "These were educated people, and globalists. I wrote a major theme for them based on Arabic music, and some Western music, with ascending and descending scales that are also found in Indian music. The Wind Trader theme makes a big statement when they appear at the Metkayina reef. It's a pretty grand affair."

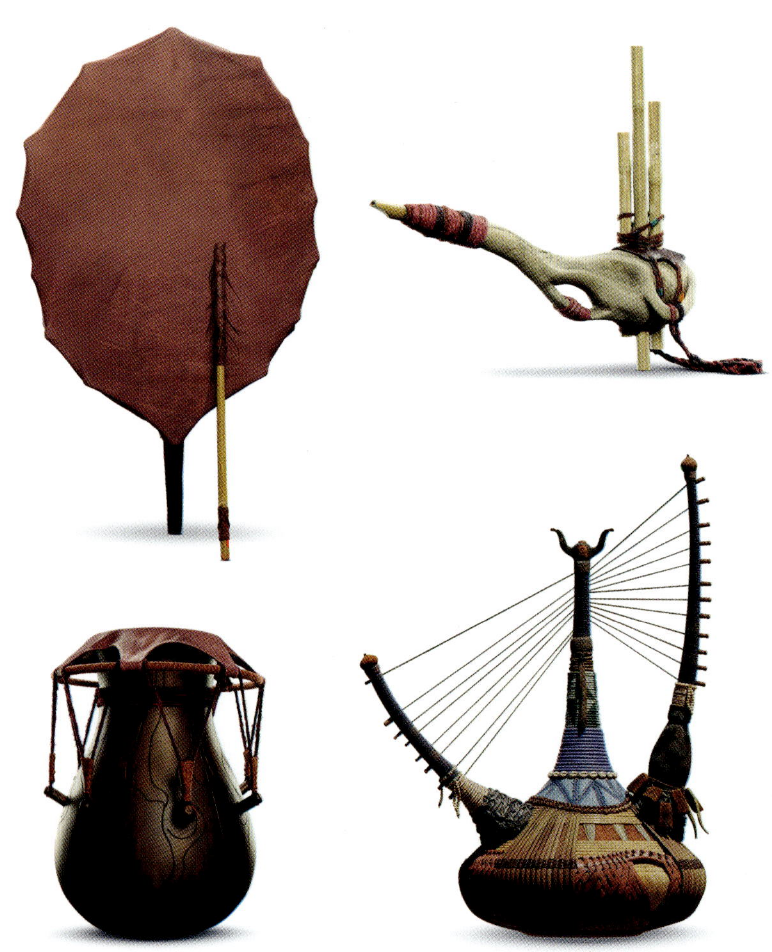

Sound design for the Wind Traders' aerial environment began with supervising sound effects editor Brent Burge—a veteran of *The Way of Water*—and sound effects editor Hayden Collow, working with Cameron's editors at Stone Street Studios and Park Road Post in Wellington. "Jim is very specific about rhythms," said Burge. "He has a very clear directive of how he wants sound to play. The Wind Traders were fascinating because we had not experienced their technology before." Burge's sound crew explored Tlalim gondola sounds using creaking ropes and flapping fabric that they obtained from Wellington's maritime community. "We also had a question: when Jake jumped up onto the medusoid, was the membrane wet? We worked through all those details with Jim, creating sounds for surfaces and sound elements that went with them."

The Sully family's journey with the Tlalim, as originally scripted, featured scenes of the Wind Traders performing on ethnic musical instruments. Simon Franglen sketched ideas for these props, which Dylan Cole's design team and Weta Workshop refined, and then the property department printed in 3D for use on the performance-capture stage. "They were stringed instruments, drums, and some simple winds," said Franglen. "The stringed instrument was like a West African kora, but it had to be portable and capable of being strapped into the rigging. We used that in a scene for what we called 'The Wind Traders Jig.' Some of the performance-capture people were good musicians, including Jon Landau's son, Jamie Landau, who is a producer now but he started his career in bands. I also sampled those instruments and used them in the jig."

Opposite page: To devise instruments for the Tlalim, composer Simon Franglen supplied concepts for ethnic instruments that Dylan Cole's design team and Weta Workshop refined, before the property department output as 3D-printed props for use on the performance-capture stage. Clockwise: a standing drum; a wind instrument; a stringed instrument; a hand drum.

Overleaf: Recom Quaritch treks across the volcanic plains of the Mangkwan territory.

Above: For scenes of merriment on board the Wind Traders' gondola, Simon Franglen composed a boisterous 'Wind Traders Jig' that the filmmakers used in audio playback on the performance capture stage. Weta Workshop concept art.

Below: An instrument used in the "Wind Traders' jig" scene, inspired by the West African kora.

To contrast with the joyful happiness of the Tlalim clan, the sound team created a distinctive new war-cry for the Mangkwan. "Our dialogue editor Martin Kwok had the really good idea to bring in punk rock and heavy metal singers for the Ash People," recalled Gwen Whittle. "They could make Ash cries without destroying their voices. It was so aggressive, unlike the [Omatikaya] 'yip-yip-yip'; it's more a growling 'rawwr.'"

Musical themes for the Mangkwan and their leader, Varang, reflected the Ash People's obsessions with weapons and metal. "The Ash People want to burn the world down," said Simon Franglen. "I gave them a frenzy and an absolute absence of any culture." The Mangkwan theme featured a Mongolian morin khuur—a viola-sized, bowed-spike lute—which Franglen combined with Western stringed instruments and synthetic bass. Varang received a theme based on Mongolian 'Long Song,' a female choral texture of extended, high-pitched vocalizations.

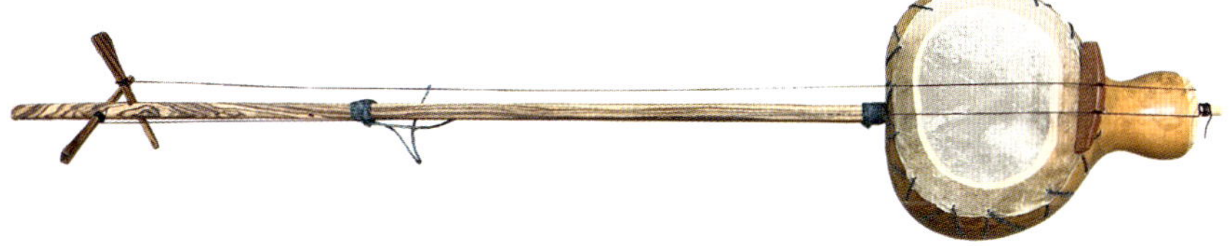

Varang's alliance with Quaritch inspired the development of the Recom Colonel's theme when addressing his obsessive rivalry with Jake Sully. "I've always looked at Quaritch and Jake as two sides of the same coin," noted Franglen. "They are both Marines, the Colonel and the Corporal, and it doesn't matter how far we go through the story, underneath it all, the Colonel feels that the Corporal has betrayed him. Quaritch also feels betrayed by the RDA, and he goes rogue. But Quaritch and the Sully clan are also tied together. Neytiri killed Quaritch [in human form], so she is the death of him. Spider is a son both to Quaritch and the Sullys. I considered all of those connections while I was writing Quaritch's theme for A2 and A3. And then, at the end of A3, the family theme and Quaritch's theme interlock. During the fight on the rocks above the Flux Devil, we play the two themes on top of each other, and they come together."

The final battle at the Cove of the Ancestors featured a culmination of sound design. The Tulkun Council included patriarchs and matriarchs of a magnitude larger and more sonically imposing than the young bull Payakan, characters who communicate with thunderous low frequency vocalizations that visibly vibrate the surface of the ocean. The final combat featured savage flurries of tsyong, and tumultuous Flux Devil sounds. The editorial crew layered sound cues for emotional resonance. "The Flux Devil had to have an evolving, rolling presence," noted Brent Burge. "It was magnetic, so there was an electrical element. But it had to have a rhythm, otherwise it became a 'constant' that you no longer hear. It all came down to the quality of the sounds. They all had to work with music and dialogue, supporting the story. Sometimes we had to take sounds away to find what worked emotionally. It was so important to find sounds that created an emotional attachment to what was happening on screen."

Musically, the conclusion of *Fire and Ash* represented a thematic progression. "*Avatar* was fundamentally a love story between Jake and Neytiri," observed Simon Franglen. "*The Way of Water* was about family, and loss. *Fire and Ash* is about two things. One is: what are you willing to give up for your family? The other is a phoenix-type idea of burning everything down and what comes out of that. *Fire and Ash* is about transformation. Spider is physically transformed, but all the characters are growing. Quaritch is transformed from a human in an alien body to an outcast. He is transformed by his connection with Varang. Even the Ash People grow from ragtag marauders to a powerful clan, hell-bent on retribution. And, through all that, Jake transforms."

The score for *Fire and Ash* amounted to approximately four hours of music—adding to the 15 hours of theme park music, and 10 hours of demos, five hours of orchestral recordings, and the three hours of music that Franglen had composed for *The Way of Water*. The composer and Lightstorm continue to plot their musical trajectory for the upcoming Avatar films.

Opposite page: In October 2024, at the Royal Albert Hall, London, *Avatar* screened to a sold-out audience who were the first to witness the film with live orchestral accompaniment.

Above: Simon Franglen (left), James Cameron, and Sigourney Weaver greet the Albert Hall crowd with conductor Ludwig Wicki and members of the London Philharmonic Orchestra.

At the end of the pipeline for Weta, they still had to render every scene in stereoscopic 3D. This required rendering each frame twice for a left eye and right eye—the basis of the stereo depth illusion. The Lightstorm team would then do a final grading pass on all the Weta renders, fine-tuning the 3D and color for every shot. This included mastering the entire film, end to end, in different formats such as the 1.35:1 wide screen aspect ratio, and the taller 16:9 ratio that would be used in many cinemas, especially the premium Giant Screen and IMAX theaters. They also mastered the film separately for different 3D formats, which have very different light levels between standard 3D and premium formats like DolbyVision, which employs the much brighter laser projectors.

Theatrical presentations of the films—in 3D, IMAX, and DolbyVision laser projection, have set the bar for the premium theatrical experience. "What I think is really exciting about this is the potential it shows for the cinema experience," Jon Landau observed to the 2010 Fox Studio crowd. "It's not just about *Avatar*. It rekindles the belief of what all movies can do, it draws people out of their homes in a day and age when home technology is getting better, and it proves that the cinema experience can still be magic. Jim always puts into his scripts what great writers do in their literature. It's a metaphor for the world in which we live. And it asks us to beg questions about how we live our lives. That's why this movie resonates."

The filmmakers acknowledged their science-fiction epic's deeper themes of colonization, military subjugation of indigenous peoples, the rape of the natural world by extractive industries, and corporate greed. "We made an environmental film that was a huge hit with a general audience," remarked James Cameron. "However, I also learned that even when people line up around the block to see your movie, there's a limit to how movies change people's behavior."

Evidence of Cameron's ecological interests appeared in a documentary on the *Avatar* Blu-ray that featured the filmmaker, his wife Suzy Amis, and actors Sigourney Weaver and Joel David Moore visiting the Xingu River people of Brazil, whose habitat was threatened by the development of Belo Monte hydroelectric dam. Tragically, environmental efforts failed and the project flooded 150 square miles of rainforest. Cameron remained undaunted and instead resolved to continue his focus on giving back to indigenous communities and environmental efforts. "I put together a small team—it still, today, only consists of three people—to channel funding to projects on a targeted basis to help them accomplish their goals," Cameron explained. "That's why it's called the Avatar Alliance Foundation. We allied with other charitable groups, like Amazon Watch and Nia Tero, to empower their resources." Since Cameron's endowment, the foundation has been self-funding, and low-profile. "We want it to have impact, and we stay out of the limelight. Sometimes, if you draw attention to the problems, you can do good. Other times, you can do more harm than good. You've got to stay the course. And some causes you just can't win. It is heartbreaking."

The experience continues to resonate with key members of the design team. "Jim's films tie in to what we feel we're on the planet to do," stated Richard Taylor from his office at Weta Workshop. "They are in the DNA of everything we've tried to create with our workshop, in our imperatives for design and fabrication. We can create wildly fantastical creatures, if required. But we love underpinning our work in Jim's plausible ecologies. These films project a sense of belief that the Na'vi truly exist out there on the other side of the universe. We relish Jim's belief in that reality. It was so endorsing, so enriching, and so empowering to be connected with that world."

For visual effects, the world-building of Avatar represents an achievement that, in many ways, filmmakers have been building to since the advent of digital technology revolutionized their creative process. "*Avatar* required us to build an entire world," observed Joe Letteri. "That was apparent in Jim's treatment when I read that in 2005. It was so vivid that I remember thinking, 'I want to see this movie.' We had to figure out how to make it, because we wanted to see it. That was a lot of motivation behind it. For me, *Avatar* represented taking all those pieces that we had learned from everything that had come before and pulling it together into one big world."

While the world-building of Avatar is epic in its technical scope—the filmmaking has remained a human endeavor. "In all my movies before Avatar," James Cameron reflected, "the film was the most important thing. But I learned not only from Avatar but also my expedition work, what's important is the quality of the experience on a day-to-day basis. It's the people that you work with. There's a small group of people that understands how hard this process is, and we share that bond.

"After the first *Avatar*, I debated whether I should do any more. But a big factor for me was getting to work again with the people that I enjoyed working with. Jon Landau, Richie Baneham, performers and stunt team, everybody—we have what we call 'the Avatar family,' and it has meaning for us. Whenever we get back together, even for a short pickup shoot, there's the feeling of a family reunion. Life moves on, people have children, but it's a family we can count on. They always come back."

Above: Producer Jon Landau (center) with Cameron and their team during live-action set scouts at Stone Street Studios in Wellington, New Zealand, May 2019.

> "These films project a sense of belief that the Na'vi truly exist out there on the other side of the universe."
>
> **Jon Landau, producer**

Epilogue

A year and a half before the release of *Avatar: Fire and Ash*, the death was announced of Avatar producer Jon Landau. Cameron's ally on *Titanic*, the father figure to the Lightstorm team, had been bravely battling cancer for a year. James Cameron's words spoke for all Jon's friends and colleagues:

"The Avatar family grieves the loss of our friend and leader, Jon Landau. His zany humor, personal magnetism, great generosity of spirit and fierce will have held the center of our Avatar universe for almost two decades. His legacy is not just the films he produced, but the personal example he set—indomitable, caring, inclusive, tireless, insightful and utterly unique.

"He produced great films, not by wielding power but by spreading warmth and the joy of making cinema. He inspired us all to be and to bring our best, every day.

"I have lost a dear friend, and my closest collaborator of 31 years. A part of myself has been torn away."

Jim Cameron.

SENIOR EDITOR
Alastair Dougall
PROJECT ART EDITOR
Jon Hall
DESIGN
XAB Design
PRODUCTION EDITOR
Marc Staples
SENIOR PRODUCTION CONTROLLER
Mary Slater
MANAGING EDITOR
Emma Grange
MANAGING ART EDITOR
Vicky Short
ART DIRECTOR
Charlotte Coulais
PUBLISHER
Paula Regan
MANAGING DIRECTOR
Mark Searle

First American Edition, 2025
Published in the United States by DK Publishing
1745 Broadway, 20th Floor, New York, NY 10019
Page design copyright © 2025 Dorling Kindersley Limited.
25 26 27 28 29 10 9 8 7 6 5 4 3 2 1
005–348770–Dec/2025

Published in Great Britain by Dorling Kindersley Limited

ISBN 979-8-2171-2640-8

Printed and bound in Italy

www.dk.com
www.avatar.com

ACKNOWLEDGMENTS

DK would like to thank the following for their assistance in making this book:
James Cameron, Jon Landau, Rae Sanchini, Joshua Izzo, Reymundo Perez, Maria Battle Campbell, Jamie Landau at Lightstorm Entertainment; Wētā FX; Wētā Workshop; Legacy Effects; Industrial Light & Magic; Nicole Spiegel at Disney. Nigel Wright at XAB Design.

Photographers
Los Angeles Set Photographer (A1, Sequels): Mark Fellman
Aotearoa New Zealand Set Photographer (Sequels): Iva Lenard
Lightstorm EPK Photographer (Sequels): John Clisham
Black-and-White Portraits of James Cameron/Jon Landau, Photographer: Niki Boon

Additional photography by: James Cameron; Jamie Landau (Sequels); Ben Procter (Sequels); Nathan Hauggard (Sequels); Legacy Effects; Mob Scene (Sequels); Jordu Schell; Richard Schwalm; Charlie Palafox (A1); Joseph C. Pepe (A1); Stan Winston Studios (A1); Weta Workshop (A1); Peter Zaccarini.

The author would like to thank: Alastair Dougall and Jon Hall at Dorling Kindersley; Josh Izzo, Rey Perez, and Geoff Burdick at Lightstorm; and the brain trust: James Cameron, Jon Landau, Rae Sanchini.

For sharing their stories: Rick Jaffa, Amanda Silver, Shane Salerno, Josh Friedman, Dylan Cole, Ben Procter, Rick Carter, Robert Stromberg, Steve Messing, Paul Frommer, John Rosengrant, Shane Mahan, Christopher Swift, Joe Letteri, Richard Baneham, Andrew Jones, Richard Hollander, Eric Saindon, Daniel Barrett, Dejan Momcilovic, Marco Revelant, Stuart Adcock, Eric Reynolds, Ryan Champney, Steve Ingram, J.D. Schwalm, Joe Pepe, Zachary Berger, Kirk Krack, Garrett Warren, Russell Carpenter, ASC, Sir Richard Taylor, Deborah Scott, Brad Elliott, Sarah Rubano, Simon Franglen, Gwen Whittle, Brent Burge, Gary Summers, and James Cameron.

For their help behind the scenes: Lizzie Binks, Gabriela Barrientos, Amy Vavrunek, Griffin Scott, Carol Marshall, Maria Campbell, Ellen Drower, Sarah Coombs, Magnus Hjert, Markus Hagemeier, Angelina Ramsey, Ri Streeter, Jade Lucas, Jessica Wallace, Julia Gessler, David Luke, Shealyn Biron, Neil S. Bulk, Deniz Cordell, Sandra Koerte, John Knoll, Ian Kintzle, Todd Vaziri, Robert Yamamoto.

For background sources: Jody Duncan, Lisa Fitzpatrick, Tara Bennett, TyRuben Ellingson, Jordu Schell, Wanda Bryant, Jay Holben, Iain Marcks, Rebecca Keegan, David Smith, Hunter Harris, Frank Rose, Michael Coleman, Perri Nemiroff, Jim Chabin, Wim Buyens, Jim Hemphill, Peter Hammond, Emma Robertson.

And for moral support: Mark Cotta Vaz, Don Shay, Jody Duncan, Patti McMahon.

I See you.

ABOUT THE AUTHOR

Joe Fordham began his career in the UK making award-winning short films, which played on BBC TV, Channel 4 TV, BAFTA/LA and Amazon. He worked in film editing, animation, visual effects, special effects, and creature effects in London and Los Angeles. His writing includes two decades with *Cinefex* magazine, freelance journalism (*Cinefantastique*, *The Hollywood Reporter*, *American Cinematographer*) and studio licensed publishing for Titan Books. Recent and upcoming titles include *Star Trek: First Contact: The Making of the Classic Film*, *Star Trek: Picard: The Art and Making of the Series* and *Alien Film Franchise Encyclopedia*. *Making Avatar: The Way of Water, Fire and Ash* is his first book for DK.